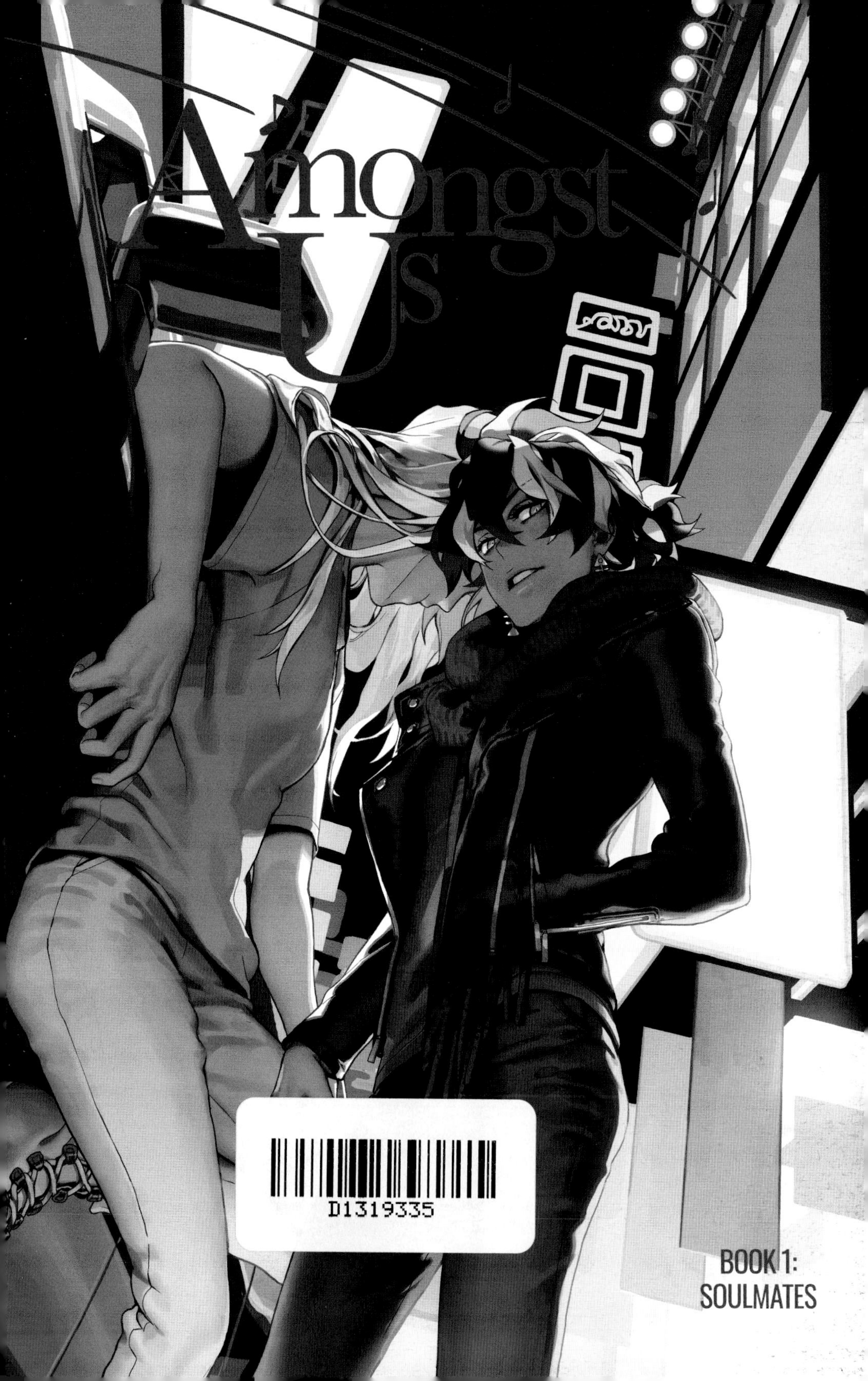
Amongst Us
BOOK 1:
SOULMATES

AMONGST US - BOOK 1: SOULMATES

Copyright © 2017 Shilin Huang
Story & Art by Shilin Huang

Published in partnership with Hiveworks Comics, LLC.
hiveworkscomics.com
thehiveworks.com
amongstuscomic.com

Seven Seas press and purchase enquiries can be sent to Marketing Manager
Lianne Sentar at press@gomanga.com. Information regarding the distribution
and purchase of digital editions is available from Digital Manager CK Russell
at digital@gomanga.com.

Print Edition Editor: Robin Herrera
Logo & Cover Art: Shilin Huang
Cover Graphic Designer: M. A. Lewife
Production Designer: Stevie Wilson
Production Manager: Lissa Pattillo
Prepress Technician: Melanie Ujimori, Jules Valera
Editor-in-Chief: Julie Davis
Associate Publisher: Adam Arnold
Publisher: Jason DeAngelis

ISBN: 978-1-63858-413-1
Printed in China
First Printing: July 2023
10 9 8 7 6 5 4 3 2 1

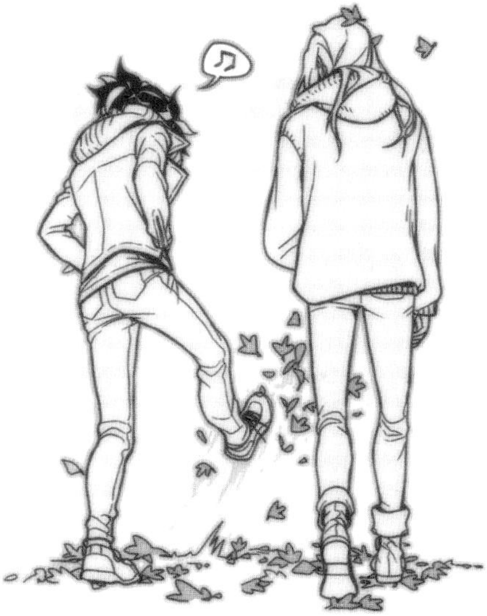
♫

Book 1: Soulmates

Table of Contents

Foreword & Dedication

If someone told me a decade ago that I'd be doing a slice-of-life story about two people in love, I probably would have laughed and called them a fool. Even though I was self-driven and self-motivated to write something about Blackbird and Veloce as a couple, I still believed a love story was not something that could be written with skill, interest, and research alone. The writer had to have lived through love, and had love to give, too. I had neither, nor was I looking for either, but some greater force must have looked at me and swore, "You are going to learn this lesson whether you want to or not," because seven years ago, I was graced with the love of my life.

She did not set out to change my world, but whether she knew it at the time or not, just her presence alone was enough to change me. She changed what I could see and feel in this same ordinary world, and what I could notice and find in this same ordinary life. A creator conveys what they are able to envision, and if it were not for her, I would not have been able to see the love I would have wanted to write so gently in this ordinary slice of life, let alone convey it.

So it would only be natural for me to dedicate this work to her. Thank you, Kristen, for opening my eyes and showing me what it means to love and feel loved.

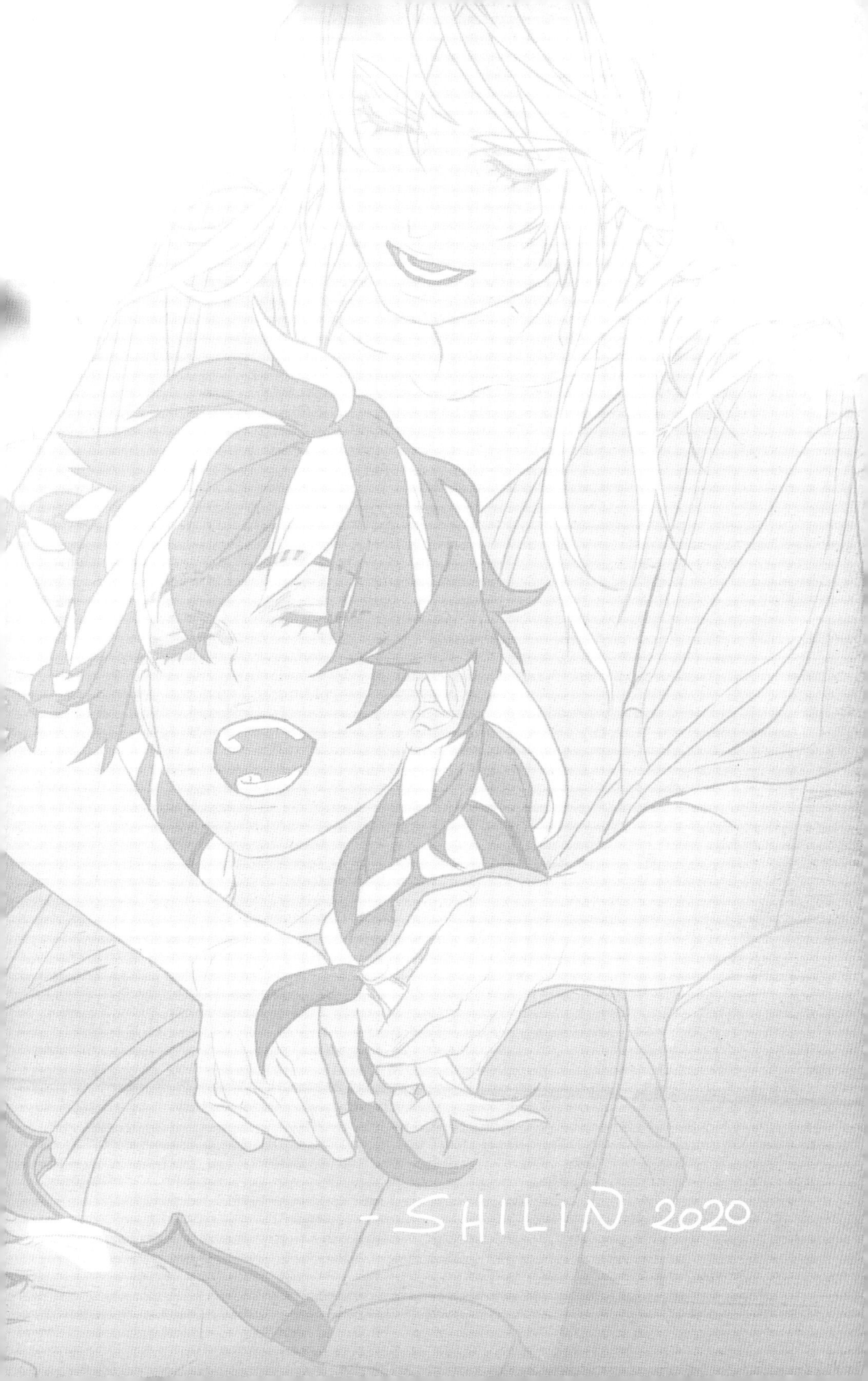
-SHILIN 2020

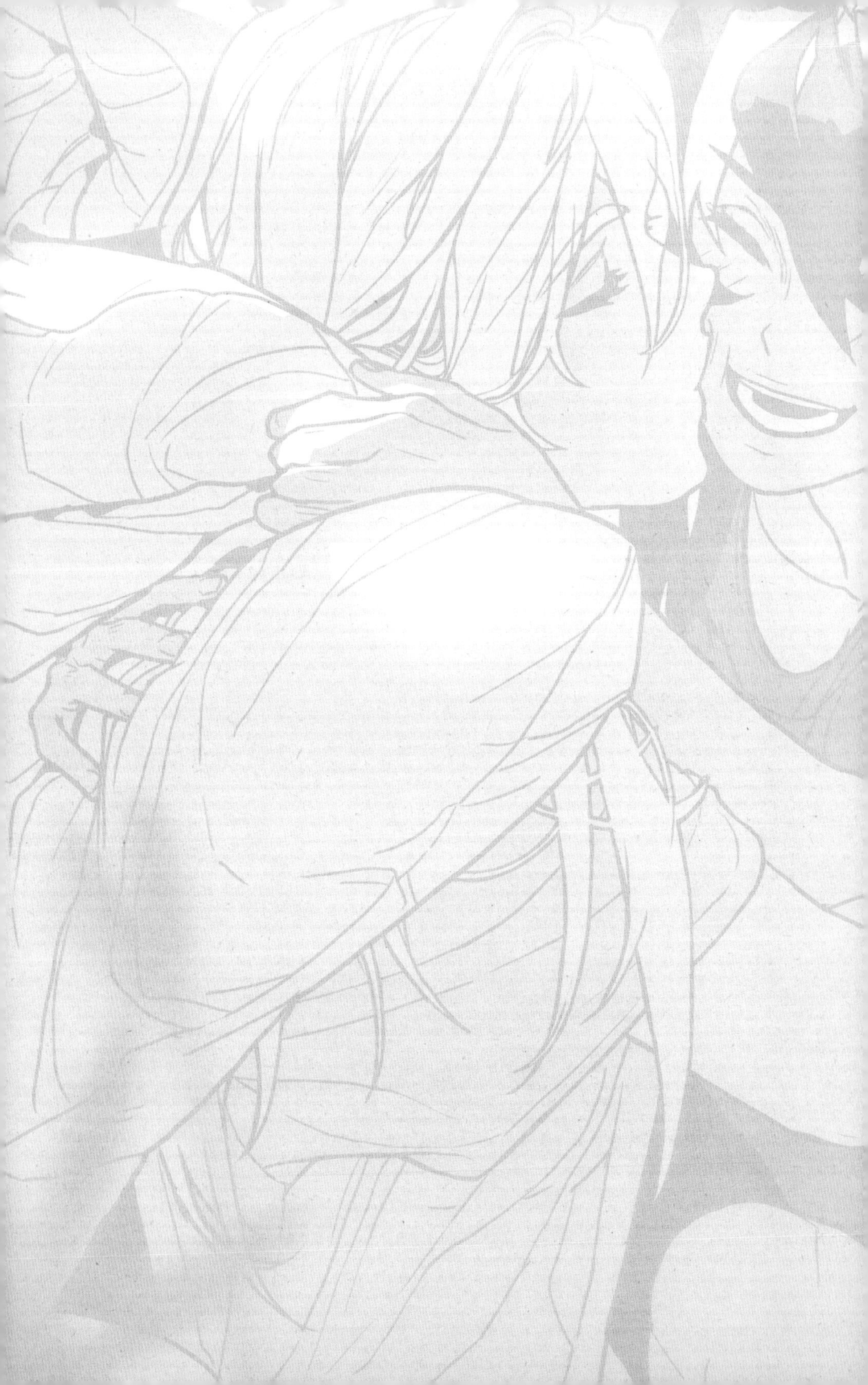

1. At the airport

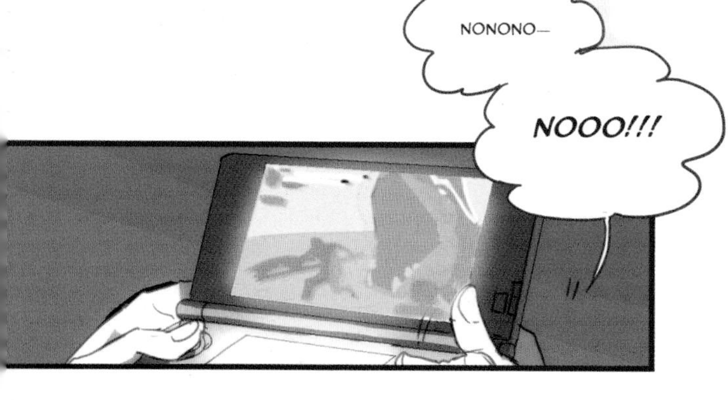
NONONO—
NOOO!!!

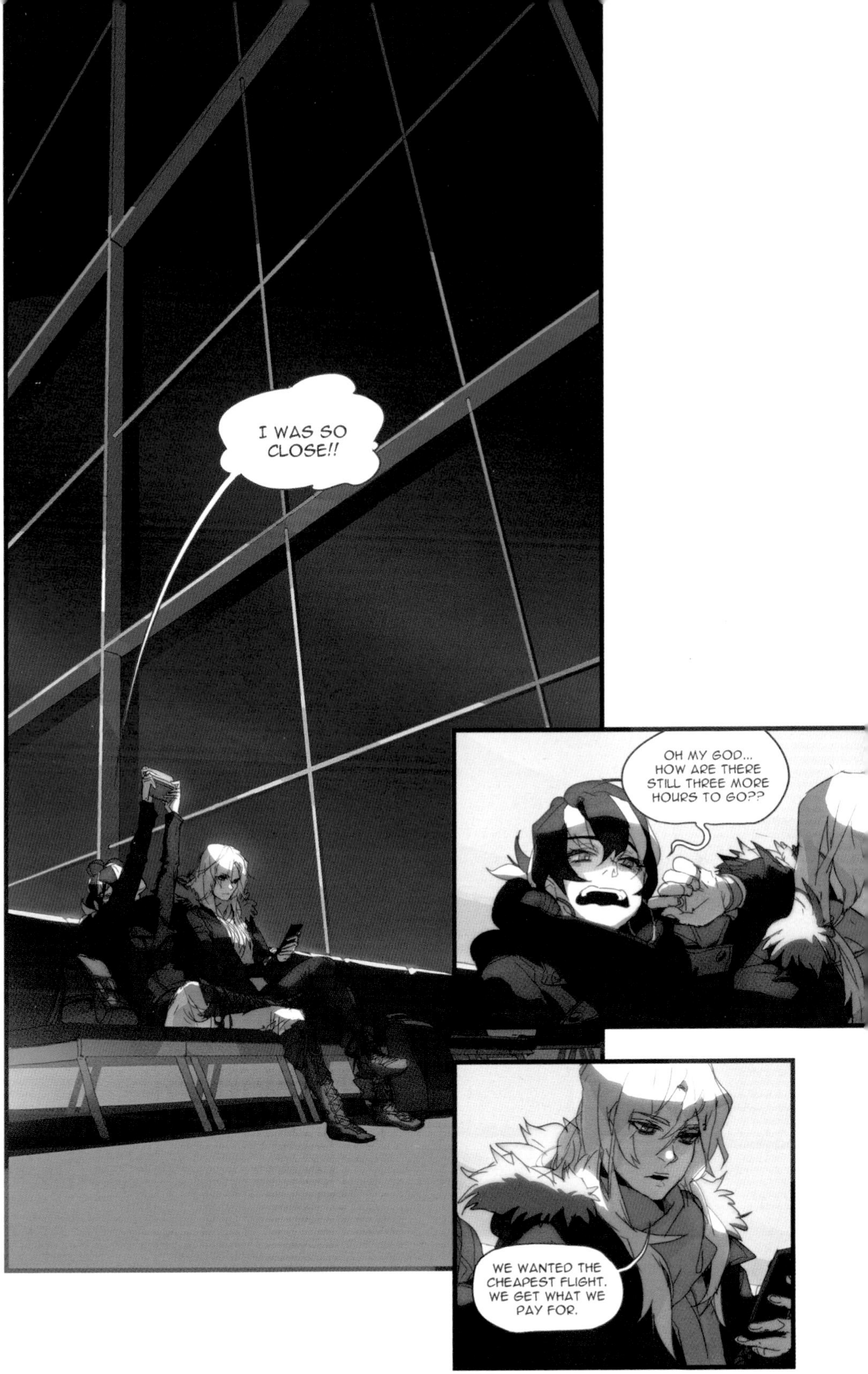
I WAS SO CLOSE!!
OH MY GOD... HOW ARE THERE STILL THREE MORE HOURS TO GO??
WE WANTED THE CHEAPEST FLIGHT. WE GET WHAT WE PAY FOR.

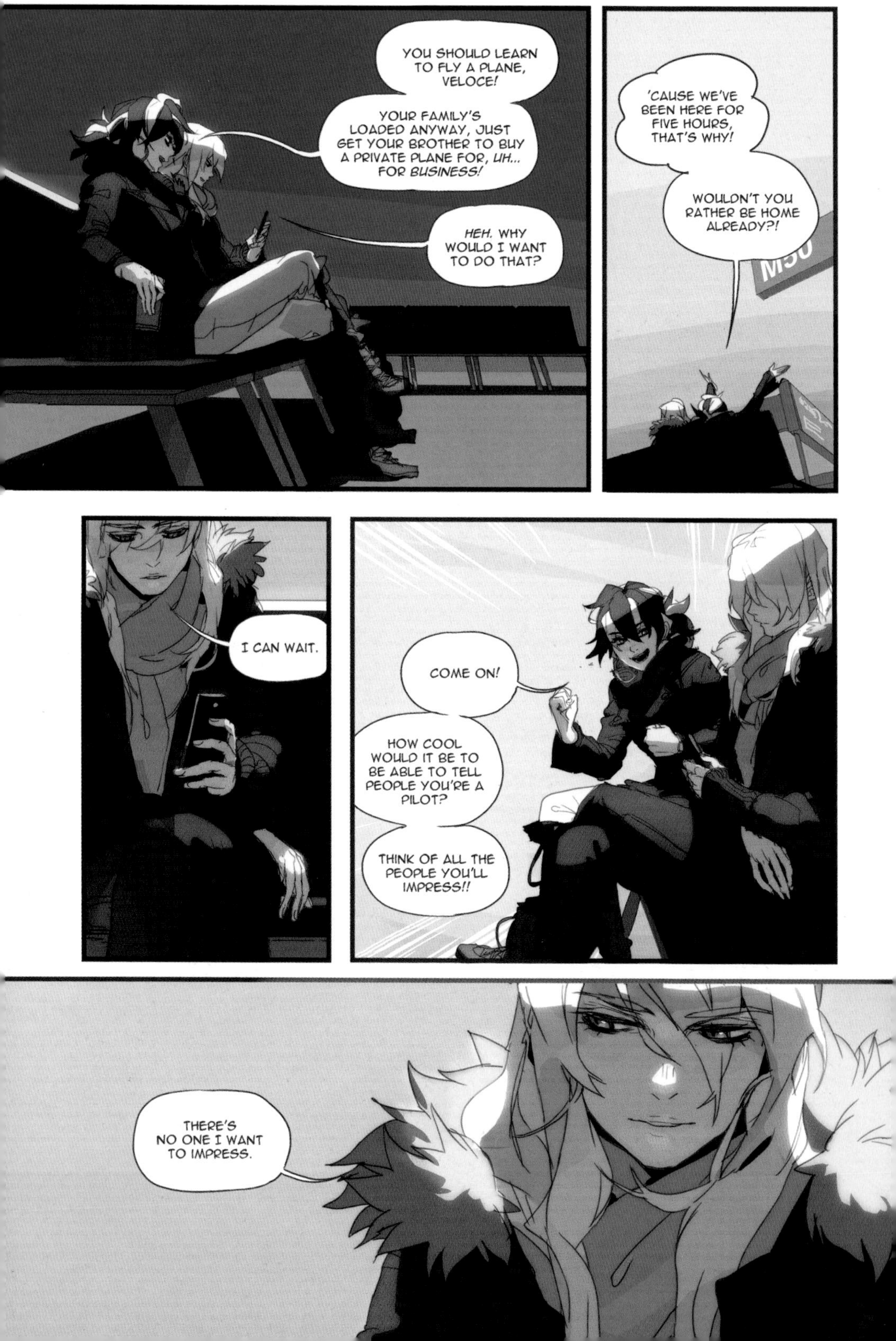
YOU SHOULD LEARN TO FLY A PLANE, VELOCE!
YOUR FAMILY'S LOADED ANYWAY, JUST GET YOUR BROTHER TO BUY A PRIVATE PLANE FOR, UH... FOR BUSINESS!
HEH. WHY WOULD I WANT TO DO THAT?
'CAUSE WE'VE BEEN HERE FOR FIVE HOURS, THAT'S WHY!
WOULDN'T YOU RATHER BE HOME ALREADY?!
I CAN WAIT.
COME ON!
HOW COOL WOULD IT BE TO BE ABLE TO TELL PEOPLE YOU'RE A PILOT?
THINK OF ALL THE PEOPLE YOU'LL IMPRESS!!
THERE'S NO ONE I WANT TO IMPRESS.

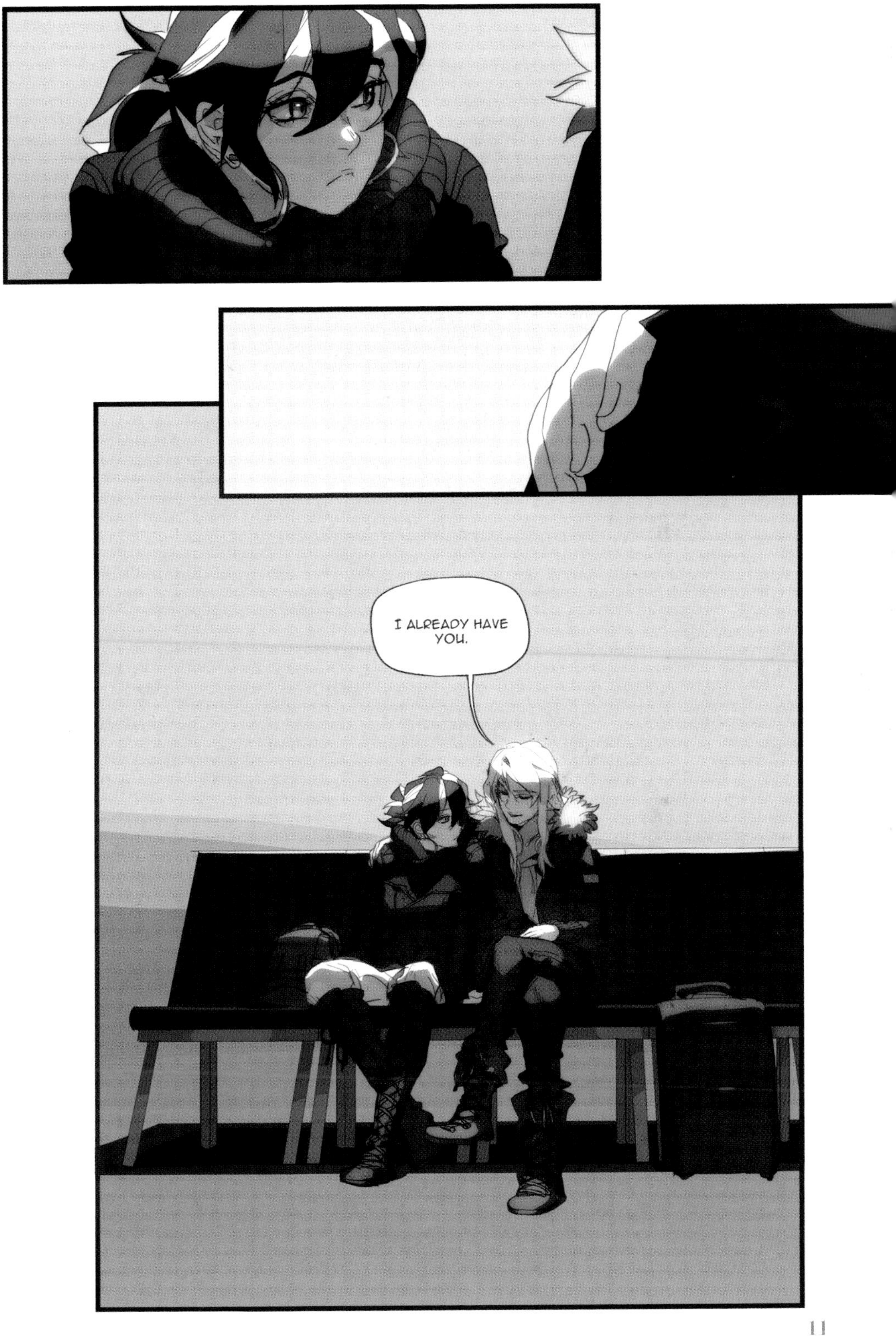
I ALREADY HAVE YOU.

2 on
the
train

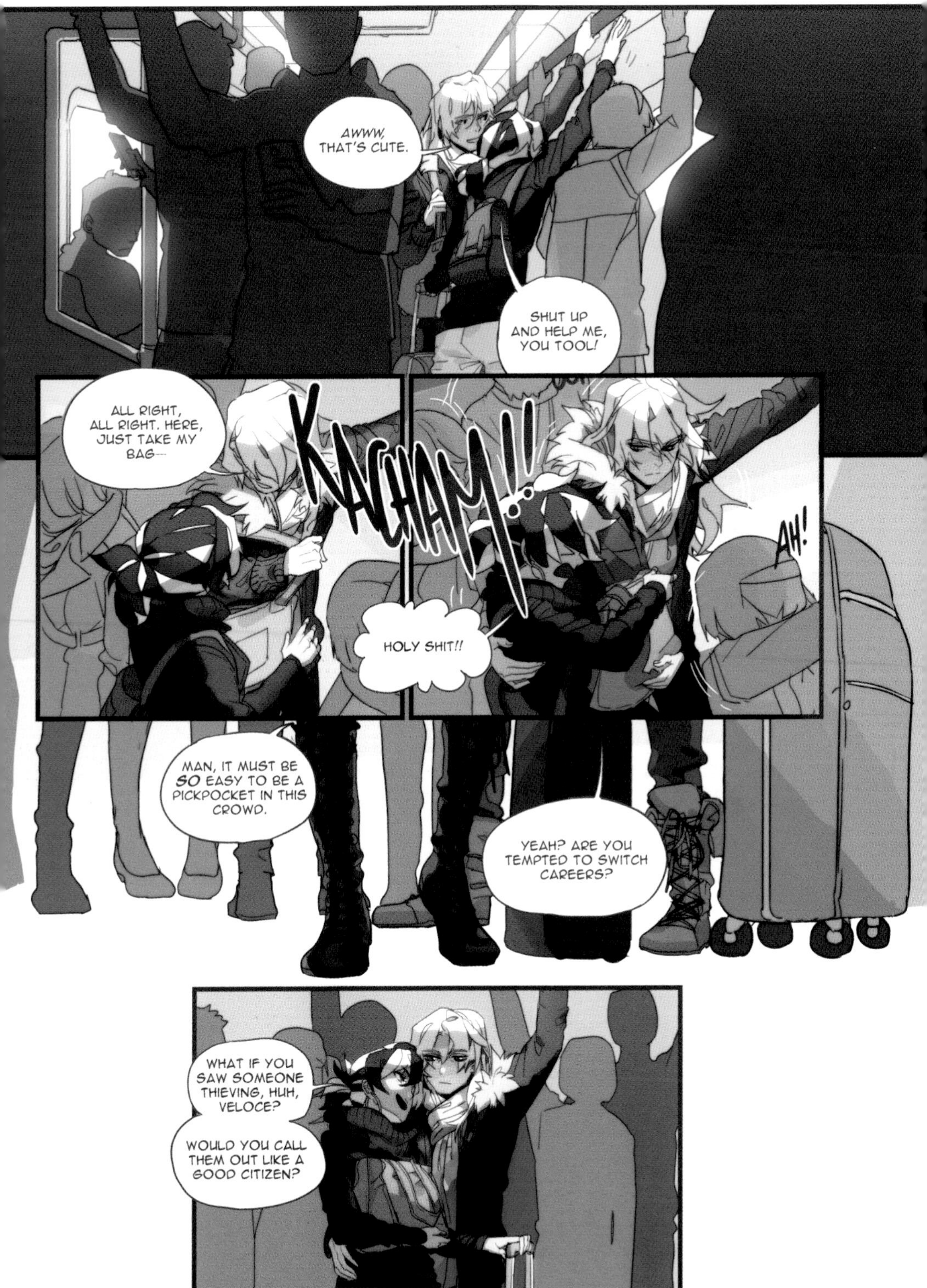
AWWW, THAT'S CUTE.
SHUT UP AND HELP ME, YOU TOOL!
ALL RIGHT, ALL RIGHT. HERE, JUST TAKE MY BAG---
KACHAM!!
HOLY SHIT!!
AH!
MAN, IT MUST BE SO EASY TO BE A PICKPOCKET IN THIS CROWD.
YEAH? ARE YOU TEMPTED TO SWITCH CAREERS?
WHAT IF YOU SAW SOMEONE THIEVING, HUH, VELOCE?
WOULD YOU CALL THEM OUT LIKE A GOOD CITIZEN?

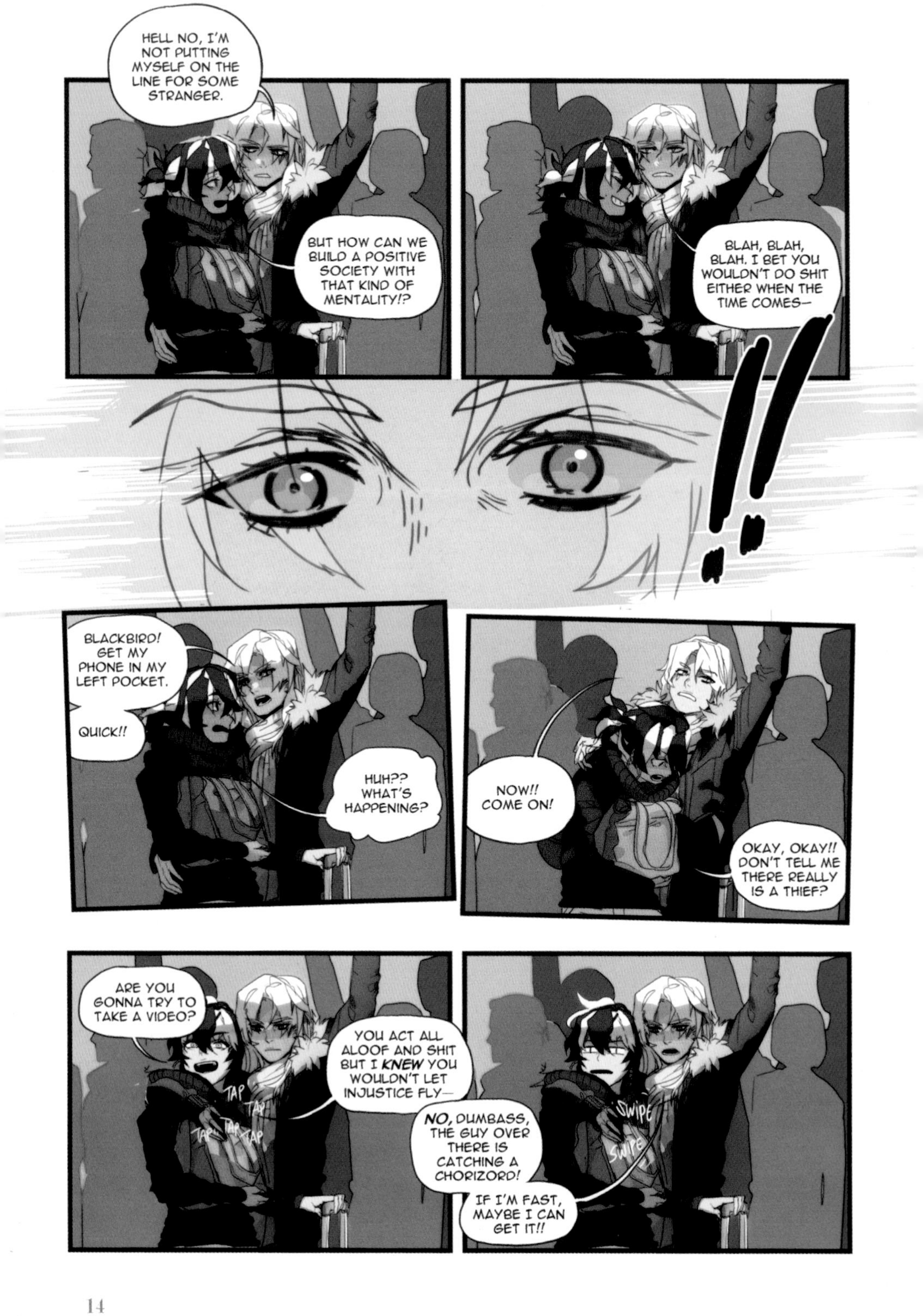
HELL NO, I'M NOT PUTTING MYSELF ON THE LINE FOR SOME STRANGER.
BUT HOW CAN WE BUILD A POSITIVE SOCIETY WITH THAT KIND OF MENTALITY!?
BLAH, BLAH, BLAH. I BET YOU WOULDN'T DO SHIT EITHER WHEN THE TIME COMES—
!!
BLACKBIRD! GET MY PHONE IN MY LEFT POCKET.
QUICK!!
HUH?? WHAT'S HAPPENING?
NOW!! COME ON!
OKAY, OKAY!! DON'T TELL ME THERE REALLY IS A THIEF?
ARE YOU GONNA TRY TO TAKE A VIDEO?
YOU ACT ALL ALOOF AND SHIT BUT I KNEW YOU WOULDN'T LET INJUSTICE FLY—
TAP TAP TAP TAP TAP
NO, DUMBASS, THE GUY OVER THERE IS CATCHING A CHORIZORD!
IF I'M FAST, MAYBE I CAN GET IT!!
SWIPE SWIPE

2. Home

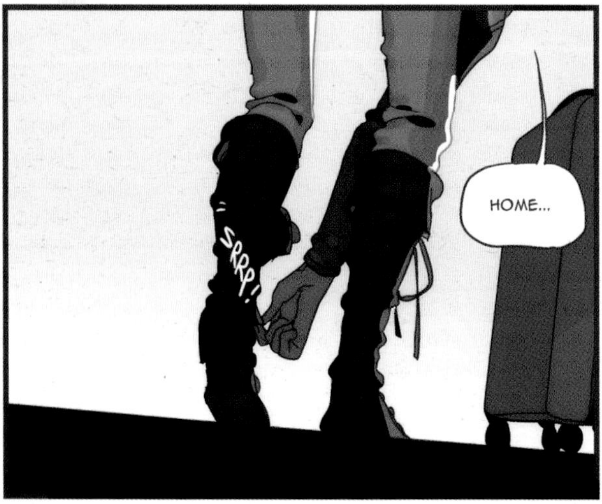
SRRP!
HOME...

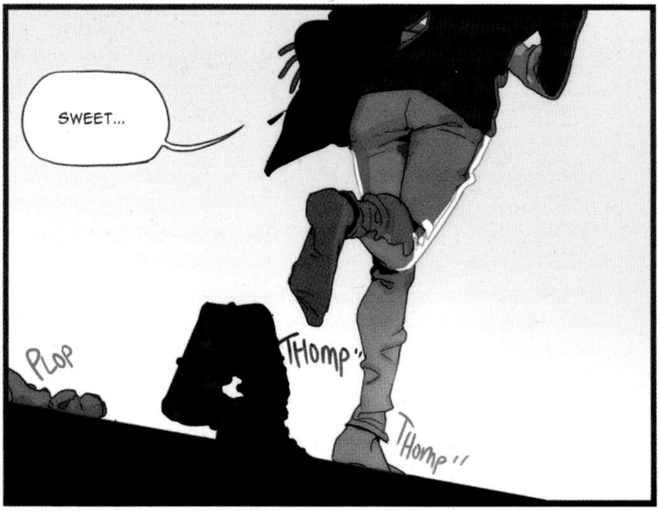
SWEET...
PLOP
THOMP
THOMP

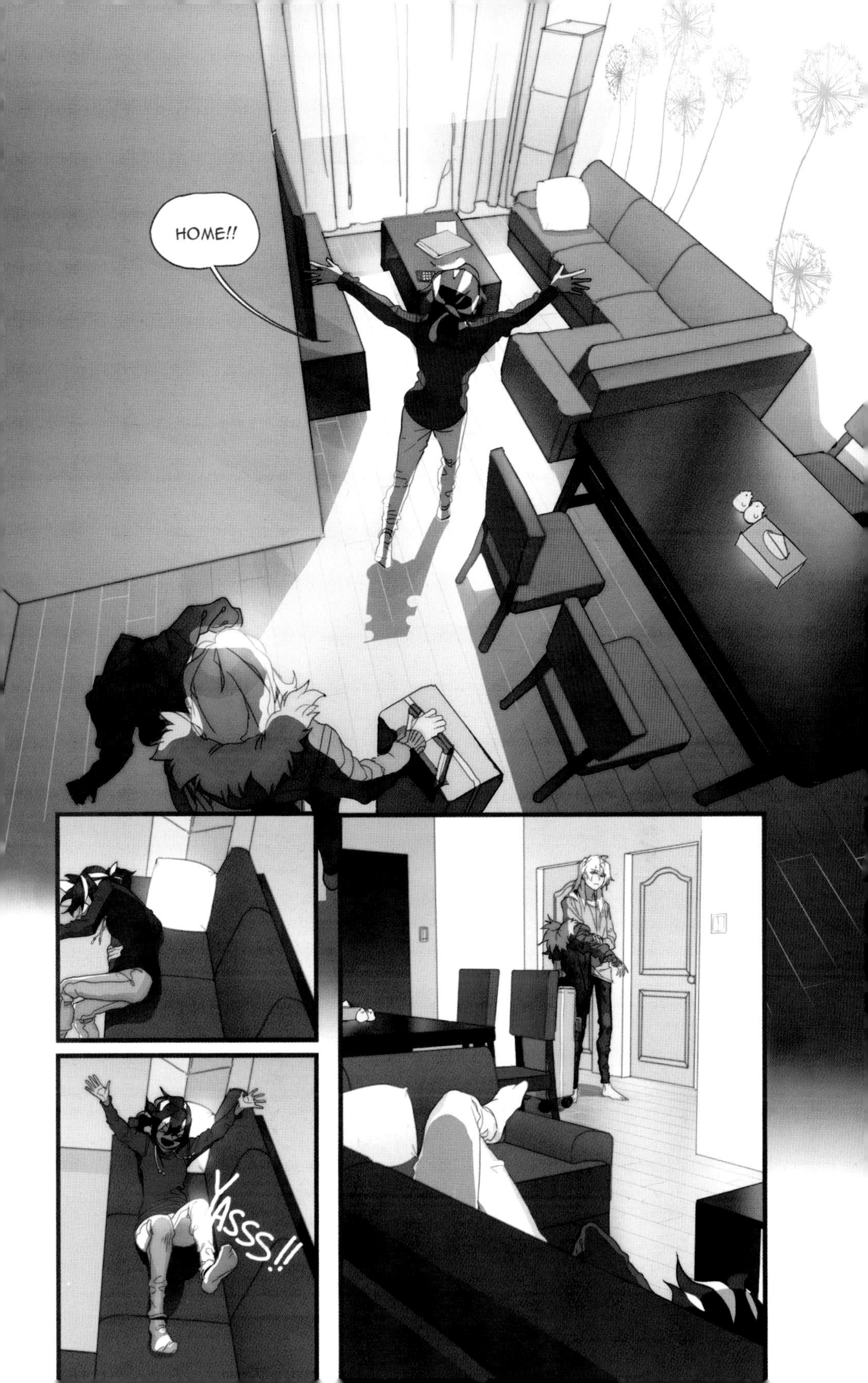
HOME!!
YASSS!!

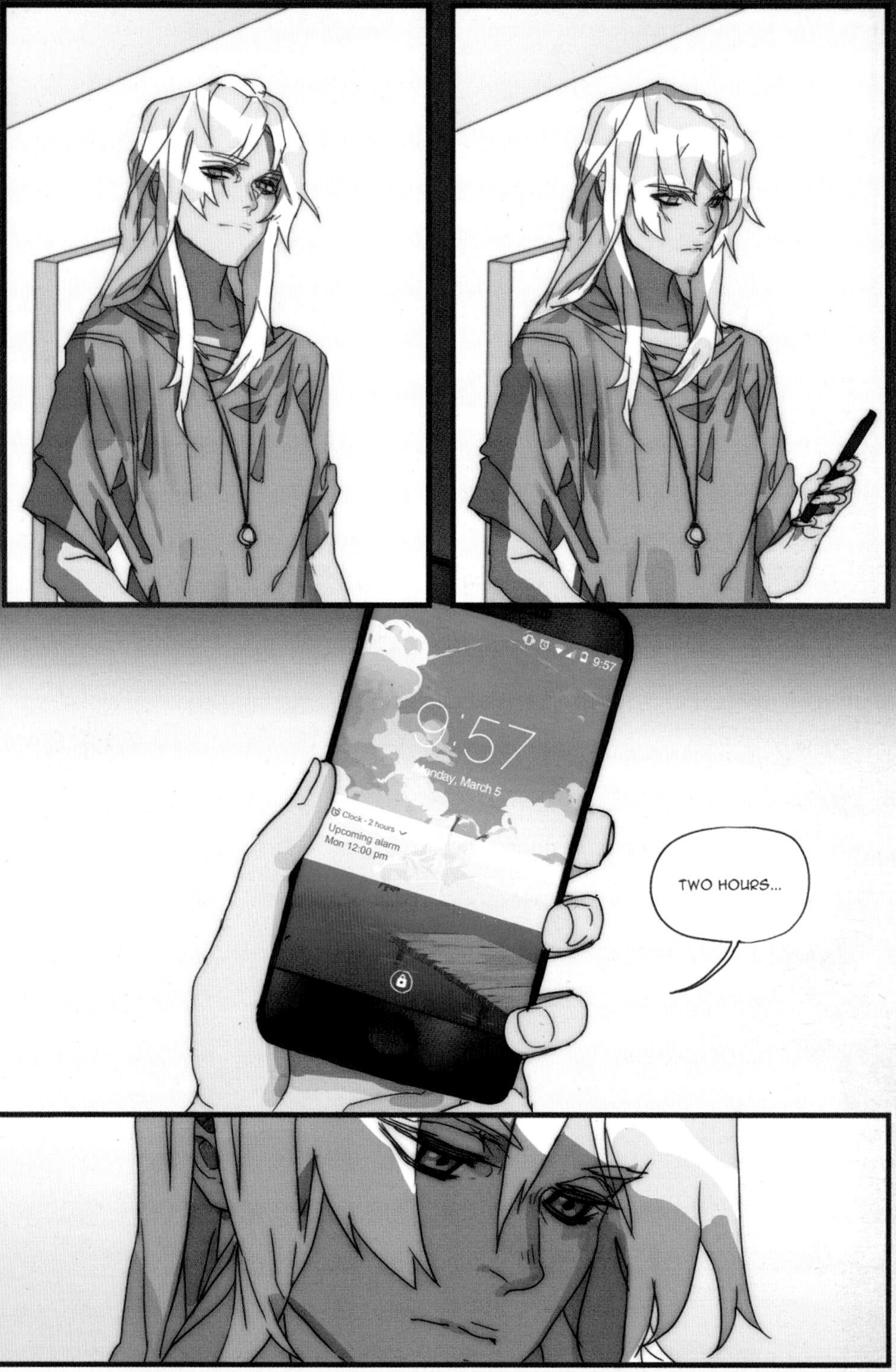
9:57
9:57
Monday, March 5
Clock · 2 hours
Upcoming alarm
Mon 12:00 pm
TWO HOURS...

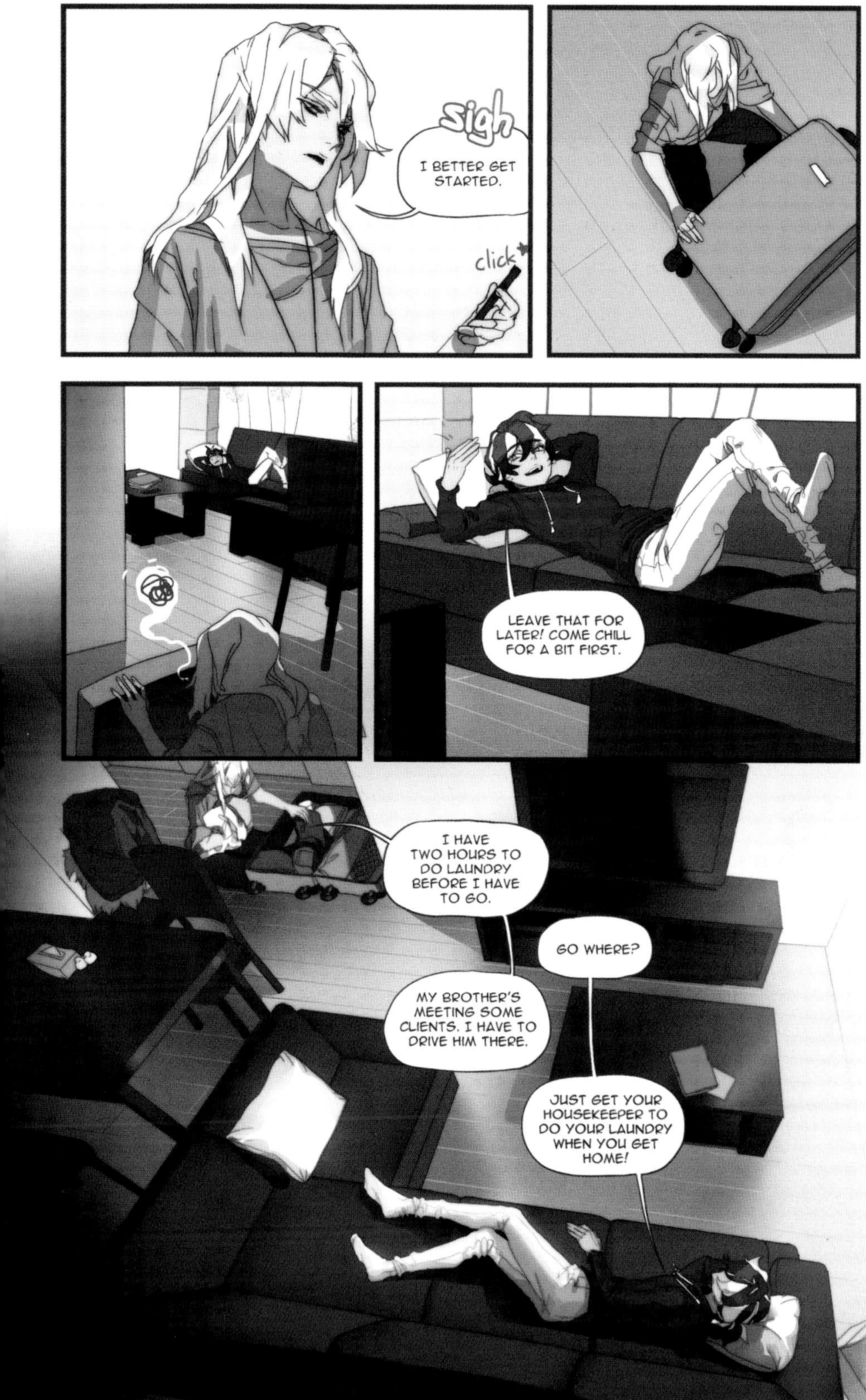
sigh
I BETTER GET STARTED.
click
LEAVE THAT FOR LATER! COME CHILL FOR A BIT FIRST.
I HAVE TWO HOURS TO DO LAUNDRY BEFORE I HAVE TO GO.
GO WHERE?
MY BROTHER'S MEETING SOME CLIENTS. I HAVE TO DRIVE HIM THERE.
JUST GET YOUR HOUSEKEEPER TO DO YOUR LAUNDRY WHEN YOU GET HOME!

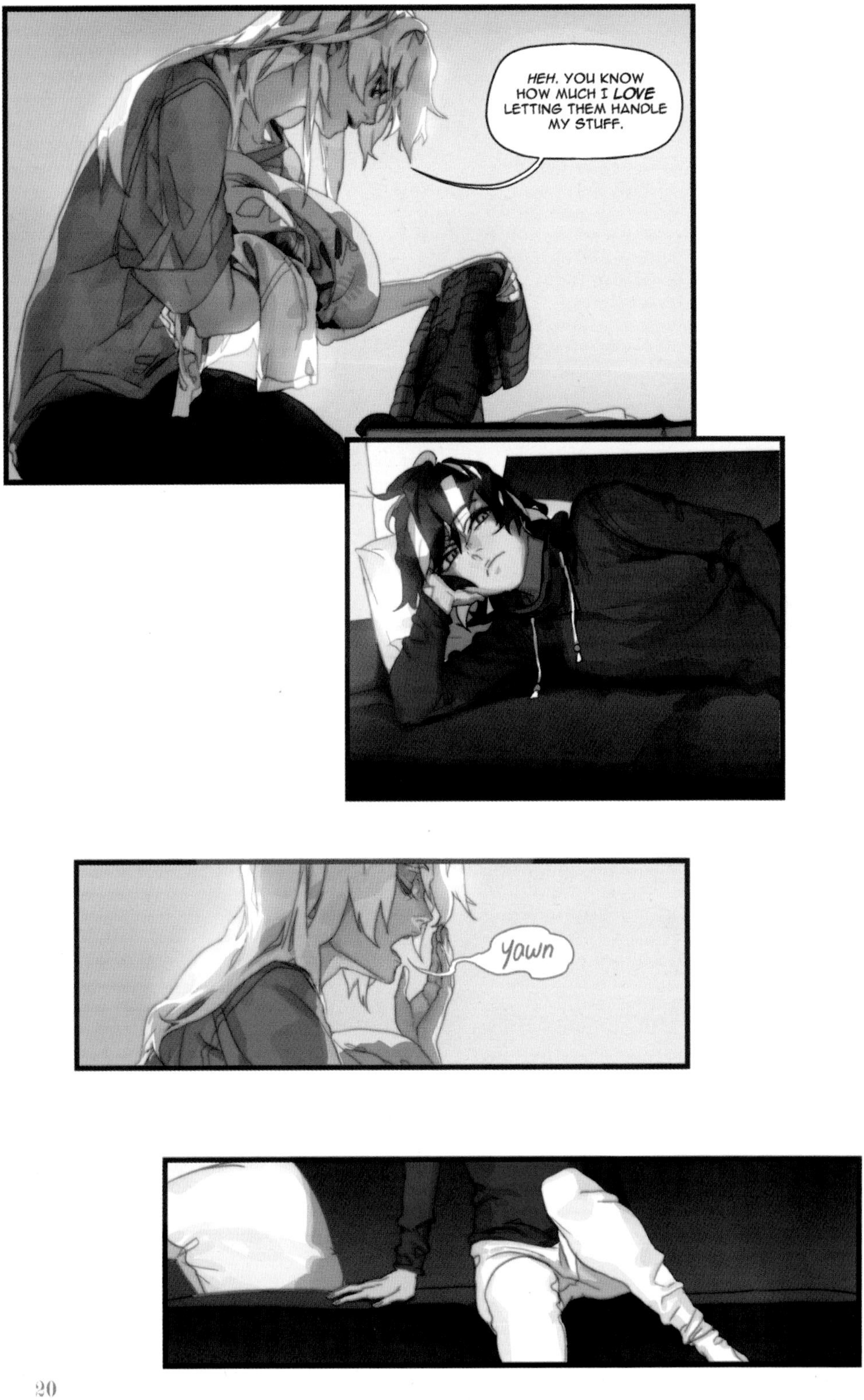
HEH. YOU KNOW HOW MUCH I LOVE LETTING THEM HANDLE MY STUFF.
yawn

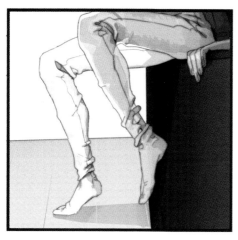

GIVE THAT TO ME.

I'LL HELP YOU JUST THIS ONCE.

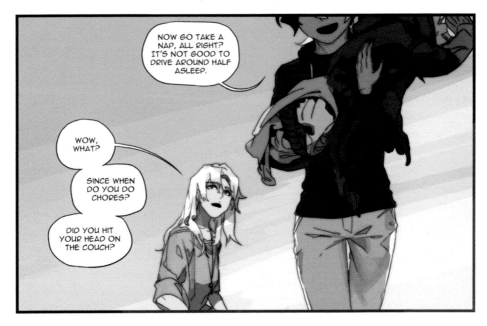

NOW GO TAKE A NAP, ALL RIGHT? IT'S NOT GOOD TO DRIVE AROUND HALF ASLEEP.

WOW, WHAT?

SINCE WHEN DO YOU DO CHORES?

DID YOU HIT YOUR HEAD ON THE COUCH?

YOU WANNA SAY THAT AGAIN?

?!!! HEY!!!

MY CLOTHES!!

yank

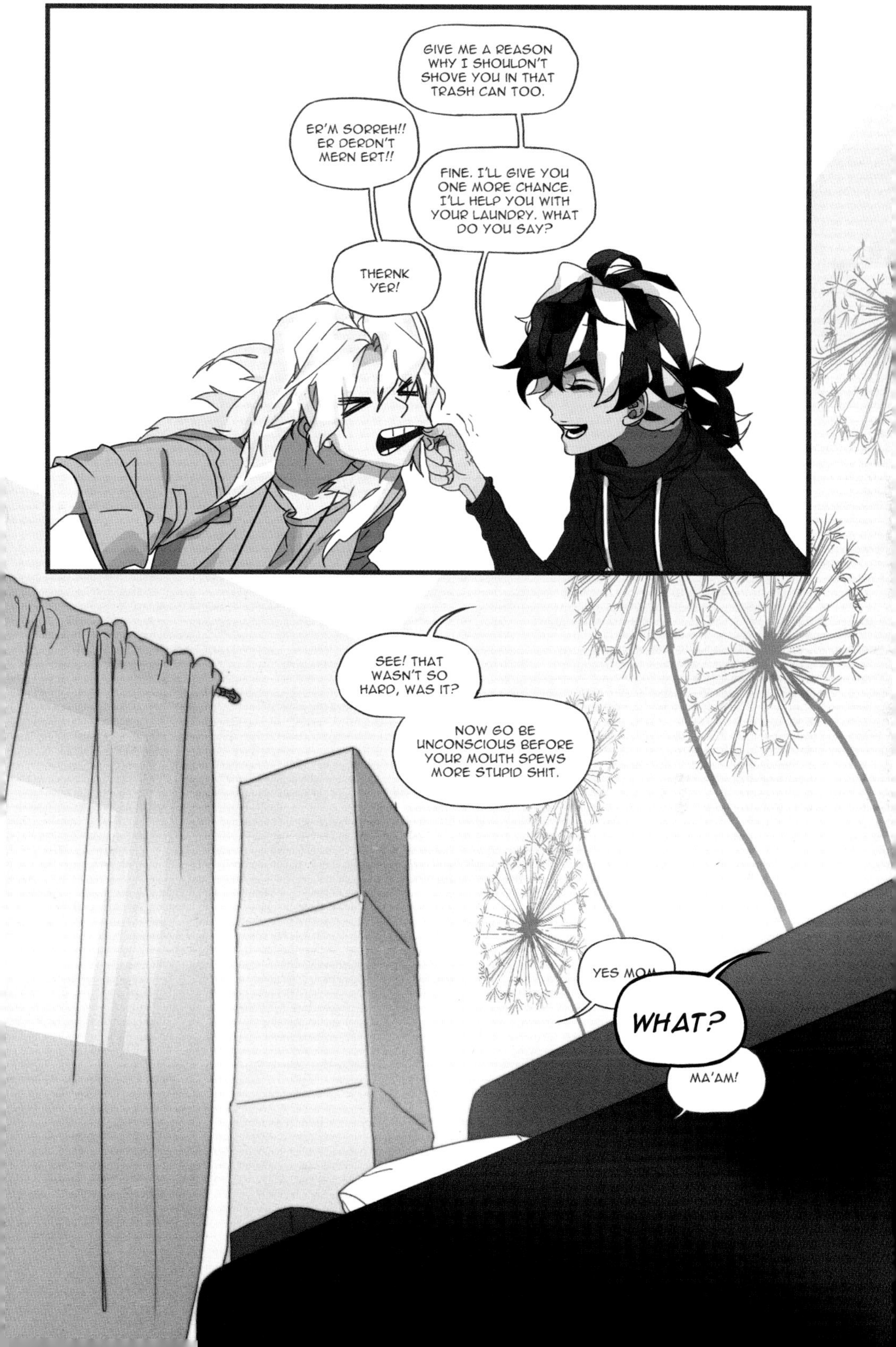
GIVE ME A REASON WHY I SHOULDN'T SHOVE YOU IN THAT TRASH CAN TOO.
ER'M SORREH!! ER DERDN'T MERN ERT!!
FINE. I'LL GIVE YOU ONE MORE CHANCE. I'LL HELP YOU WITH YOUR LAUNDRY. WHAT DO YOU SAY?
THERNK YER!
SEE! THAT WASN'T SO HARD, WAS IT?
NOW GO BE UNCONSCIOUS BEFORE YOUR MOUTH SPEWS MORE STUPID SHIT.
YES MOM
WHAT?
MA'AM!

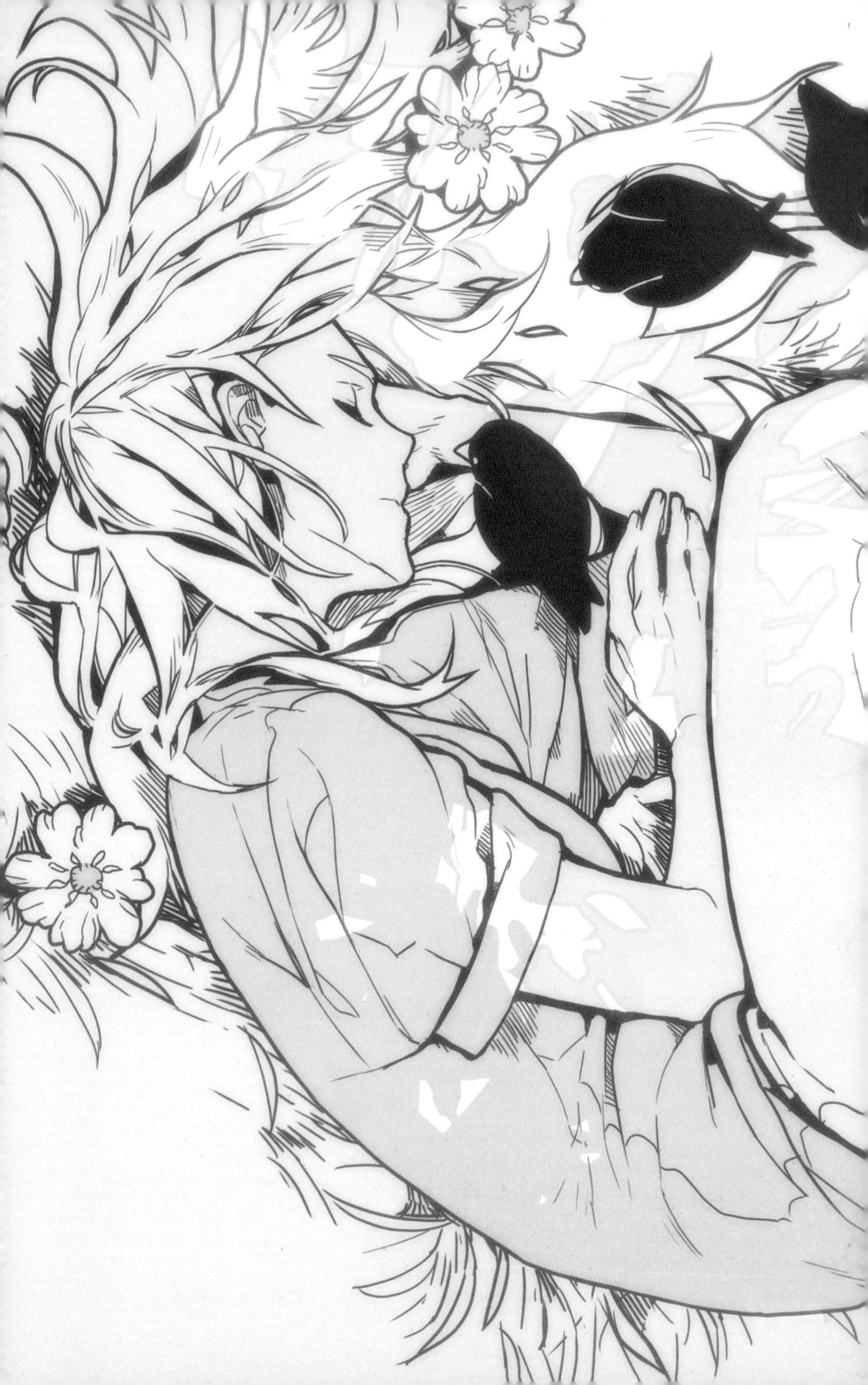

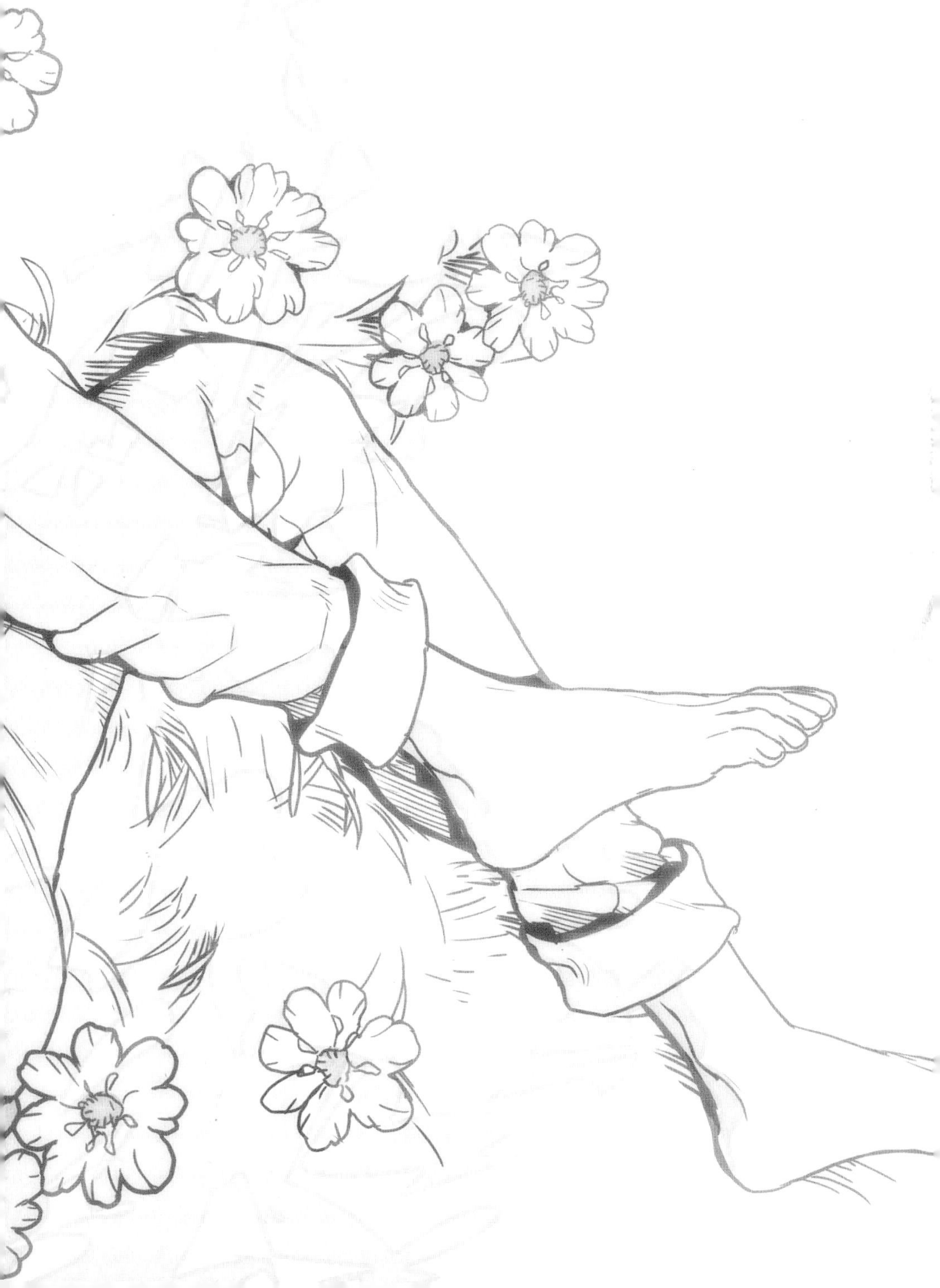

VELOCE~!

VELOCE, IT'S NOON~!

TIME TO GET UP!

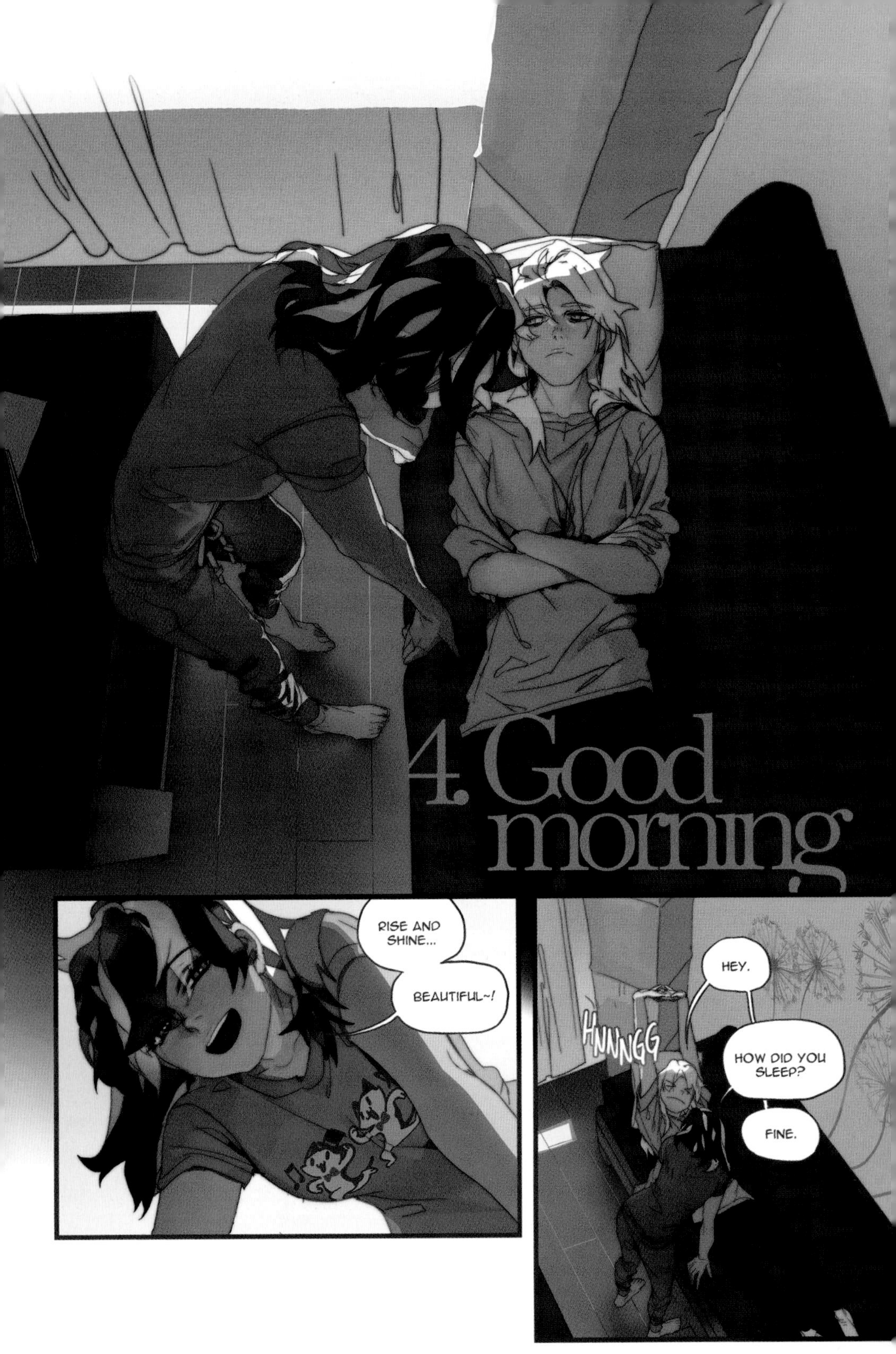
4. Good morning
RISE AND SHINE...
BEAUTIFUL~!
HNNNGG
HEY.
HOW DID YOU SLEEP?
FINE.

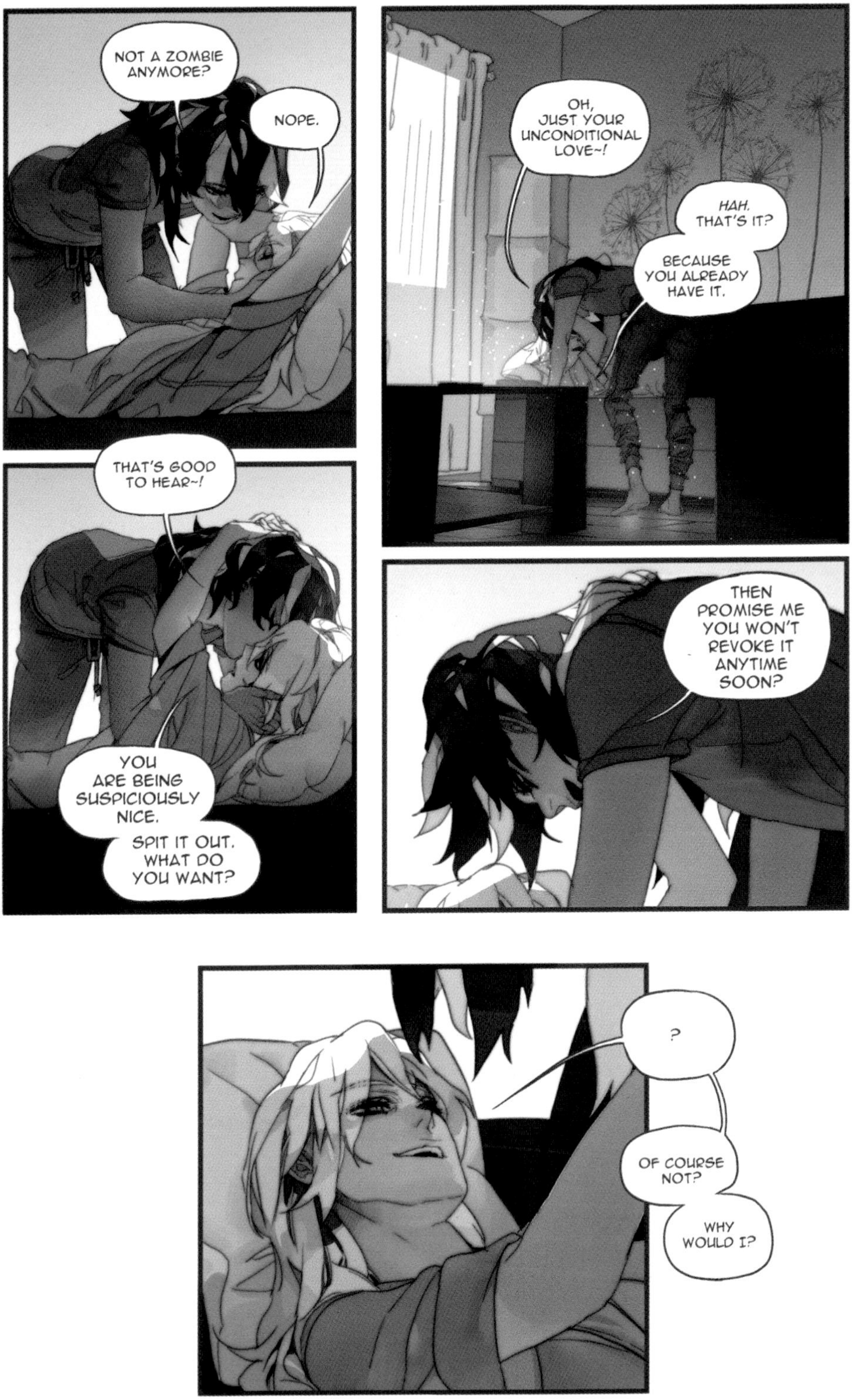
NOT A ZOMBIE ANYMORE?
NOPE.
OH, JUST YOUR UNCONDITIONAL LOVE~!
HAH. THAT'S IT?
BECAUSE YOU ALREADY HAVE IT.
THAT'S GOOD TO HEAR~!
YOU ARE BEING SUSPICIOUSLY NICE.
SPIT IT OUT. WHAT DO YOU WANT?
THEN PROMISE ME YOU WON'T REVOKE IT ANYTIME SOON?
?
OF COURSE NOT?
WHY WOULD I?

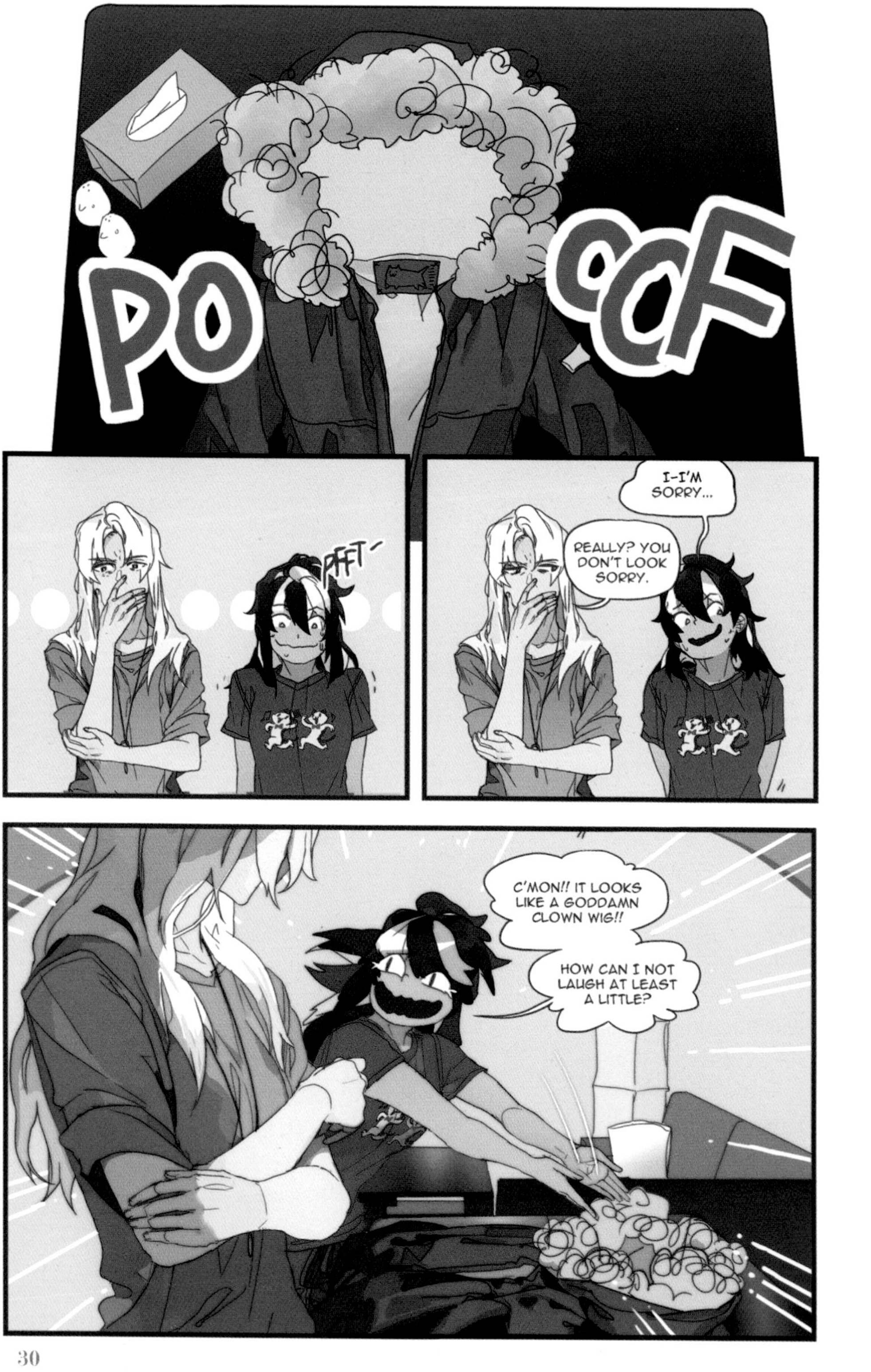
POOF
PFFT-
I-I'M SORRY...
REALLY? YOU DON'T LOOK SORRY.
C'MON!! IT LOOKS LIKE A GODDAMN CLOWN WIG!!
HOW CAN I NOT LAUGH AT LEAST A LITTLE?

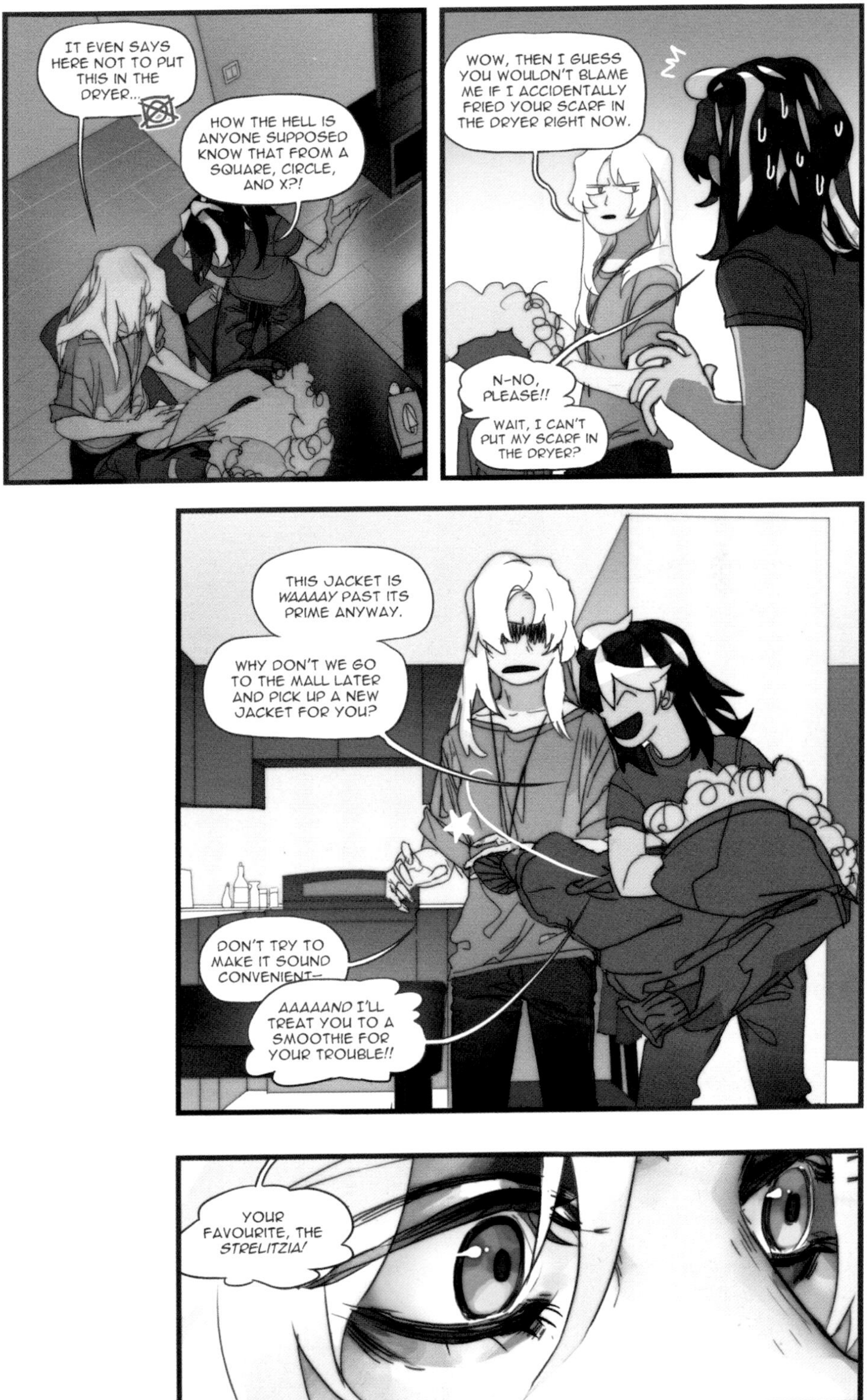
IT EVEN SAYS HERE NOT TO PUT THIS IN THE DRYER...
HOW THE HELL IS ANYONE SUPPOSED KNOW THAT FROM A SQUARE, CIRCLE, AND X?!
WOW, THEN I GUESS YOU WOULDN'T BLAME ME IF I ACCIDENTALLY FRIED YOUR SCARF IN THE DRYER RIGHT NOW.
N-NO, PLEASE!!
WAIT, I CAN'T PUT MY SCARF IN THE DRYER?
THIS JACKET IS WAAAAY PAST ITS PRIME ANYWAY.
WHY DON'T WE GO TO THE MALL LATER AND PICK UP A NEW JACKET FOR YOU?
DON'T TRY TO MAKE IT SOUND CONVENIENT–
AAAAAND I'LL TREAT YOU TO A SMOOTHIE FOR YOUR TROUBLE!!
YOUR FAVOURITE, THE STRELITZIA!

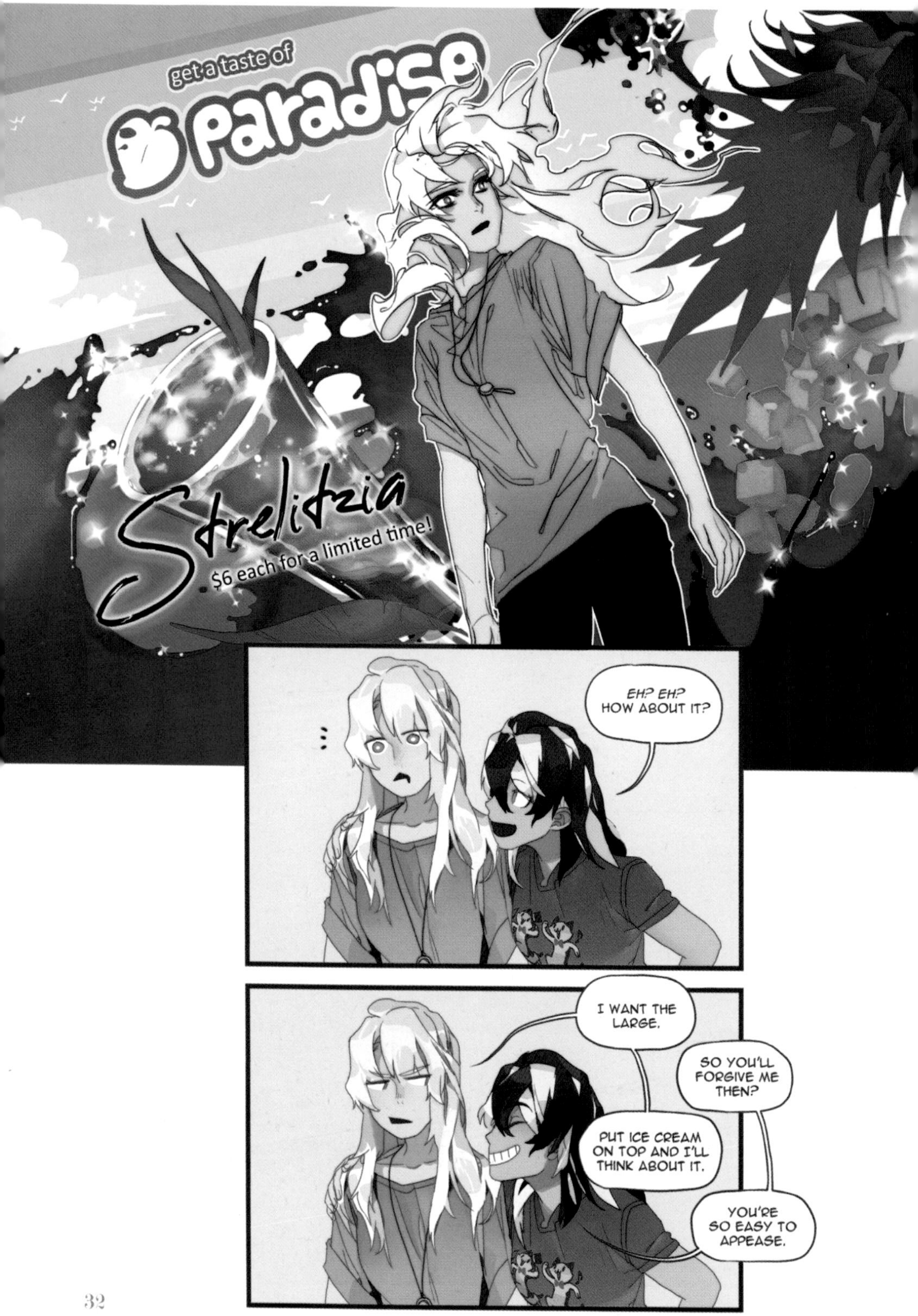
get a taste of
paradise
Strelitzia
$6 each for a limited time!
EH? EH? HOW ABOUT IT?
I WANT THE LARGE.
SO YOU'LL FORGIVE ME THEN?
PUT ICE CREAM ON TOP AND I'LL THINK ABOUT IT.
YOU'RE SO EASY TO APPEASE.

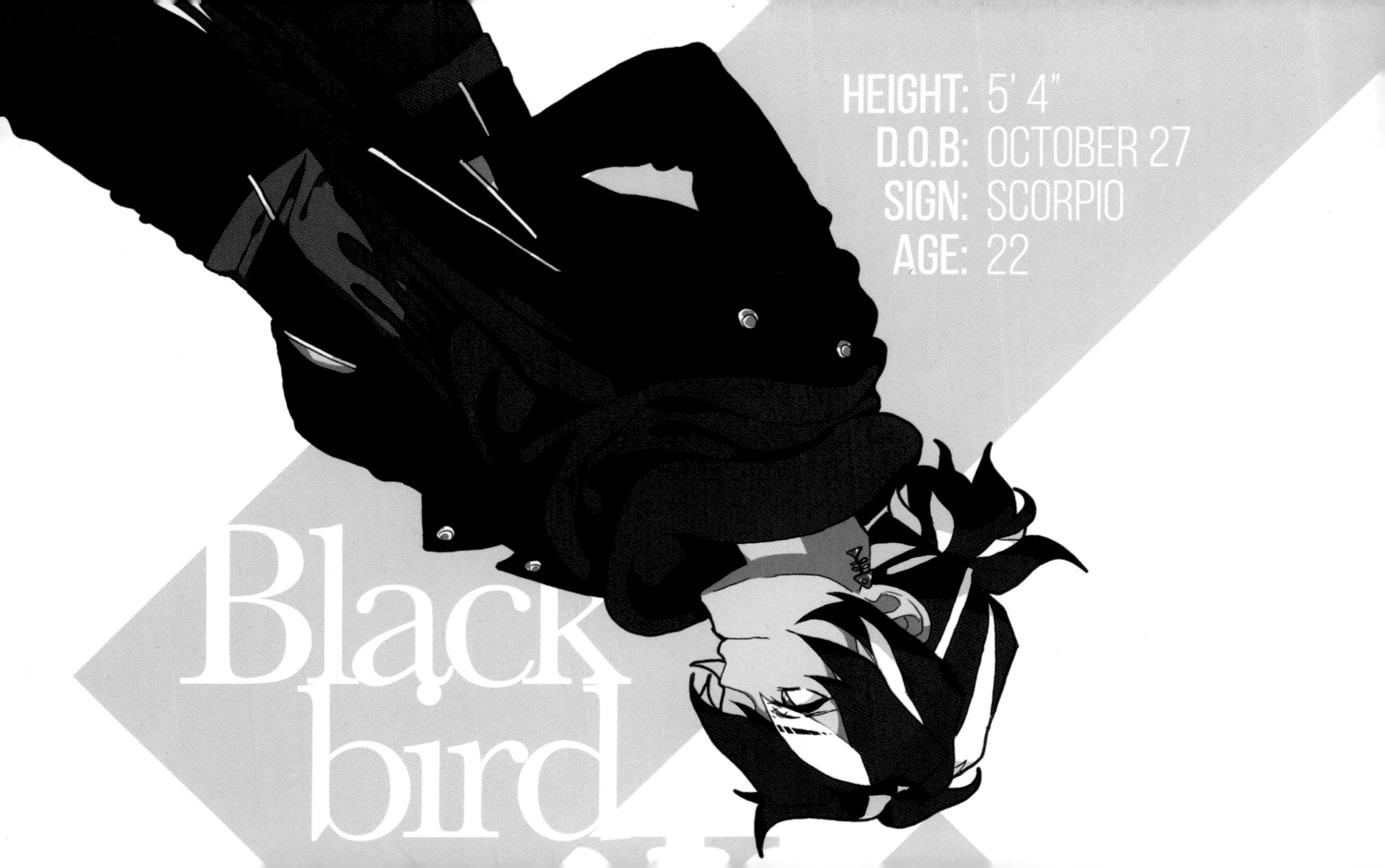
HEIGHT: 5' 4"
D.O.B: OCTOBER 27
SIGN: SCORPIO
AGE: 22
Black
bird

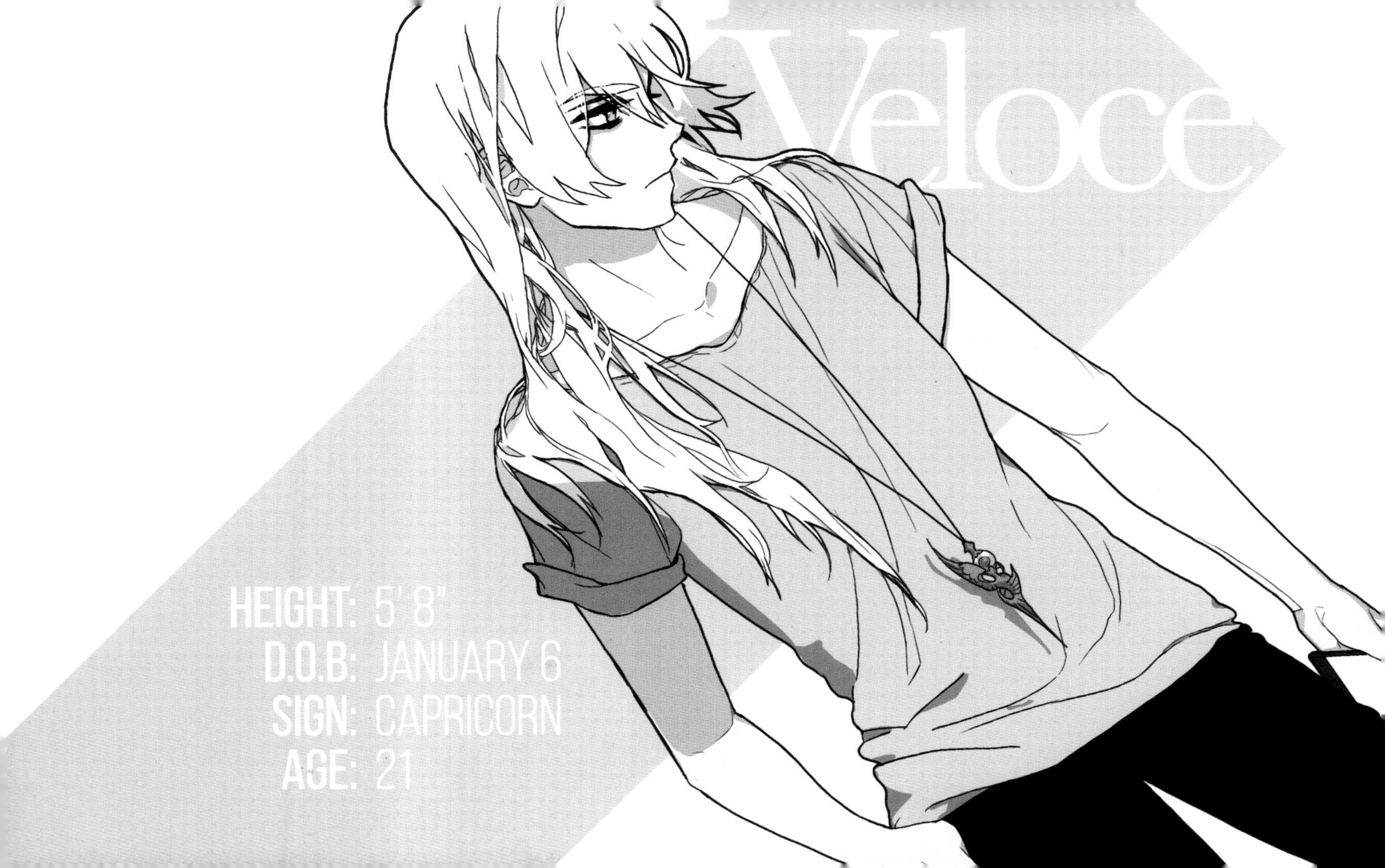
Veloce
HEIGHT: 5' 8"
D.O.B: JANUARY 6
SIGN: CAPRICORN
AGE: 21

5. At the mall

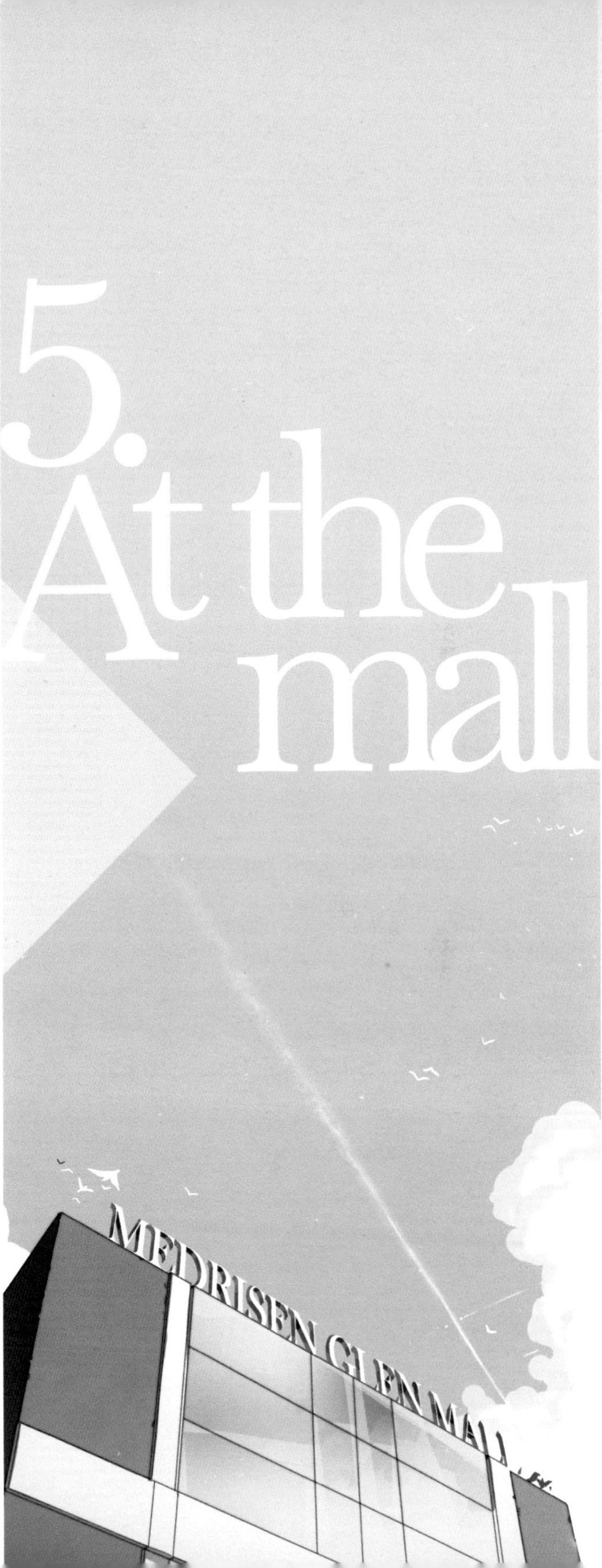
MEDRISEN GLEN MALL

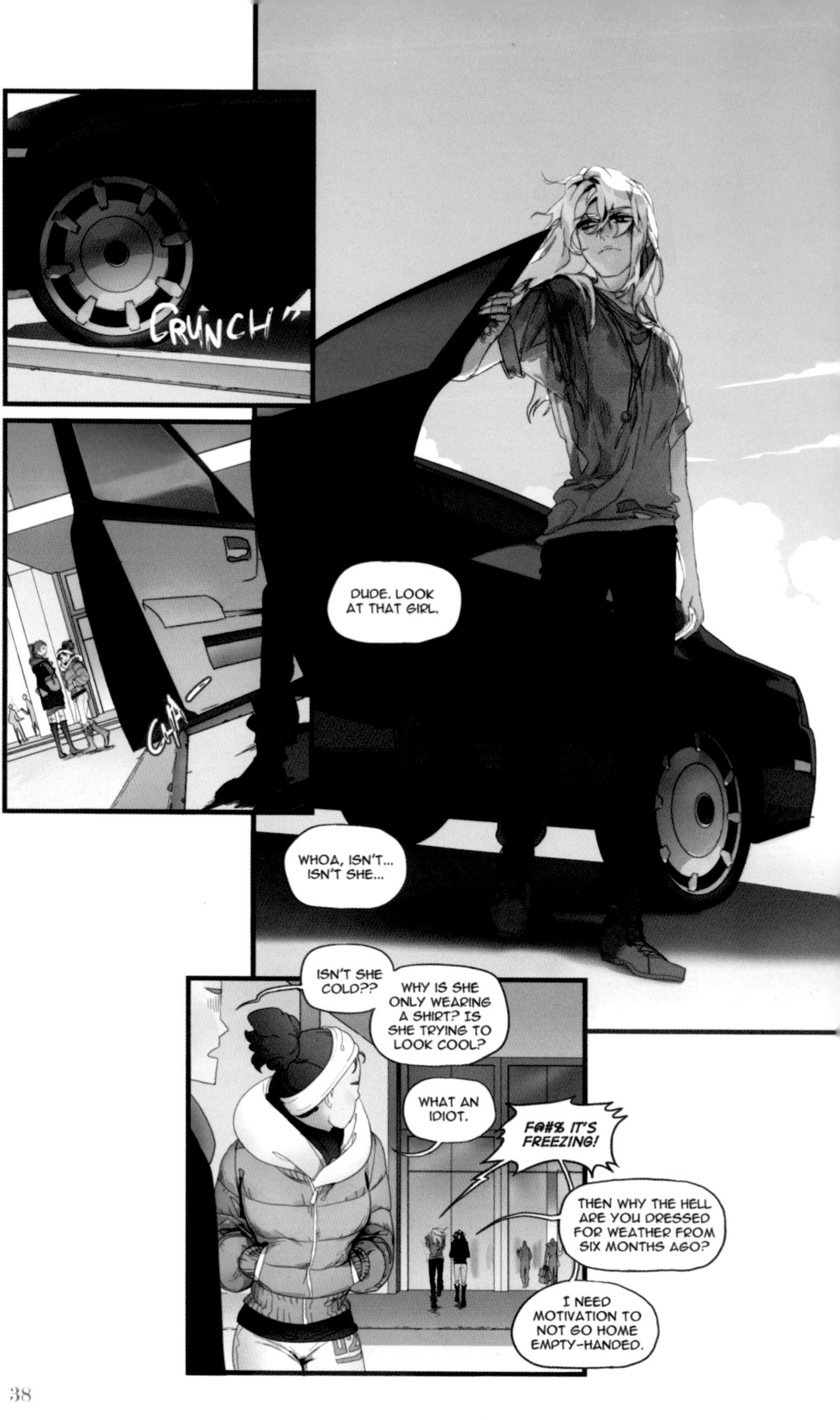
CRUNCH
CHA
DUDE. LOOK AT THAT GIRL.
WHOA, ISN'T... ISN'T SHE...
ISN'T SHE COLD??
WHY IS SHE ONLY WEARING A SHIRT? IS SHE TRYING TO LOOK COOL?
WHAT AN IDIOT.
F@#% IT'S FREEZING!
THEN WHY THE HELL ARE YOU DRESSED FOR WEATHER FROM SIX MONTHS AGO?
I NEED MOTIVATION TO NOT GO HOME EMPTY-HANDED.

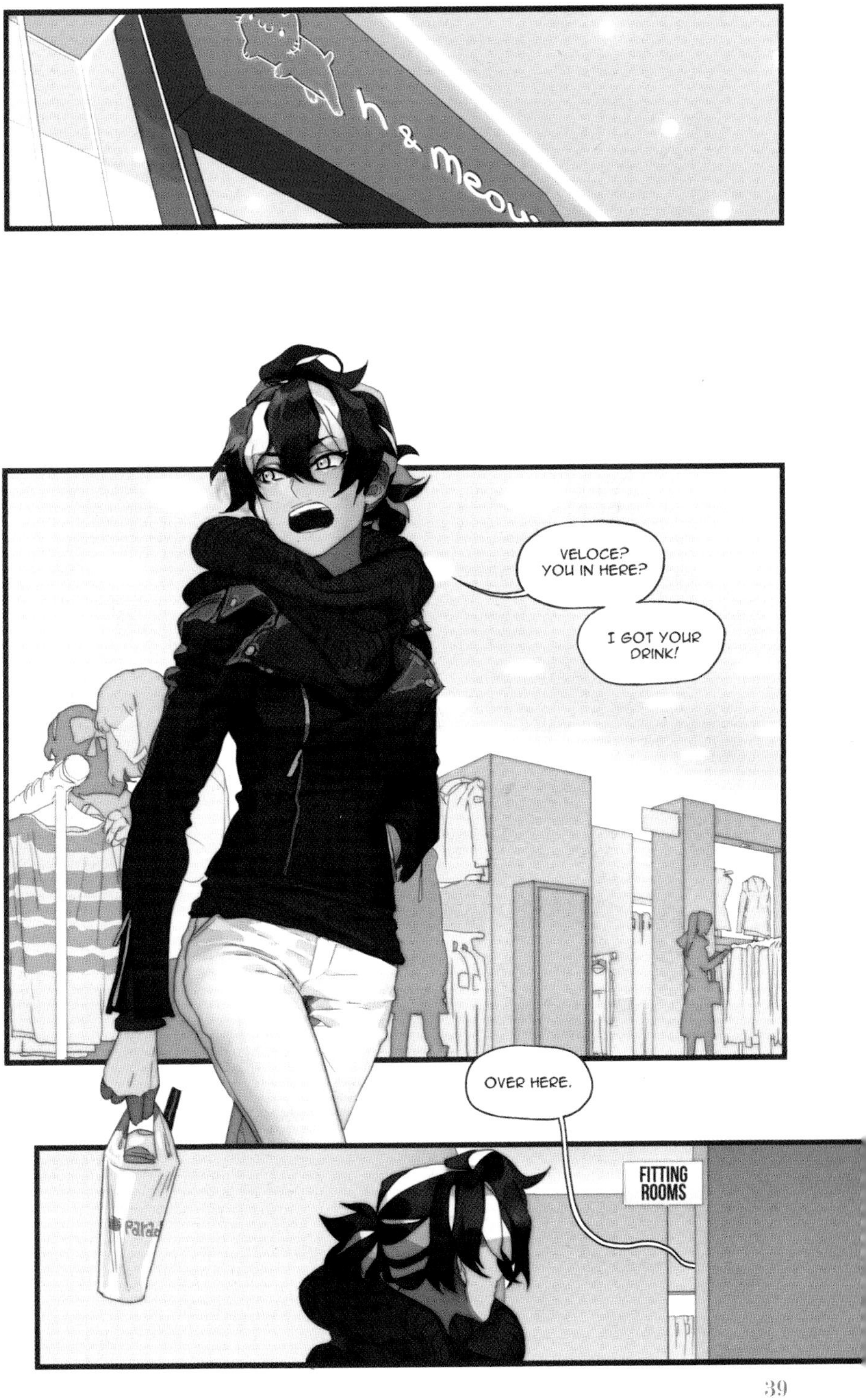
h & meow
VELOCE? YOU IN HERE?
I GOT YOUR DRINK!
OVER HERE.
FITTING ROOMS

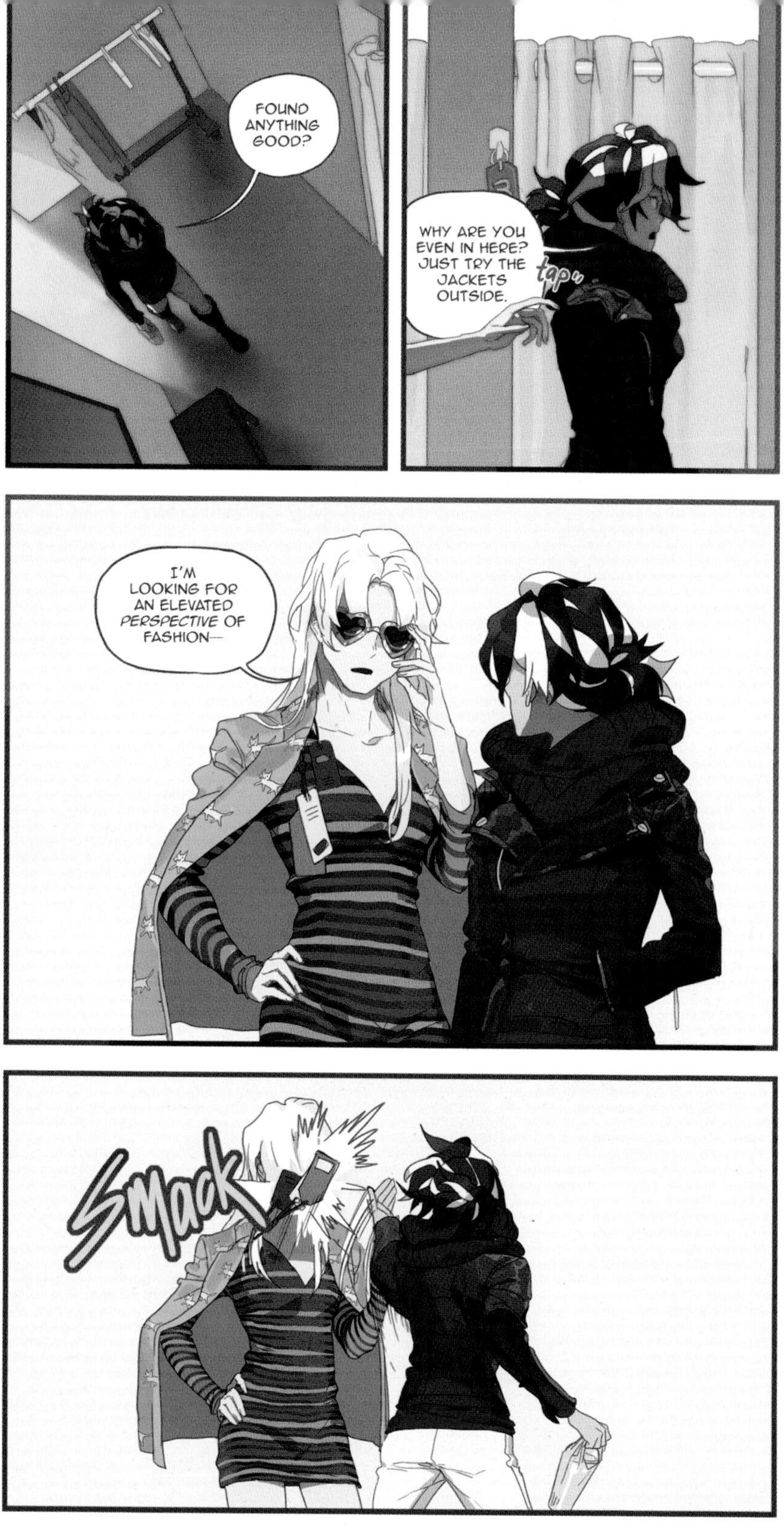
FOUND ANYTHING GOOD?
WHY ARE YOU EVEN IN HERE? JUST TRY THE JACKETS OUTSIDE.
tap
I'M LOOKING FOR AN ELEVATED PERSPECTIVE OF FASHION—
SMACK

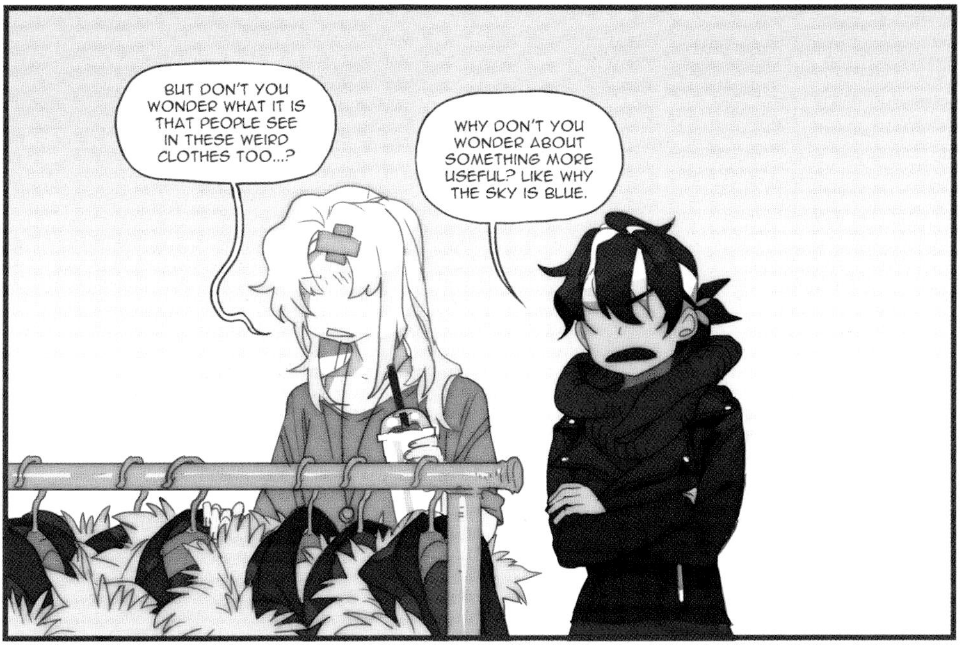
BUT DON'T YOU WONDER WHAT IT IS THAT PEOPLE SEE IN THESE WEIRD CLOTHES TOO...?
WHY DON'T YOU WONDER ABOUT SOMETHING MORE USEFUL? LIKE WHY THE SKY IS BLUE.

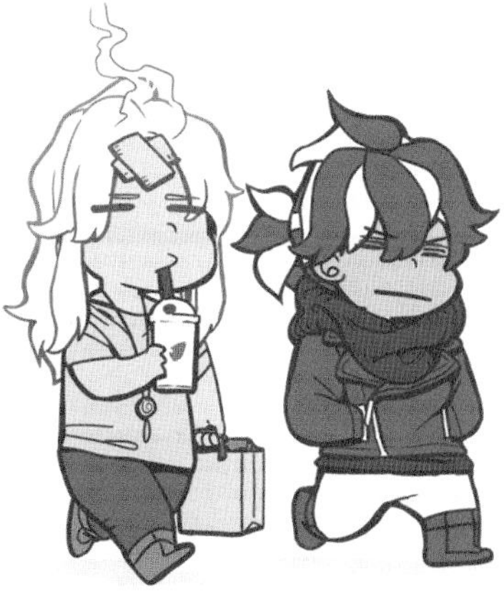

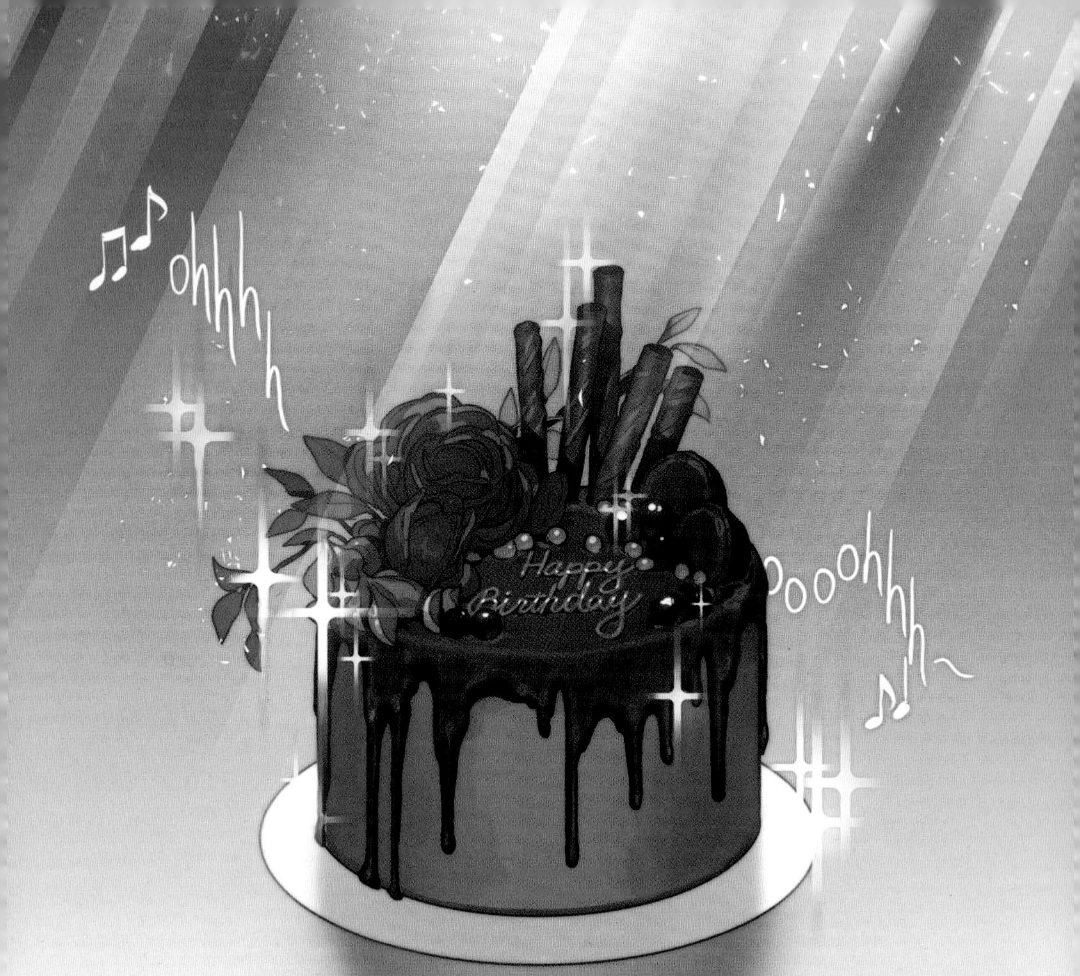
♫♪ ohhhhh
oooohhhh ♪~
Happy Birthday

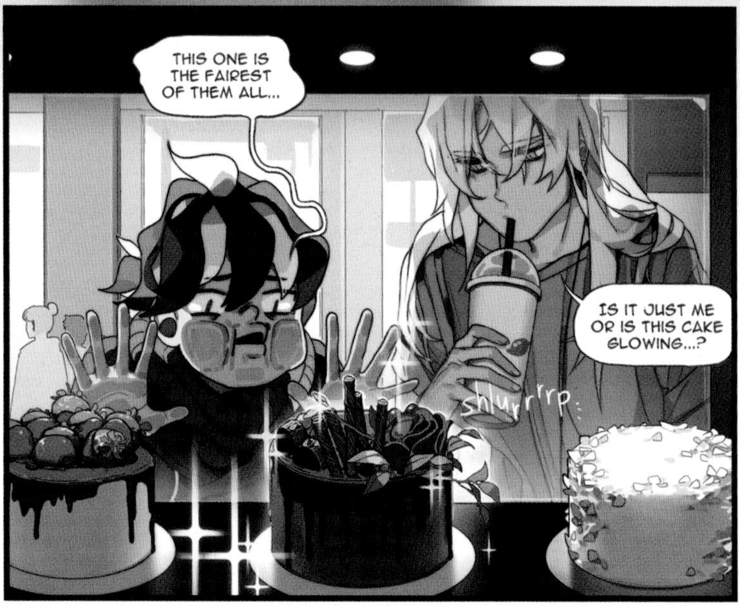
THIS ONE IS THE FAIREST OF THEM ALL...
IS IT JUST ME OR IS THIS CAKE GLOWING...?
shlurrrp

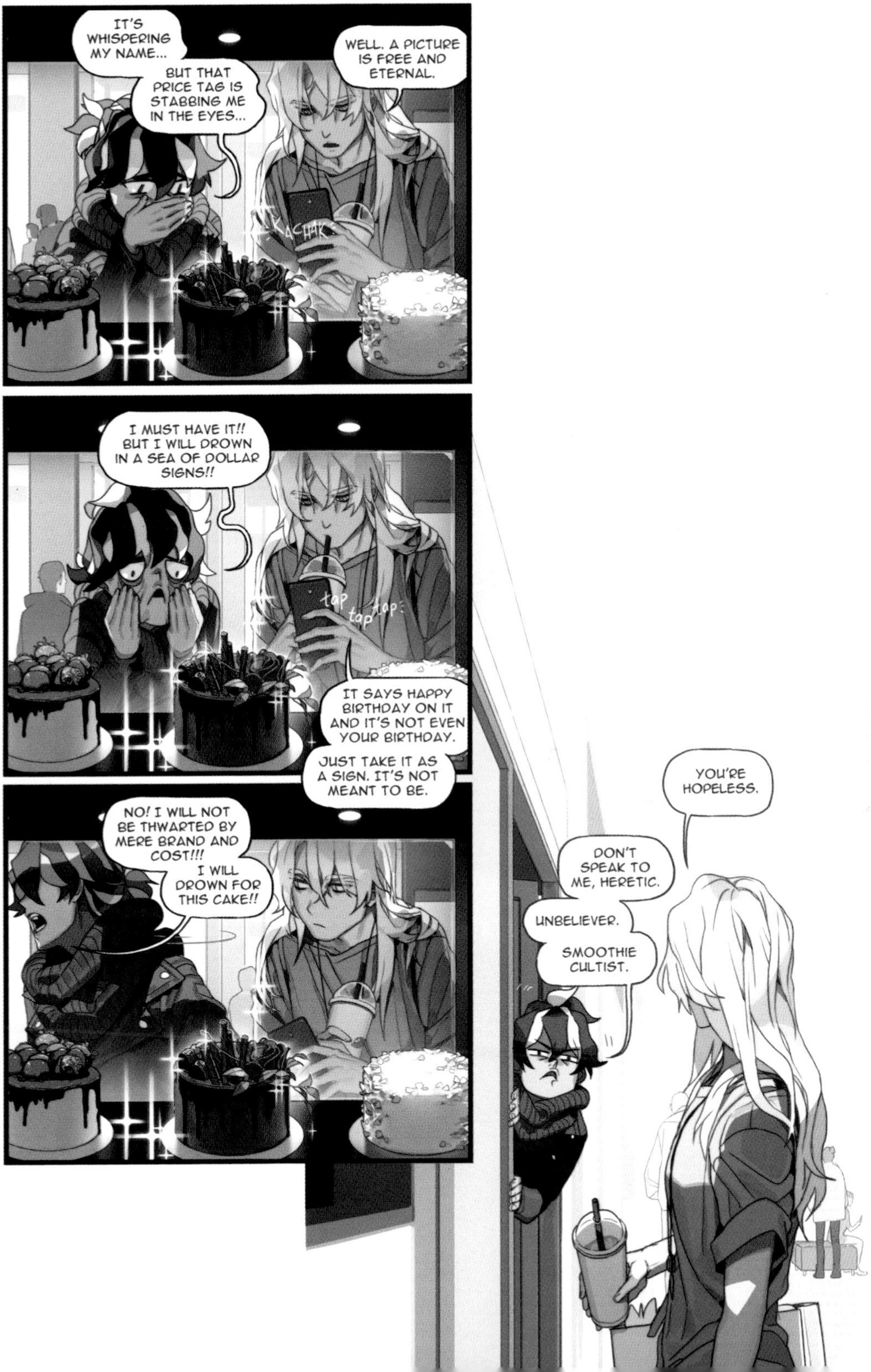
IT'S WHISPERING MY NAME...
BUT THAT PRICE TAG IS STABBING ME IN THE EYES...
WELL. A PICTURE IS FREE AND ETERNAL.
KACHAK
I MUST HAVE IT!! BUT I WILL DROWN IN A SEA OF DOLLAR SIGNS!!
tap tap tap
IT SAYS HAPPY BIRTHDAY ON IT AND IT'S NOT EVEN YOUR BIRTHDAY.
JUST TAKE IT AS A SIGN. IT'S NOT MEANT TO BE.
NO! I WILL NOT BE THWARTED BY MERE BRAND AND COST!!!
I WILL DROWN FOR THIS CAKE!!
YOU'RE HOPELESS.
DON'T SPEAK TO ME, HERETIC.
UNBELIEVER.
SMOOTHIE CULTIST.

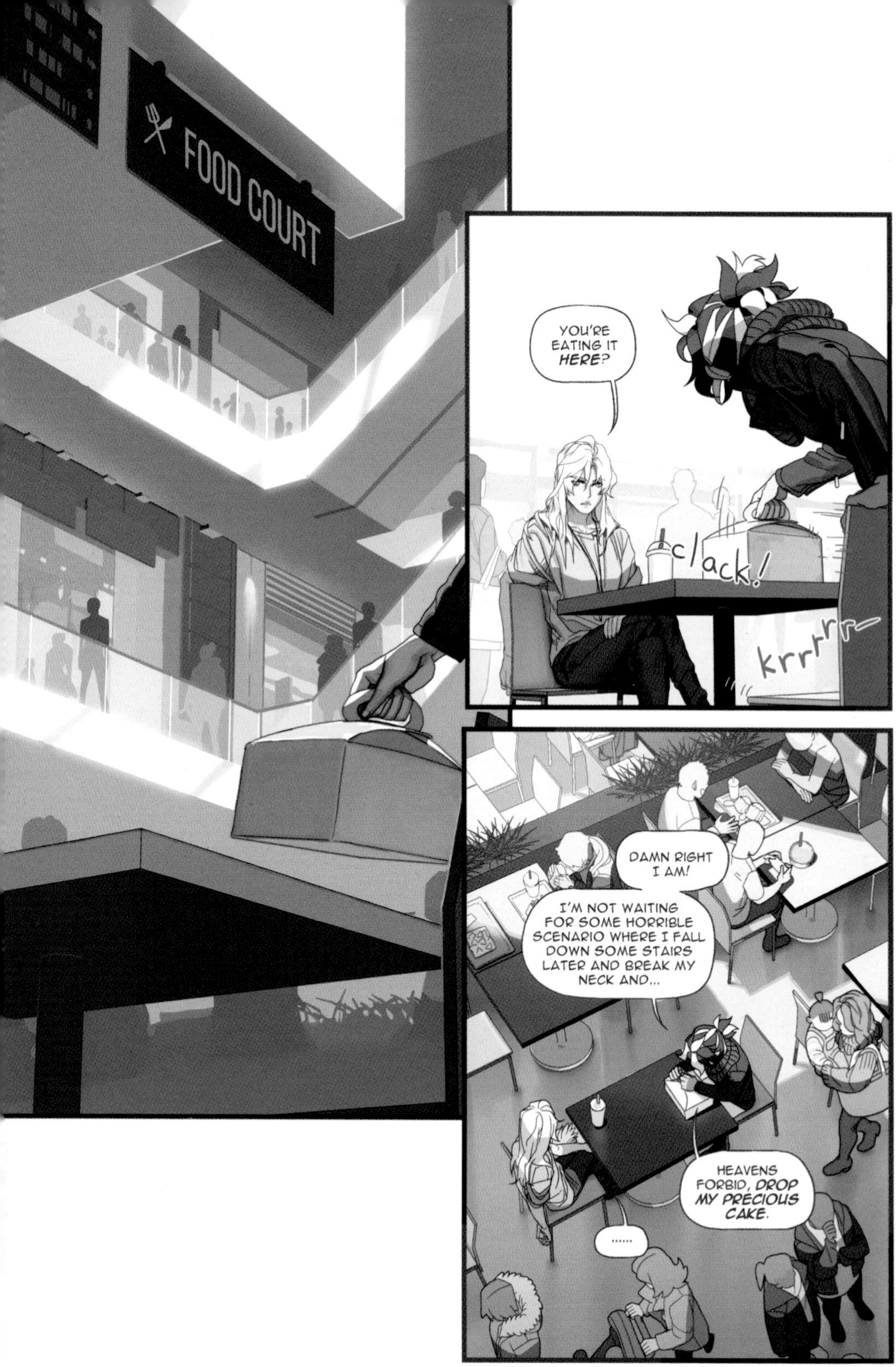
FOOD COURT
YOU'RE EATING IT *HERE*?
clack!
krrrrr–
DAMN RIGHT I AM!
I'M NOT WAITING FOR SOME HORRIBLE SCENARIO WHERE I FALL DOWN SOME STAIRS LATER AND BREAK MY NECK AND...
HEAVENS FORBID, *DROP MY PRECIOUS CAKE*.
......

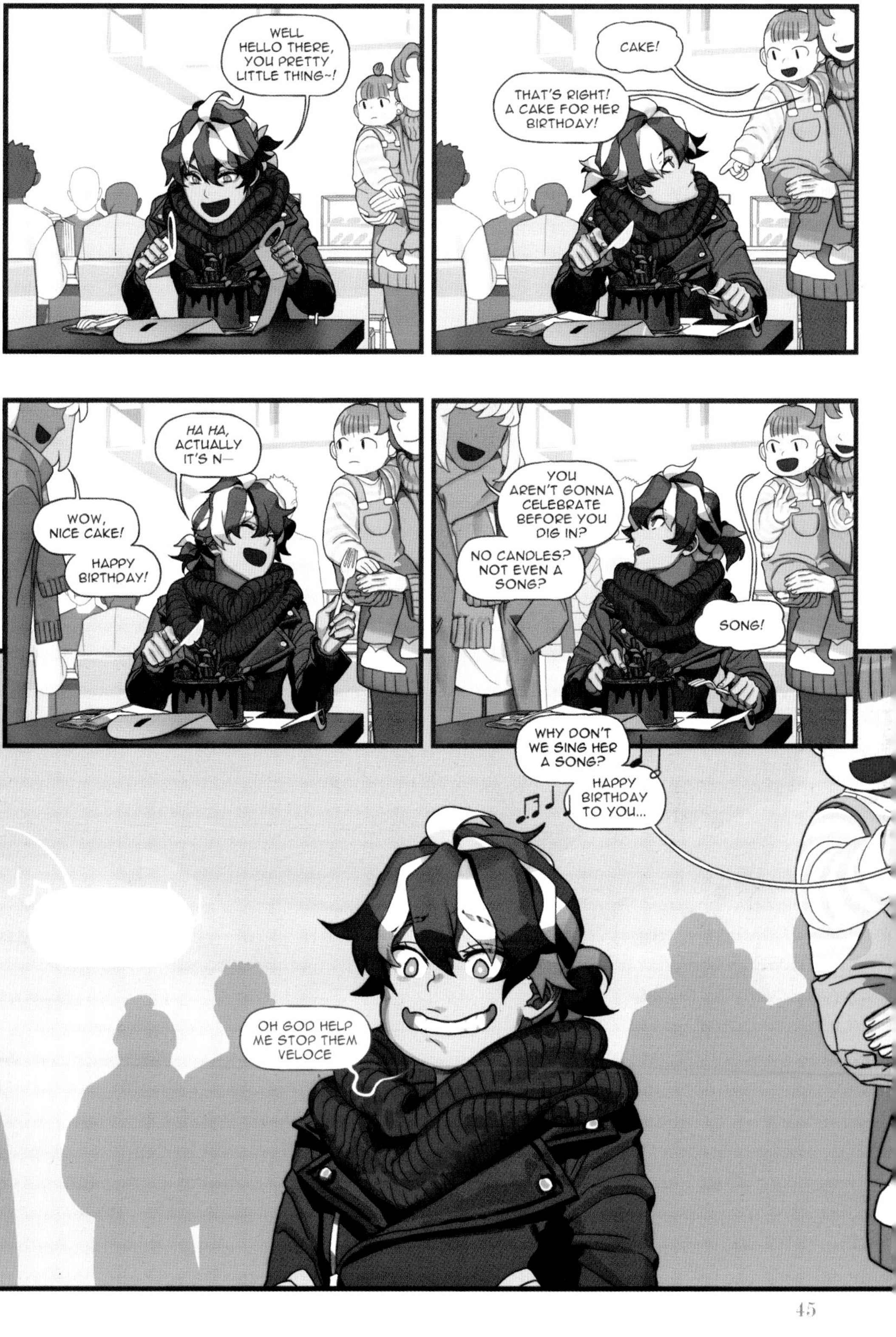
WELL HELLO THERE, YOU PRETTY LITTLE THING~!
CAKE!
THAT'S RIGHT! A CAKE FOR HER BIRTHDAY!
HA HA, ACTUALLY IT'S N—
WOW, NICE CAKE!
HAPPY BIRTHDAY!
YOU AREN'T GONNA CELEBRATE BEFORE YOU DIG IN?
NO CANDLES? NOT EVEN A SONG?
SONG!
WHY DON'T WE SING HER A SONG?
HAPPY BIRTHDAY TO YOU...
OH GOD HELP ME STOP THEM VELOCE

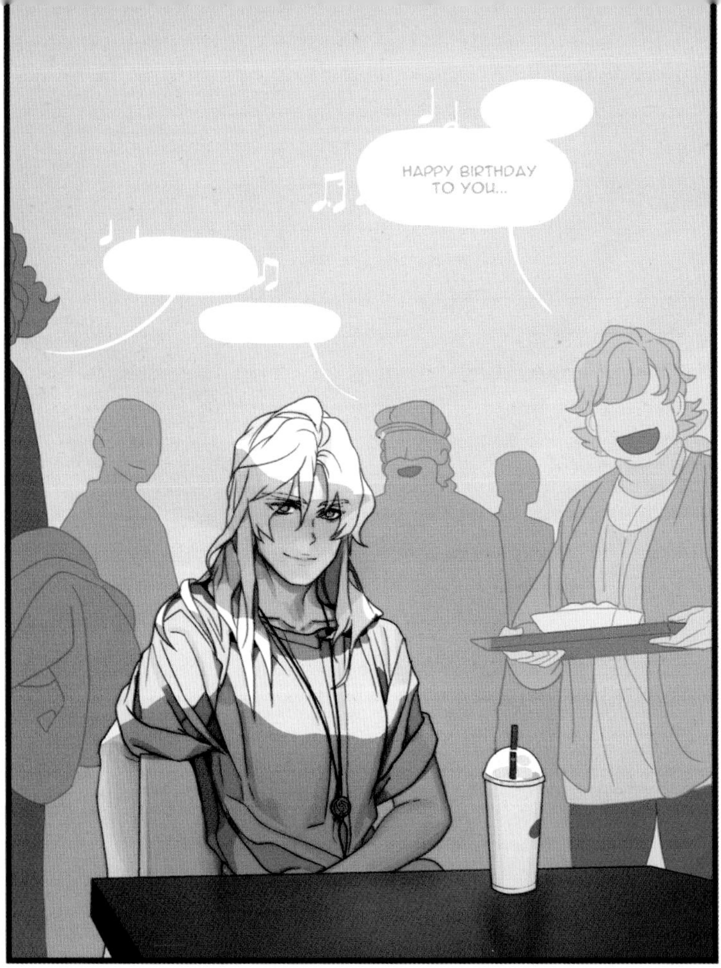
HAPPY BIRTHDAY
TO YOU...

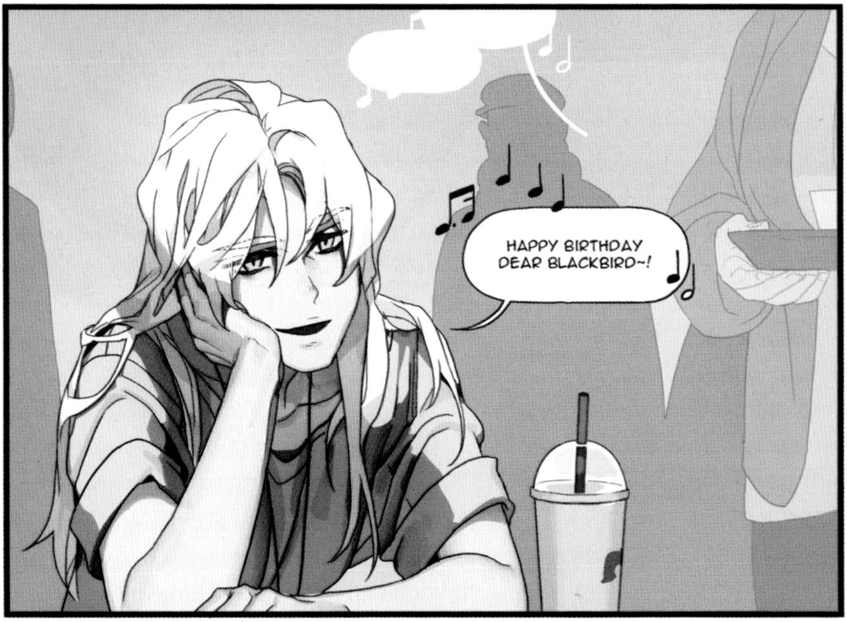
HAPPY BIRTHDAY
DEAR BLACKBIRD~!

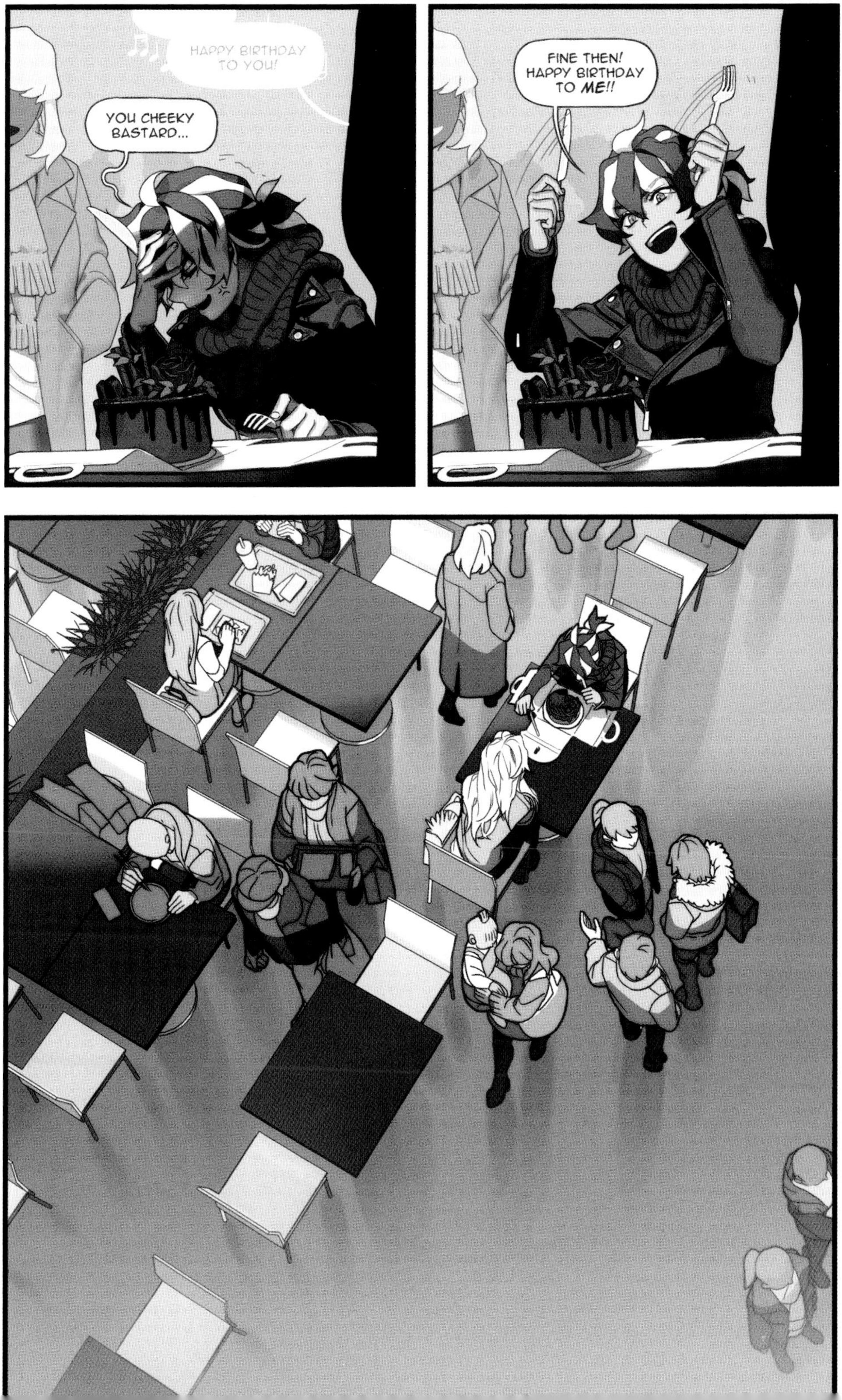
HAPPY BIRTHDAY TO YOU!
YOU CHEEKY BASTARD...
FINE THEN! HAPPY BIRTHDAY TO *ME*!!

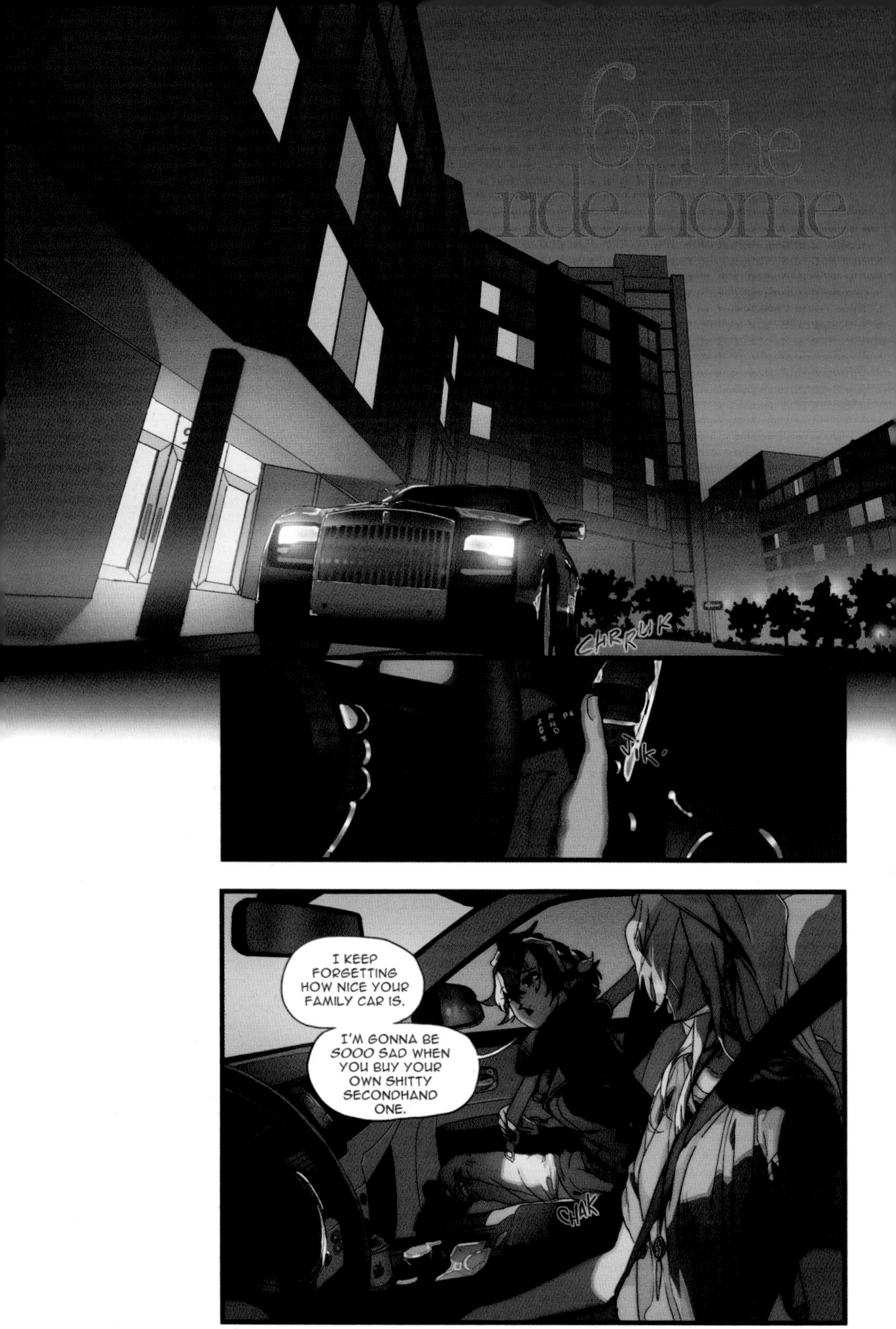
6: The ride home
CHRRUK
JIK
I KEEP FORGETTING HOW NICE YOUR FAMILY CAR IS.
I'M GONNA BE *SOOO* SAD WHEN YOU BUY YOUR OWN SHITTY SECONDHAND ONE.
CHAK

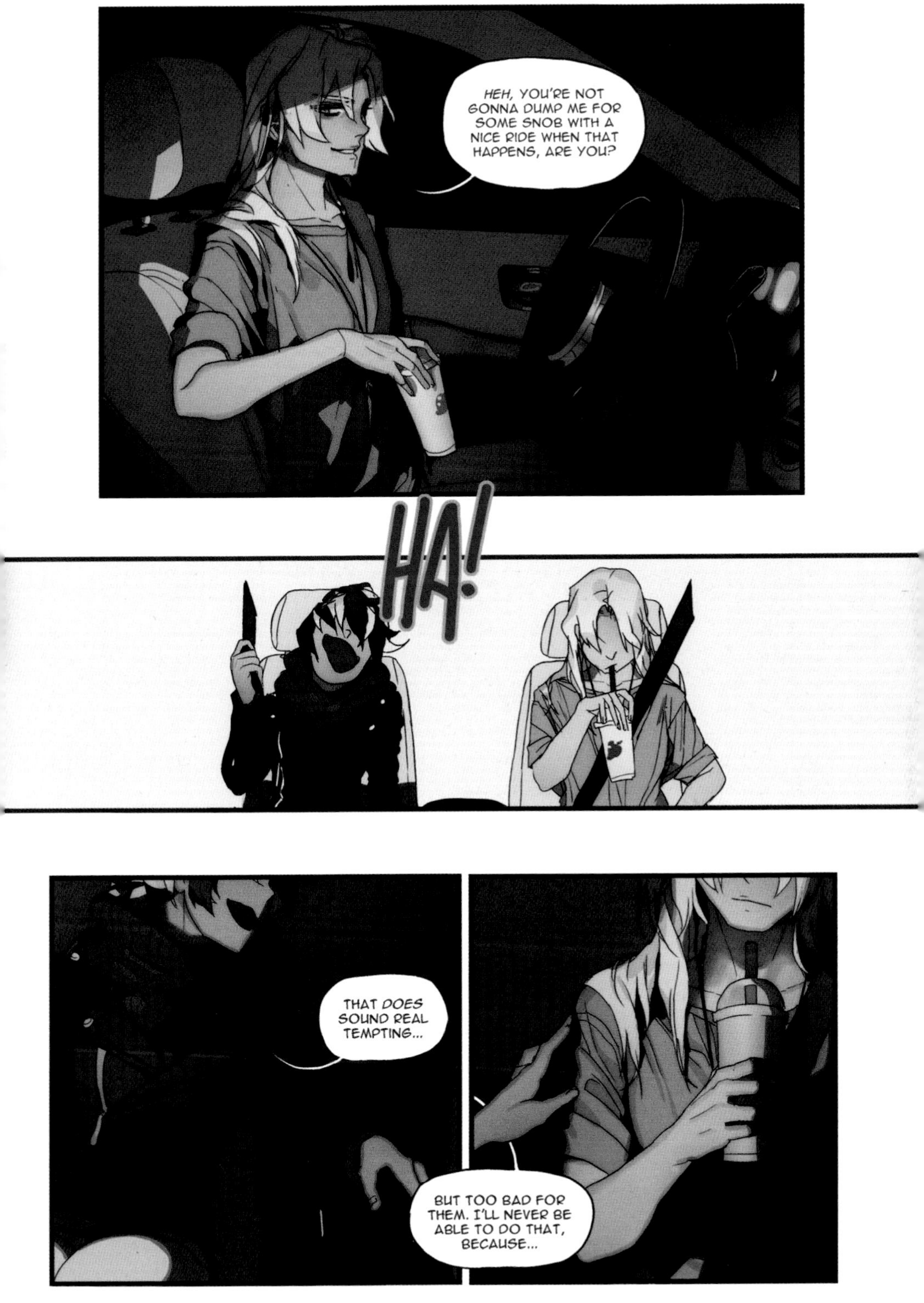
HEH, YOU'RE NOT GONNA DUMP ME FOR SOME SNOB WITH A NICE RIDE WHEN THAT HAPPENS, ARE YOU?
HA!
THAT DOES SOUND REAL TEMPTING...
BUT TOO BAD FOR THEM. I'LL NEVER BE ABLE TO DO THAT, BECAUSE...

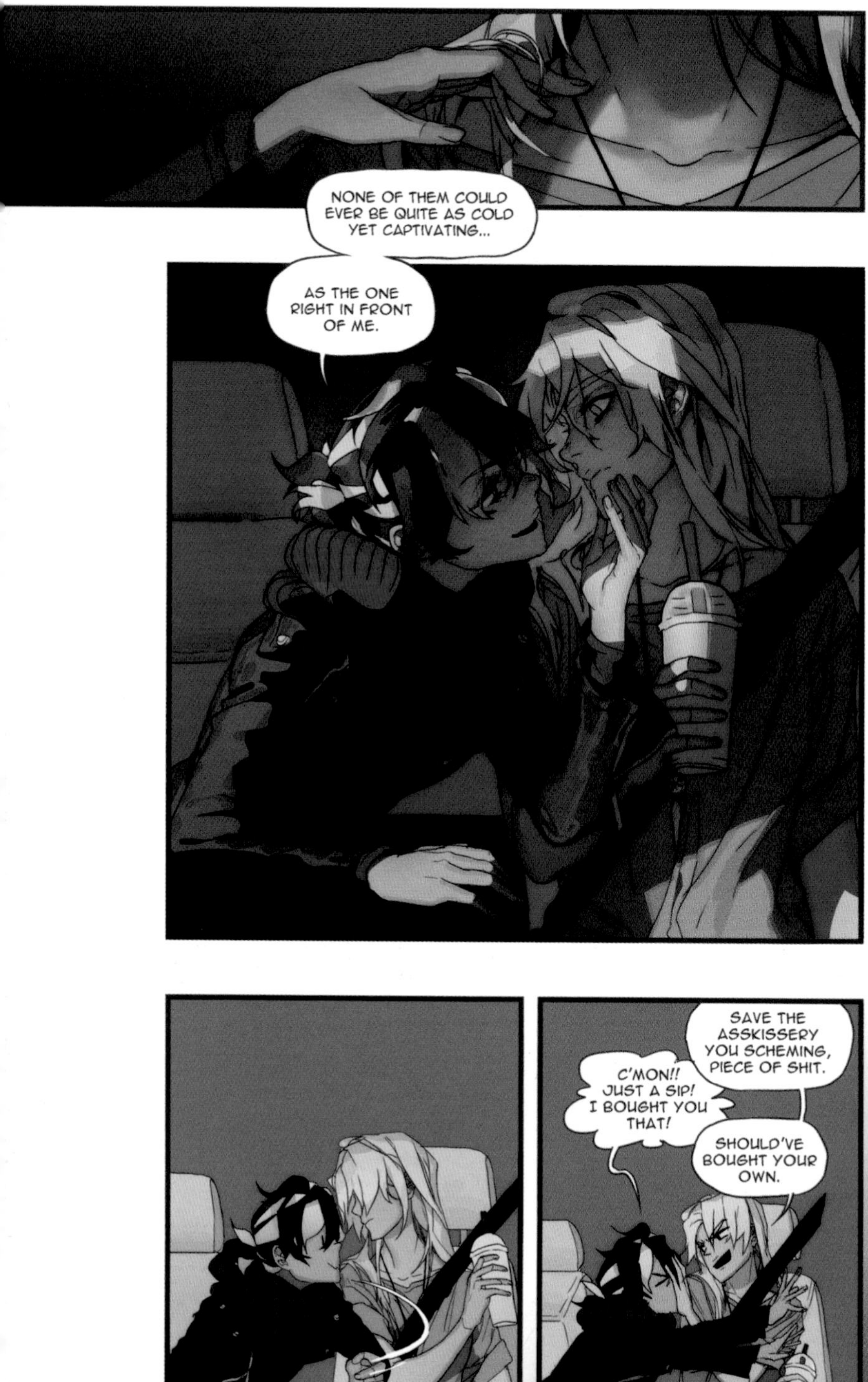
NONE OF THEM COULD EVER BE QUITE AS COLD YET CAPTIVATING...
AS THE ONE RIGHT IN FRONT OF ME.
C'MON!! JUST A SIP! I BOUGHT YOU THAT!
SAVE THE ASSKISSERY YOU SCHEMING, PIECE OF SHIT.
SHOULD'VE BOUGHT YOUR OWN.

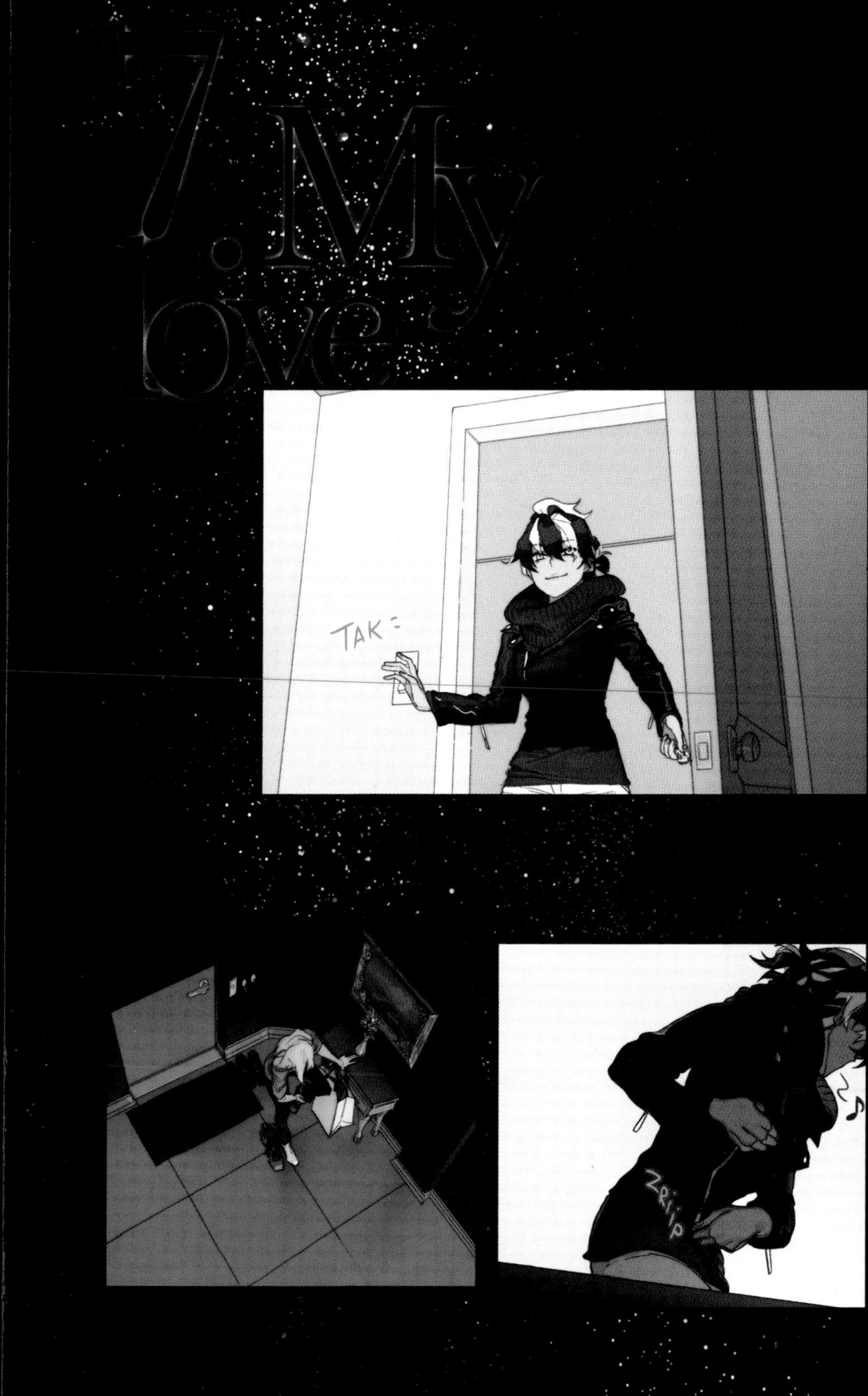
7. My love
TAK
Zriip

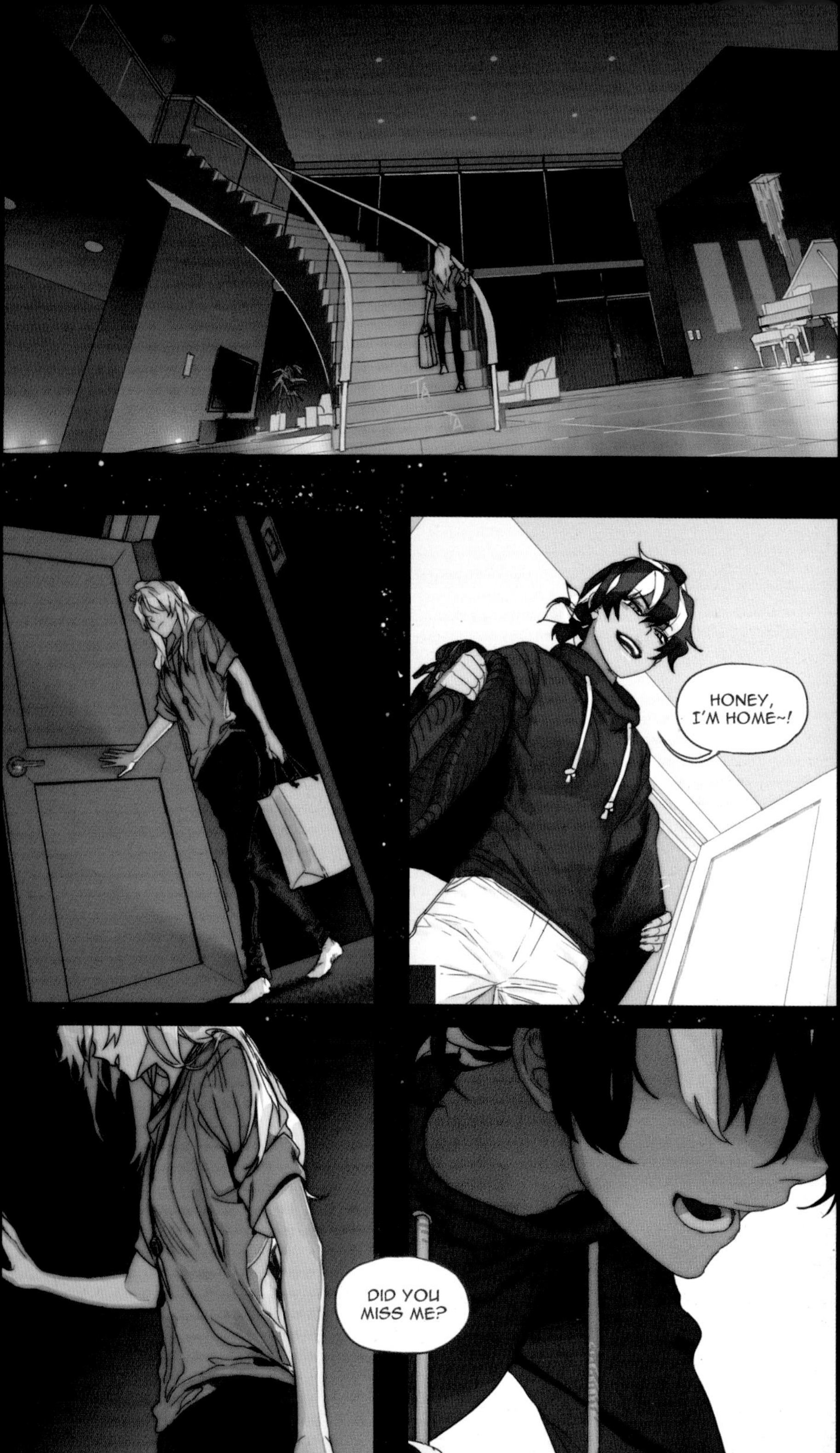
TA
TA
HONEY, I'M HOME~!
DID YOU MISS ME?

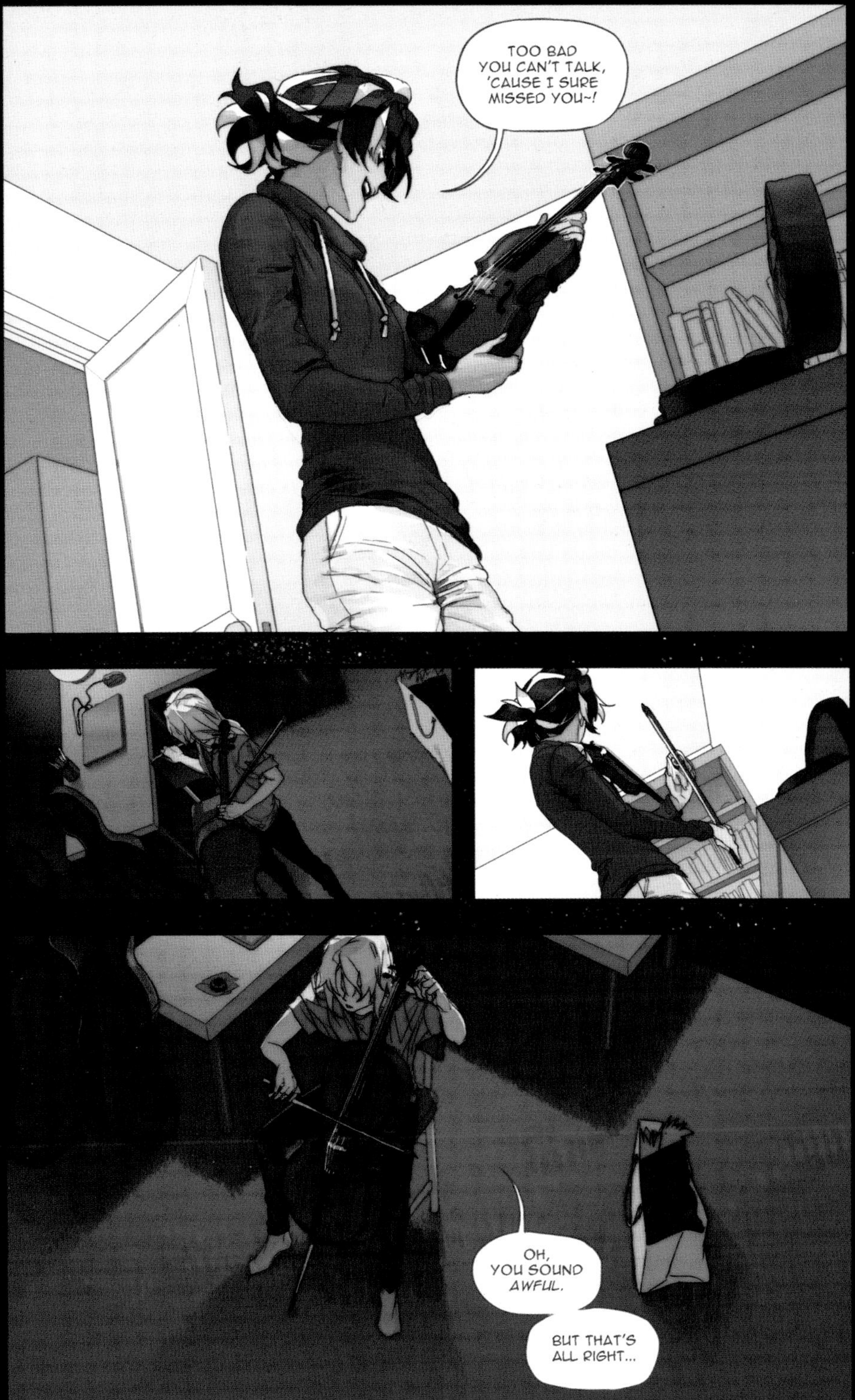
TOO BAD YOU CAN'T TALK, 'CAUSE I SURE MISSED YOU~!
OH, YOU SOUND AWFUL.
BUT THAT'S ALL RIGHT...

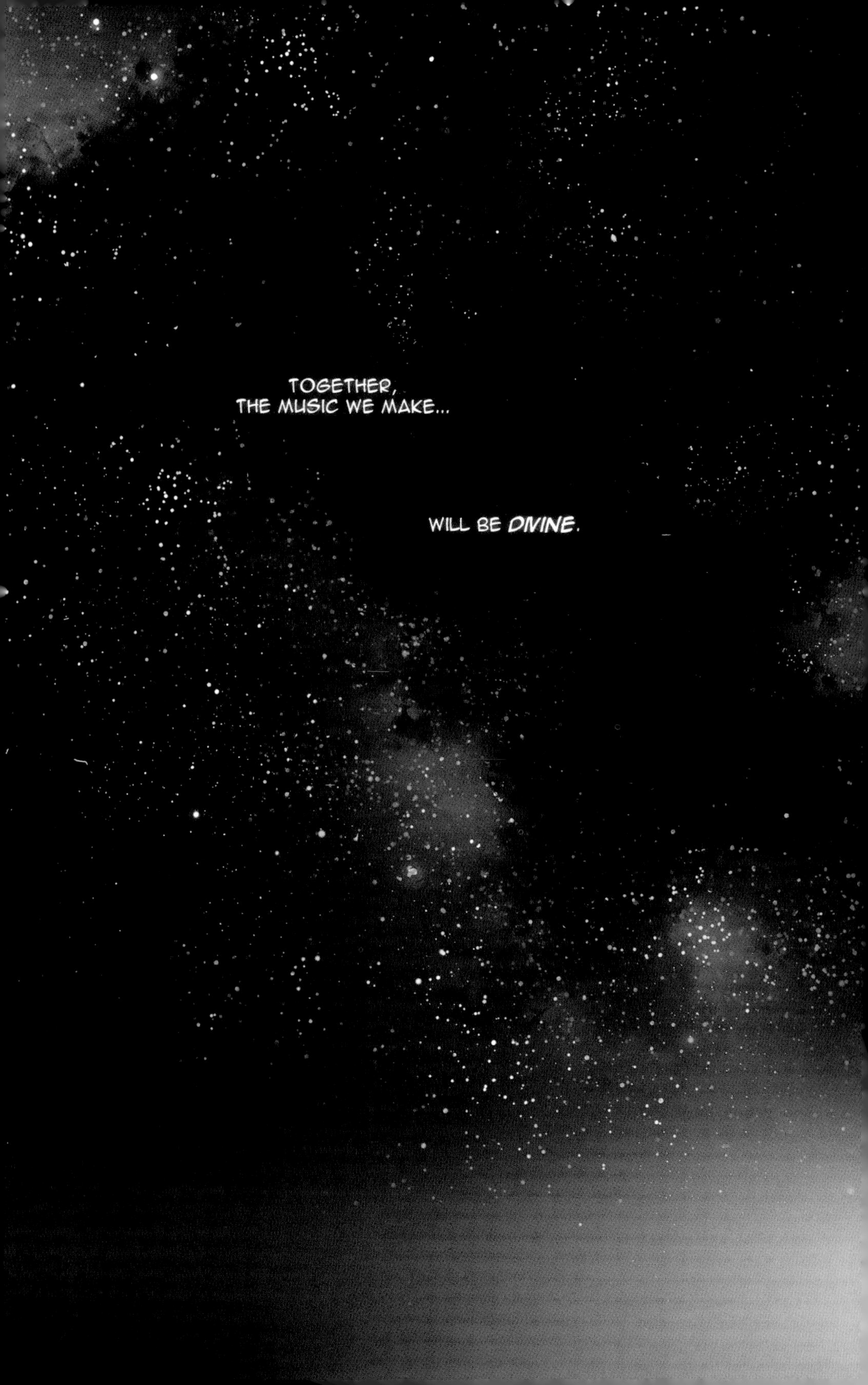
TOGETHER, THE MUSIC WE MAKE...
WILL BE DIVINE.

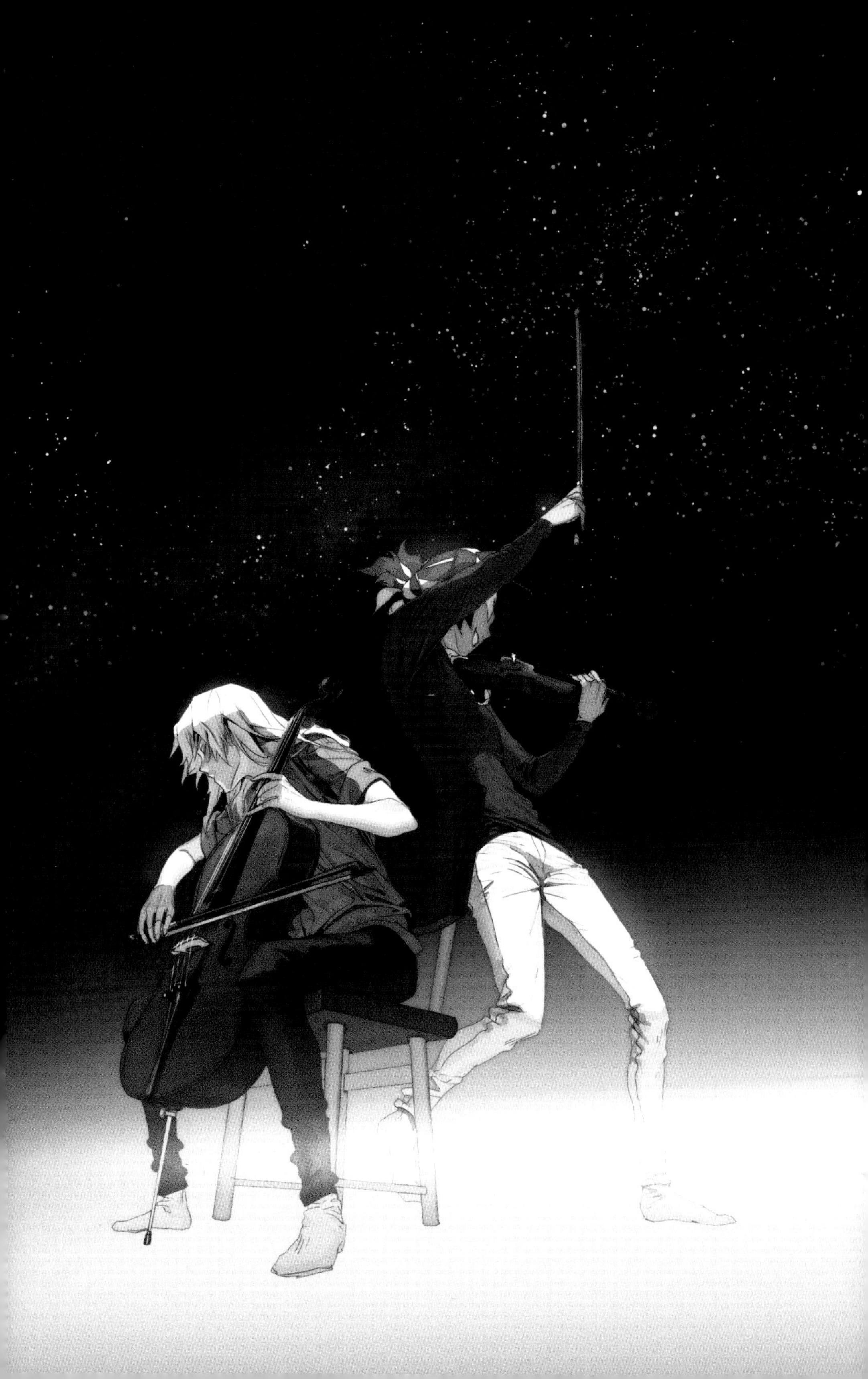

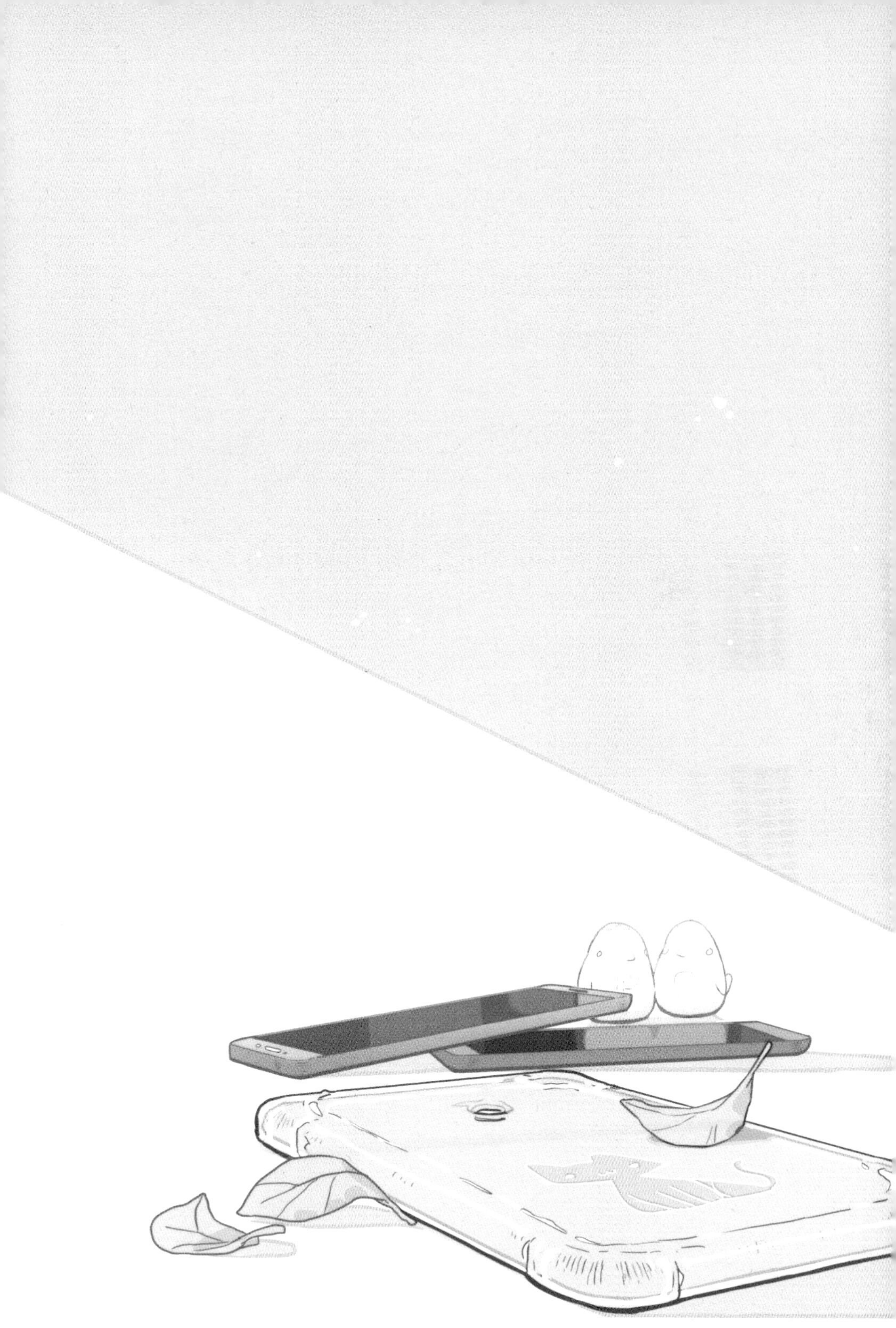

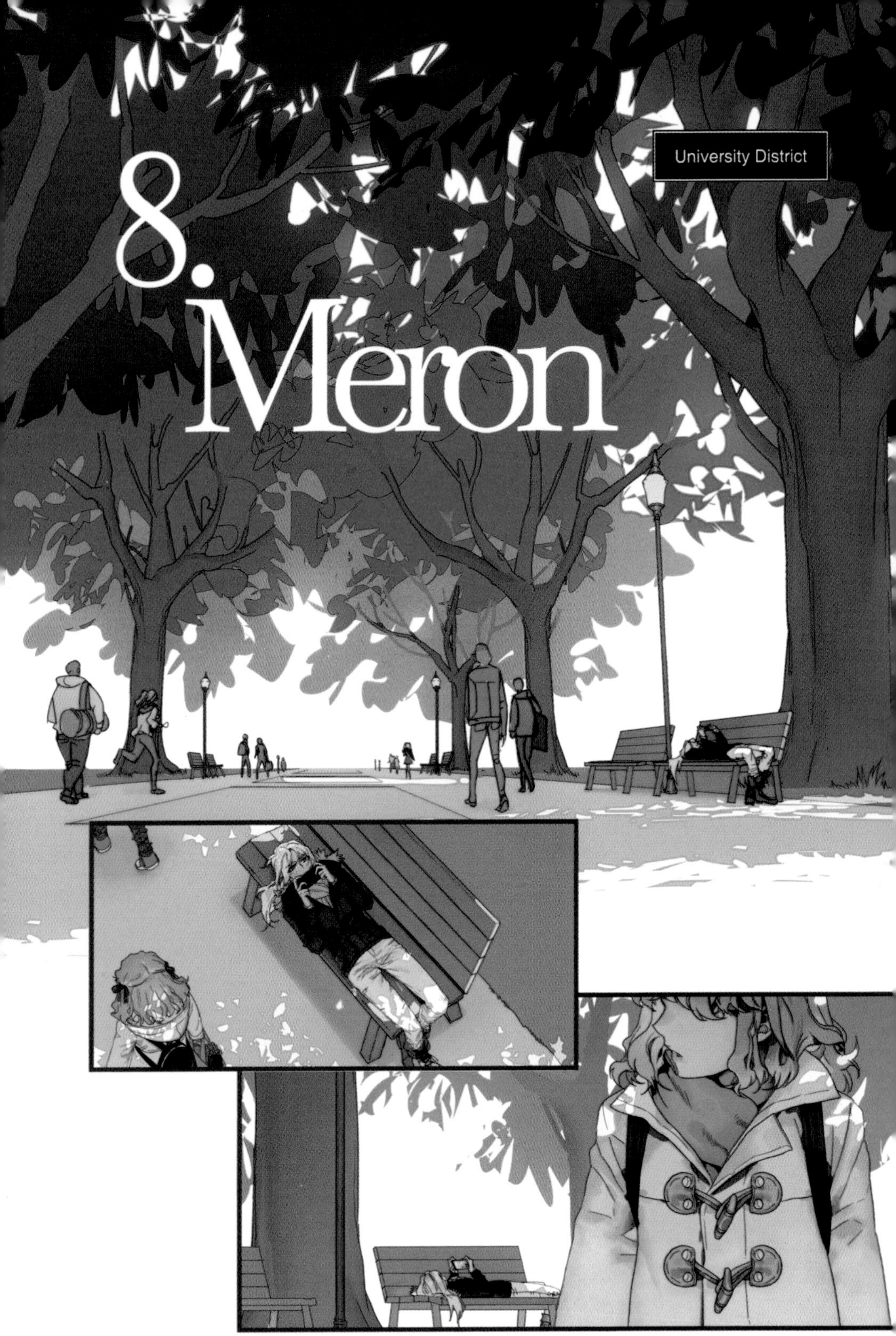
8.
Meron
University District

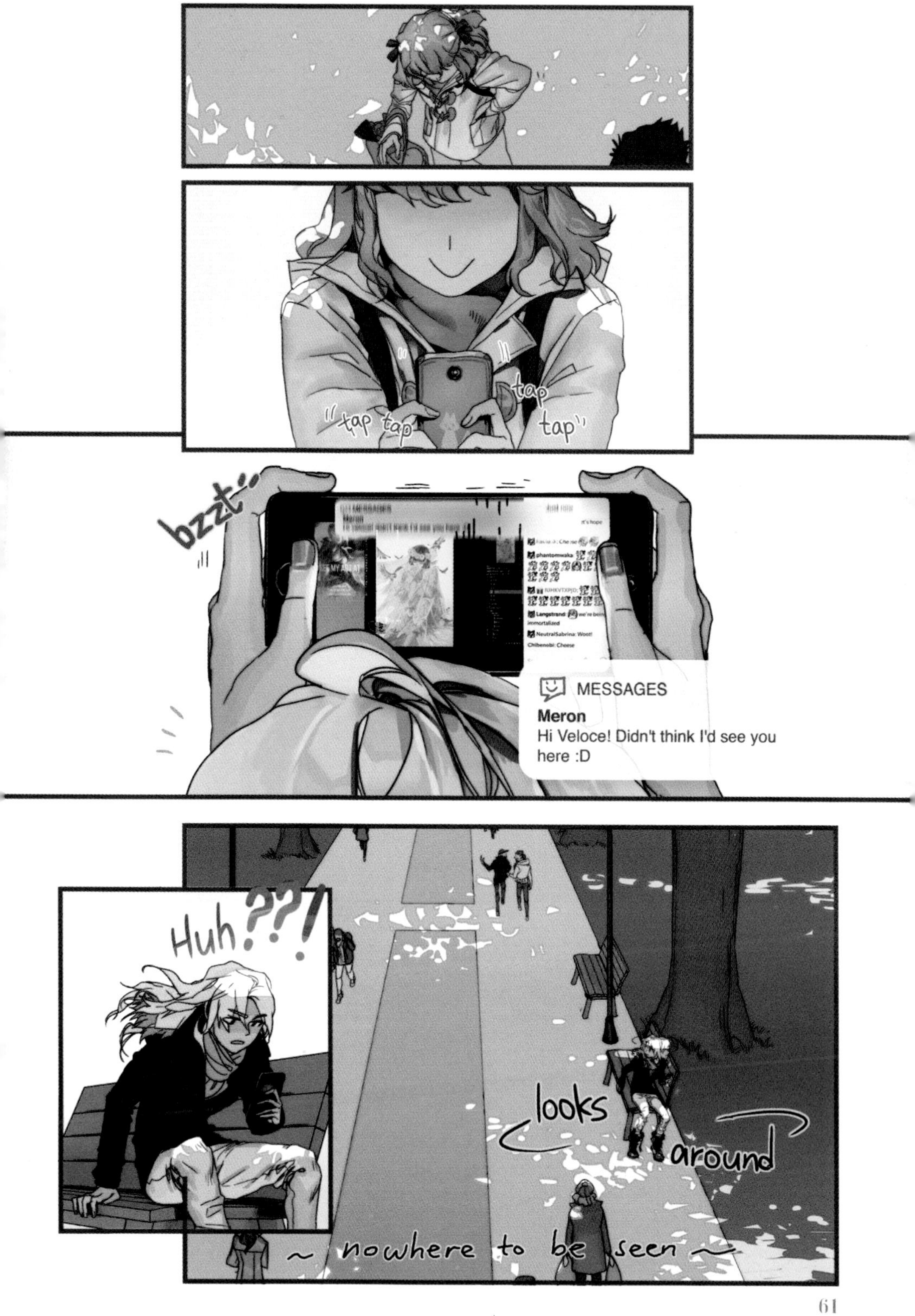
tap
tap tap
tap
bzzt
MESSAGES
Meron
Hi Veloce! Didn't think I'd see you here :D
Huh???!
looks around
~ nowhere to be seen ~

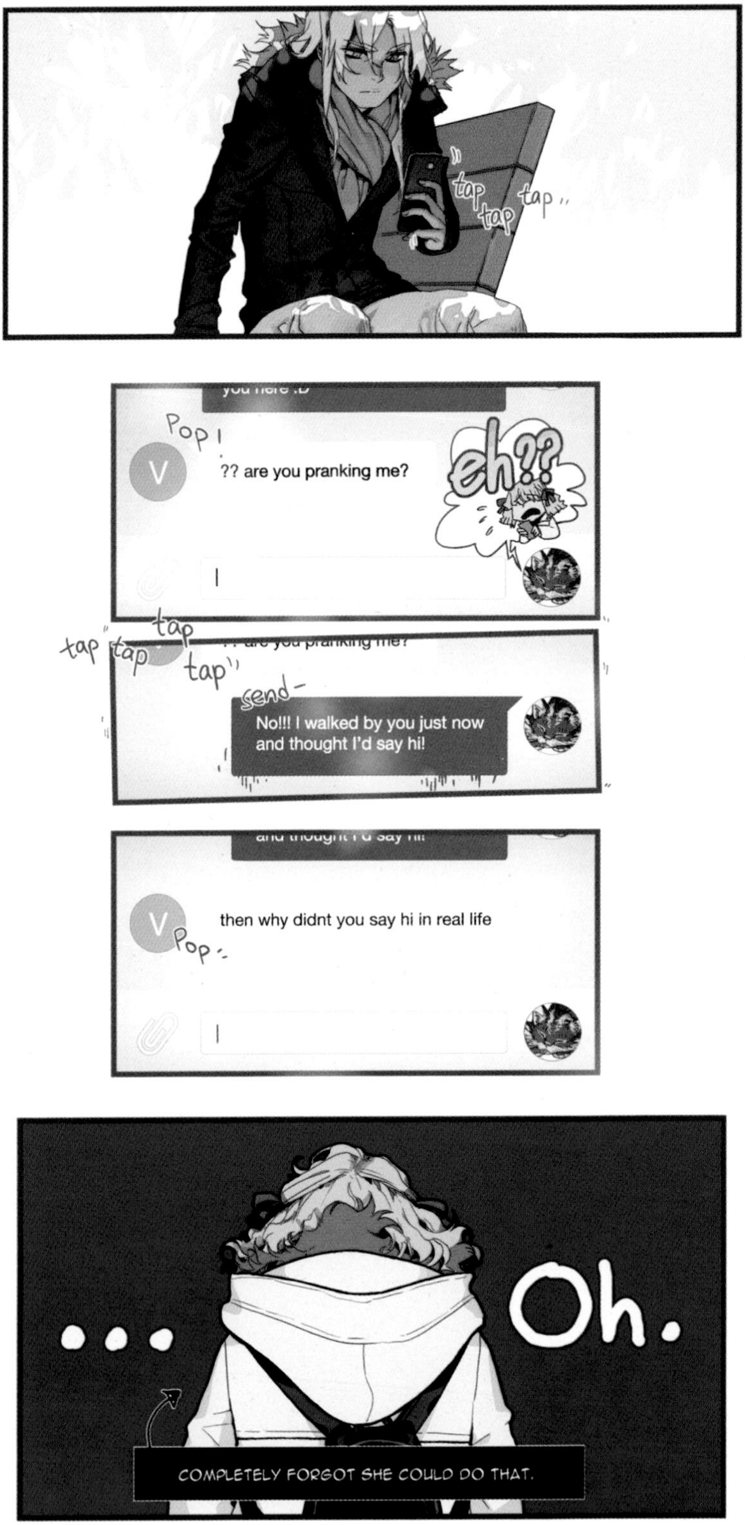
tap tap tap
Pop!
?? are you pranking me?
eh??
tap tap tap tap
send-
No!!! I walked by you just now and thought I'd say hi!
then why didnt you say hi in real life
Pop
...Oh.
COMPLETELY FORGOT SHE COULD DO THAT.

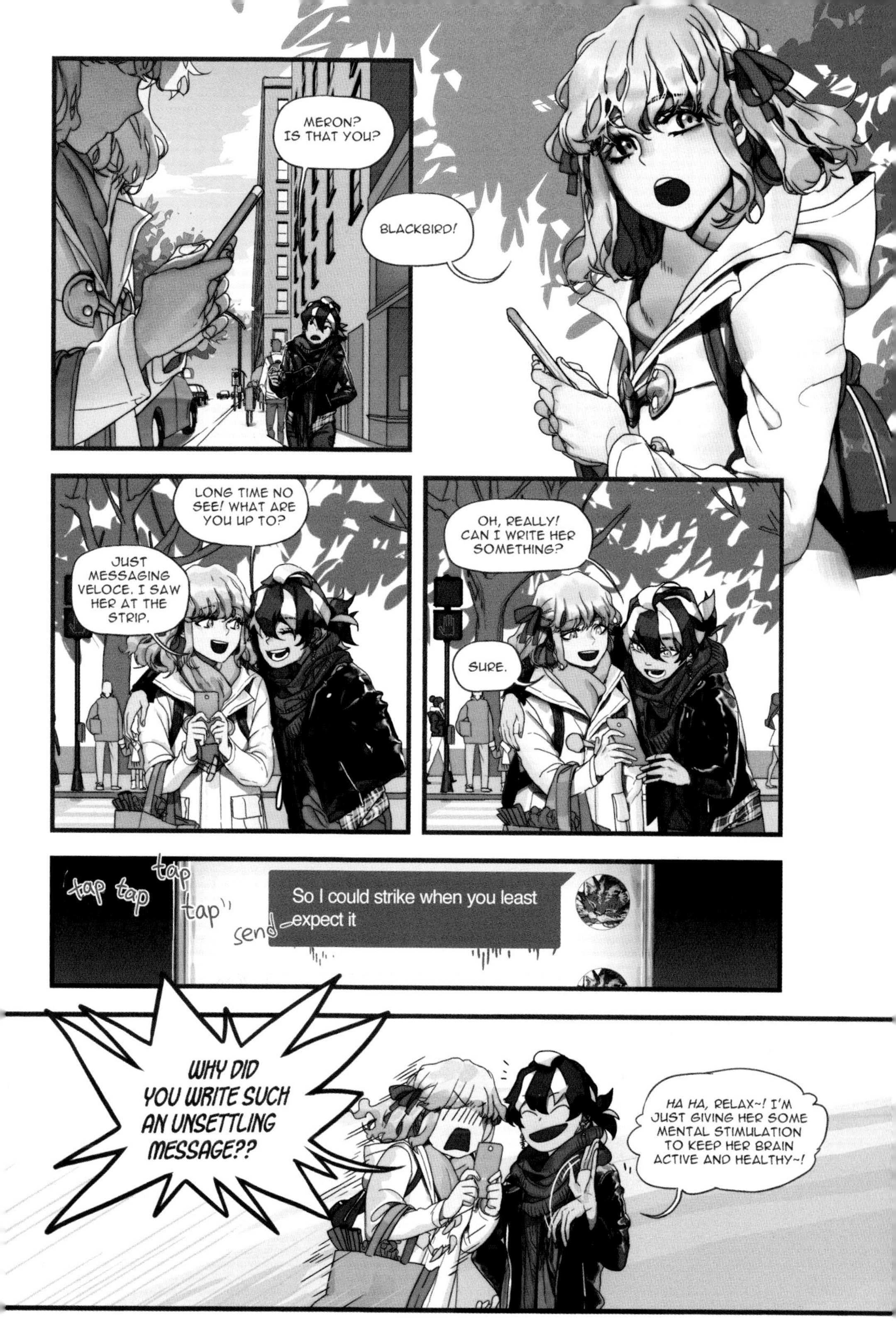
MERON? IS THAT YOU?
BLACKBIRD!
LONG TIME NO SEE! WHAT ARE YOU UP TO?
JUST MESSAGING VELOCE. I SAW HER AT THE STRIP.
OH, REALLY! CAN I WRITE HER SOMETHING?
SURE.
tap tap tap tap
send
So I could strike when you least expect it
WHY DID YOU WRITE SUCH AN UNSETTLING MESSAGE??
HA HA, RELAX~! I'M JUST GIVING HER SOME MENTAL STIMULATION TO KEEP HER BRAIN ACTIVE AND HEALTHY~!

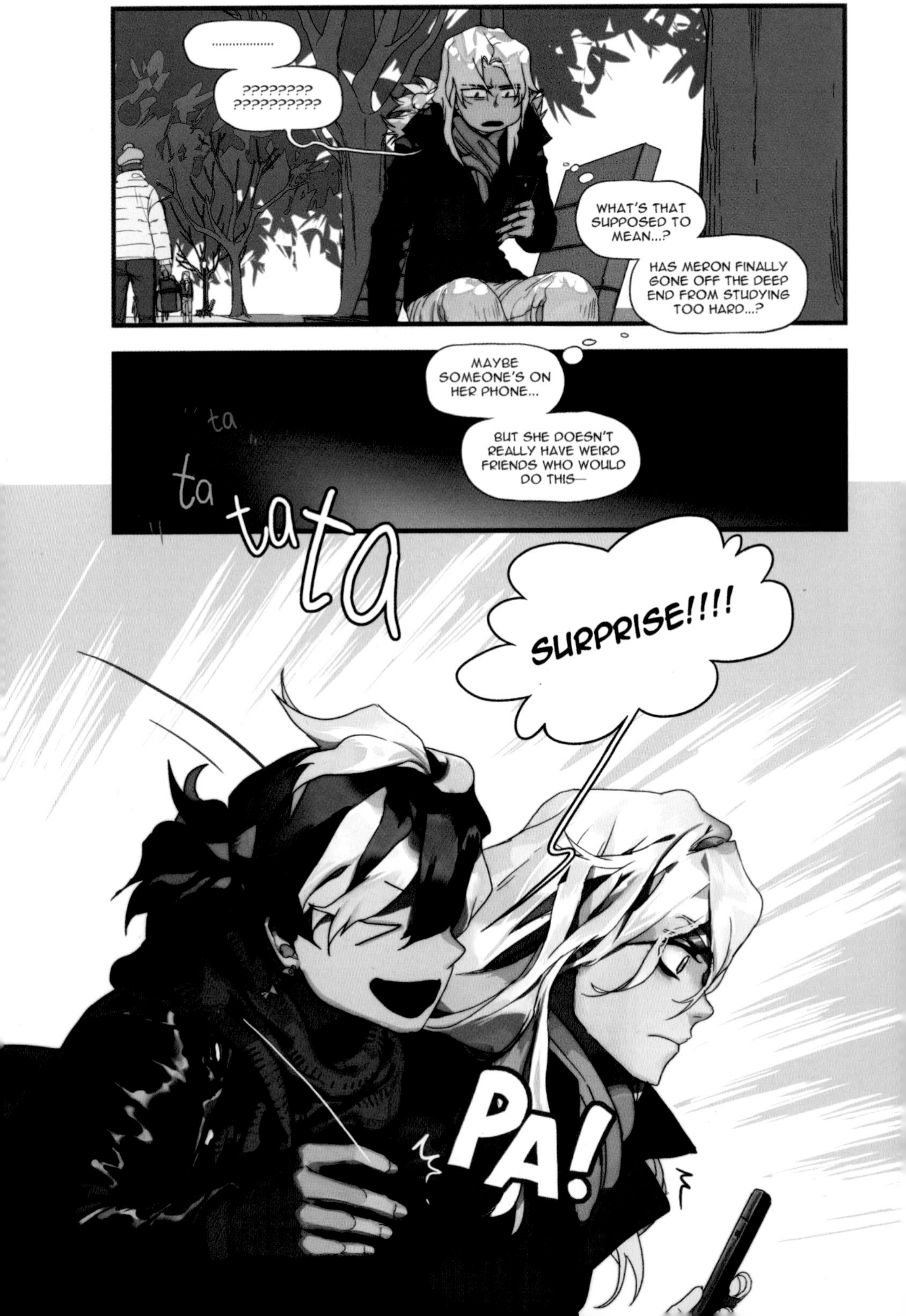

....
?????????
??????????
WHAT'S THAT SUPPOSED TO MEAN...?
HAS MERON FINALLY GONE OFF THE DEEP END FROM STUDYING TOO HARD...?
MAYBE SOMEONE'S ON HER PHONE...
BUT SHE DOESN'T REALLY HAVE WEIRD FRIENDS WHO WOULD DO THIS—
ta
ta
tata
SURPRISE!!!!
PA!

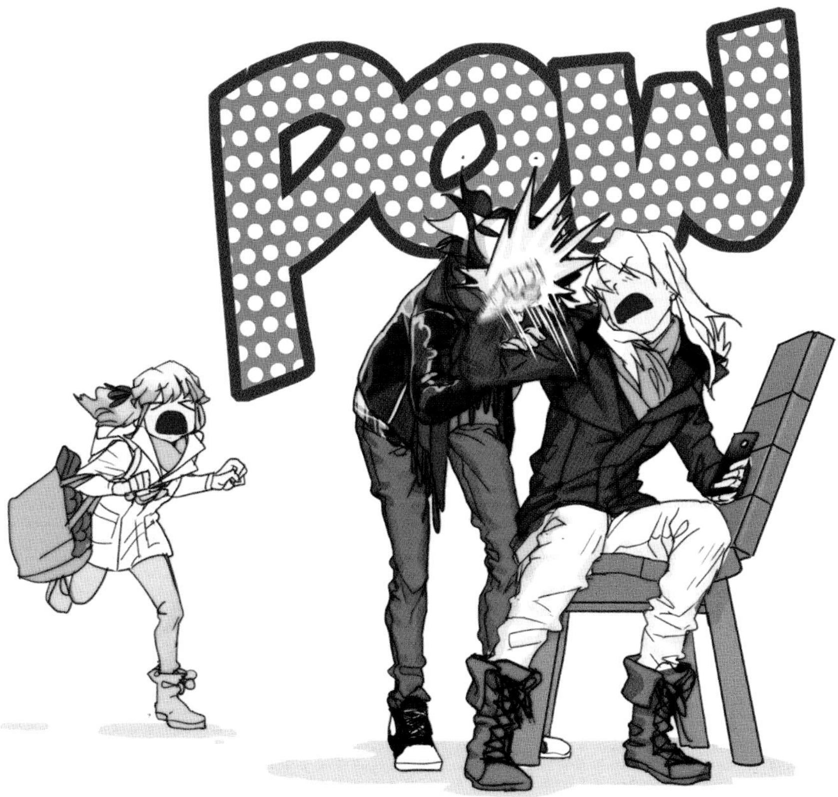
POW

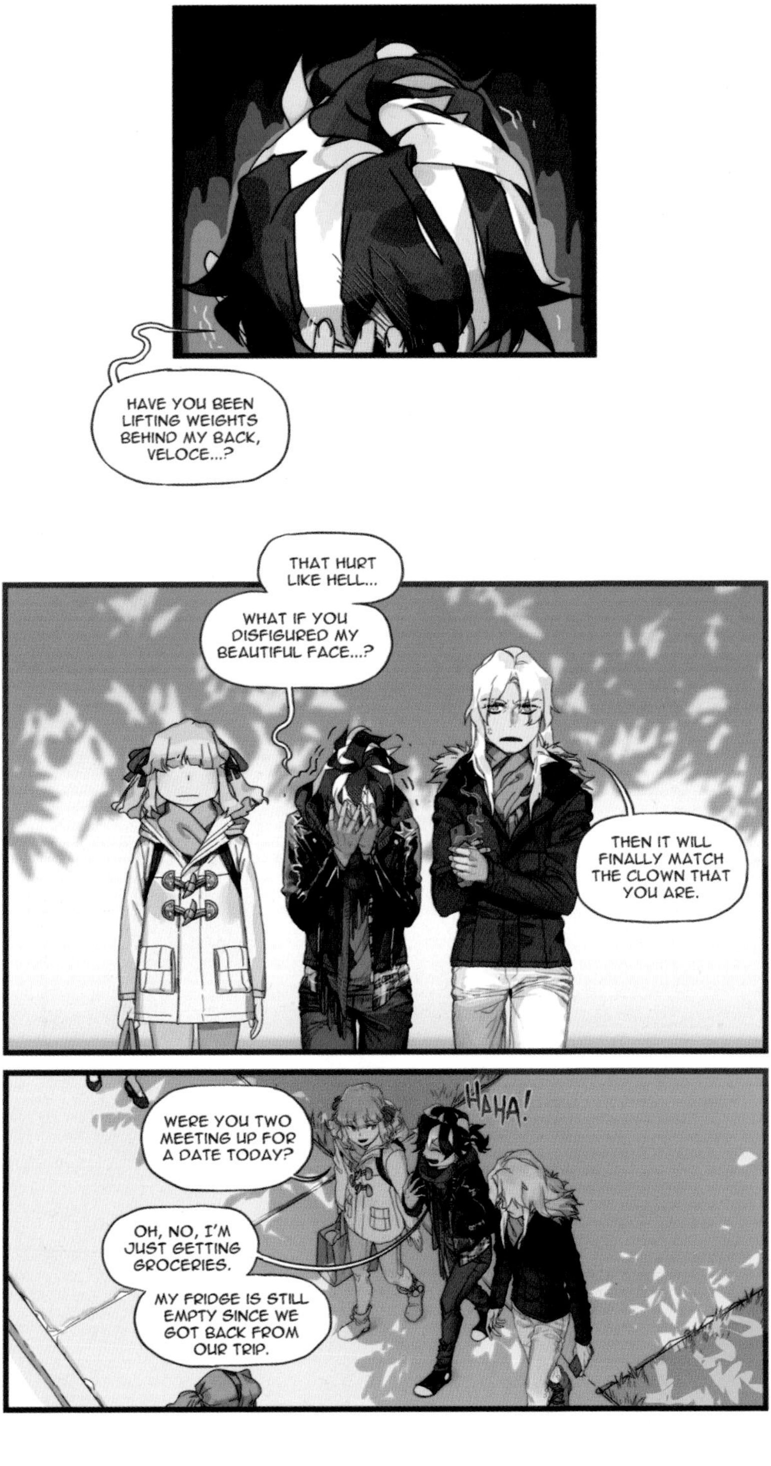
HAVE YOU BEEN LIFTING WEIGHTS BEHIND MY BACK, VELOCE...?
THAT HURT LIKE HELL...
WHAT IF YOU DISFIGURED MY BEAUTIFUL FACE...?
THEN IT WILL FINALLY MATCH THE CLOWN THAT YOU ARE.
HAHA!
WERE YOU TWO MEETING UP FOR A DATE TODAY?
OH, NO, I'M JUST GETTING GROCERIES.
MY FRIDGE IS STILL EMPTY SINCE WE GOT BACK FROM OUR TRIP.

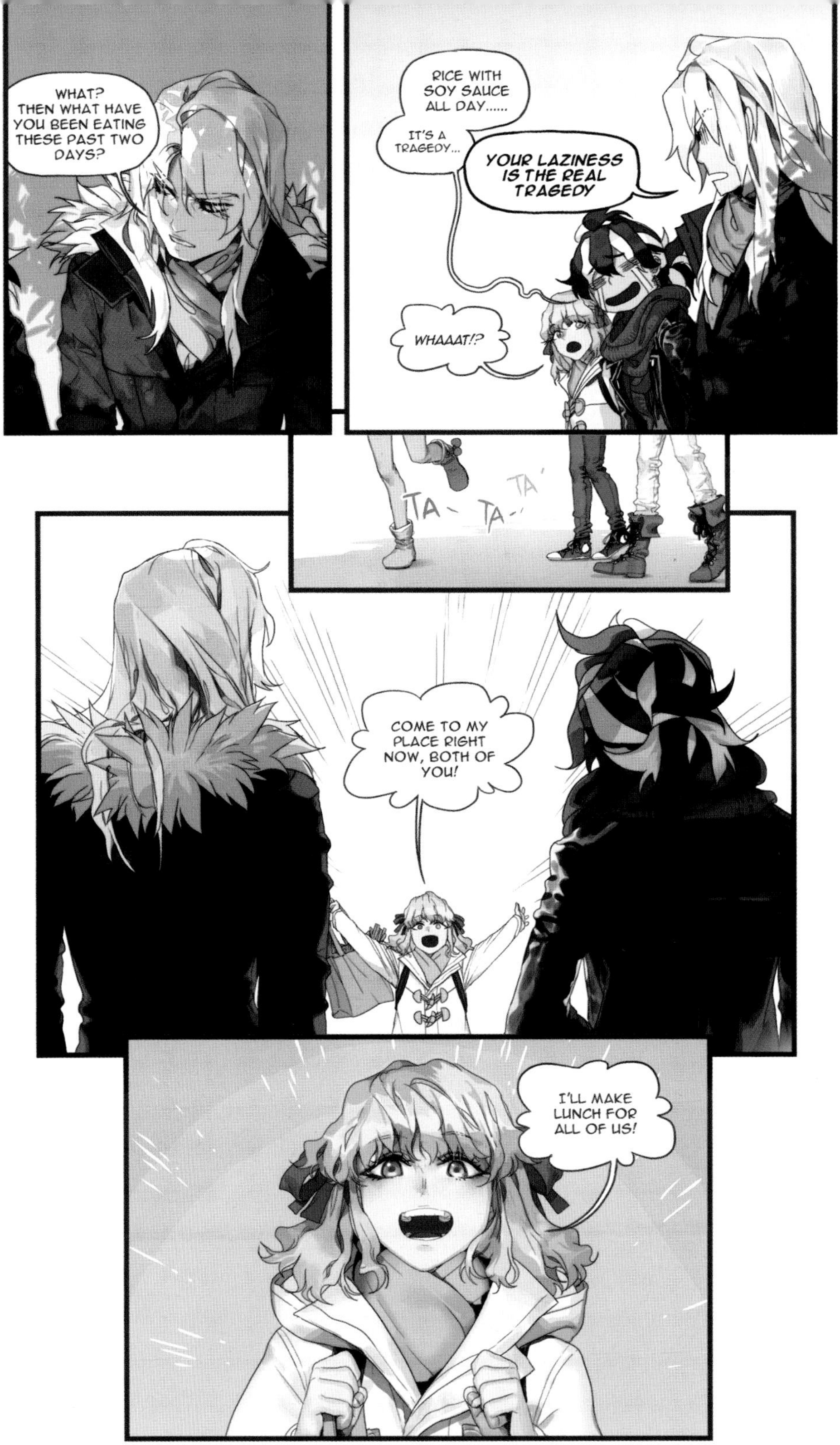
WHAT? THEN WHAT HAVE YOU BEEN EATING THESE PAST TWO DAYS?
RICE WITH SOY SAUCE ALL DAY......
IT'S A TRAGEDY...
YOUR LAZINESS IS THE REAL TRAGEDY
WHAAAT!?
TA- TA- TA
COME TO MY PLACE RIGHT NOW, BOTH OF YOU!
I'LL MAKE LUNCH FOR ALL OF US!

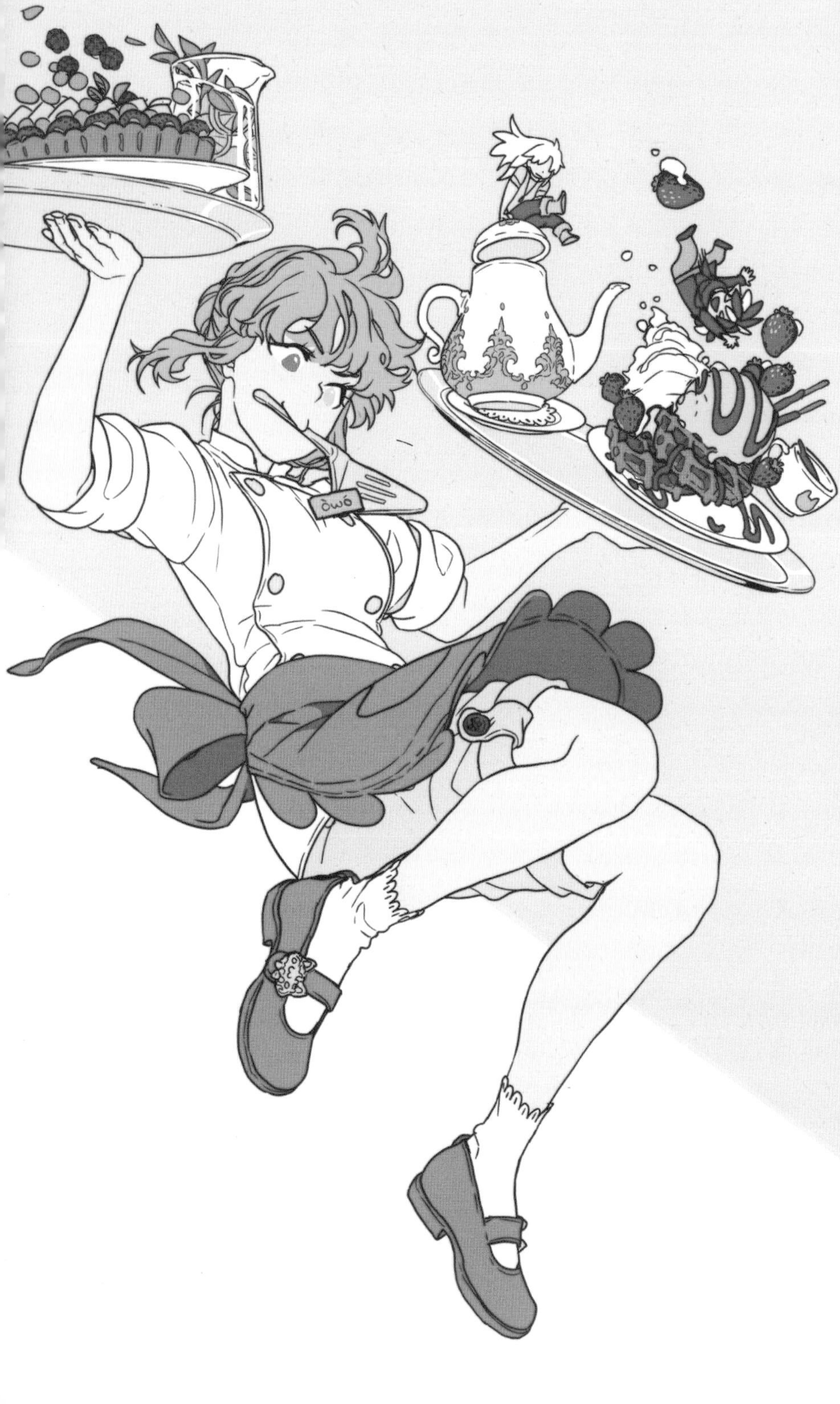
òwó

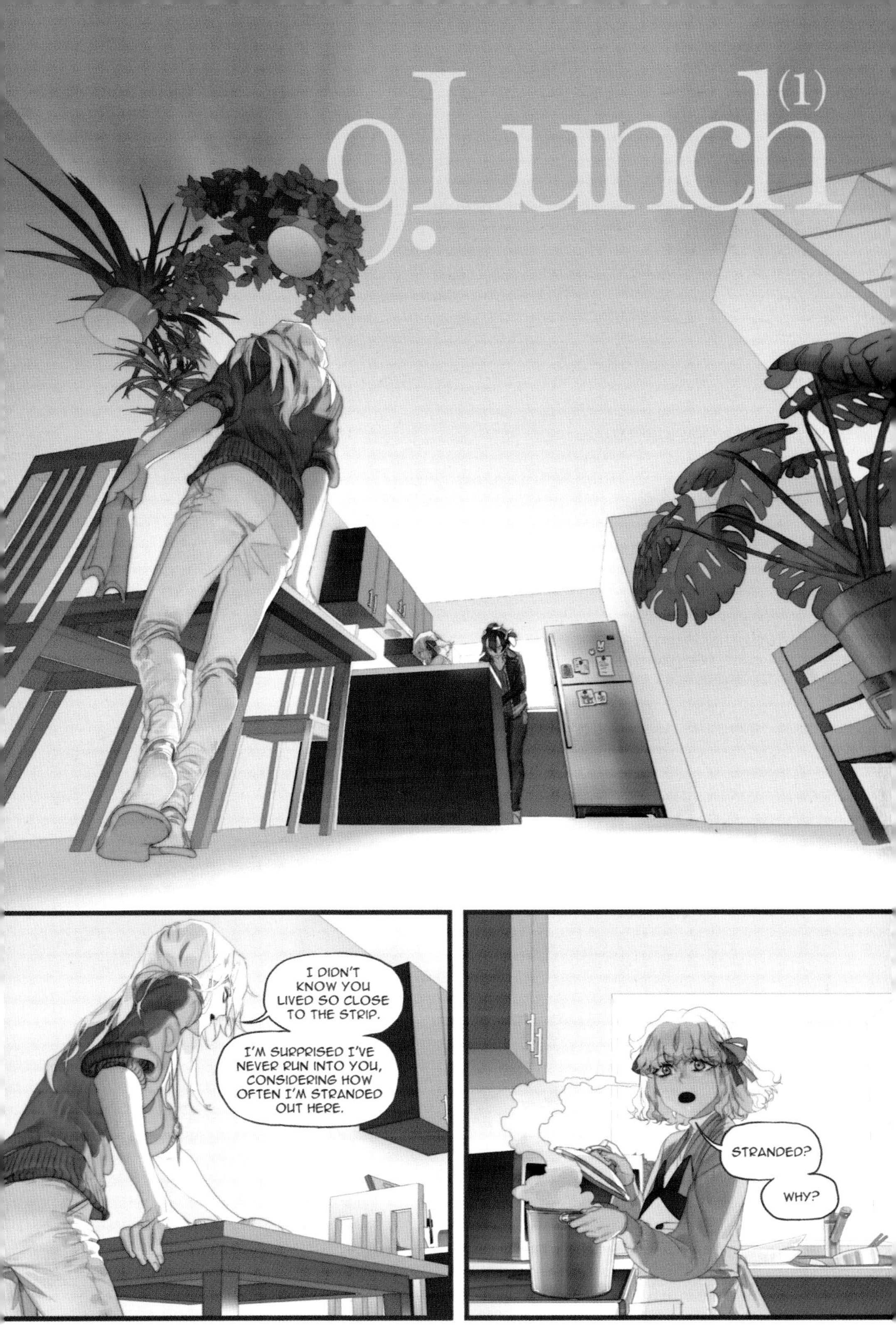
9. Lunch (1)
I DIDN'T KNOW YOU LIVED SO CLOSE TO THE STRIP.
I'M SURPRISED I'VE NEVER RUN INTO YOU, CONSIDERING HOW OFTEN I'M STRANDED OUT HERE.
STRANDED?
WHY?

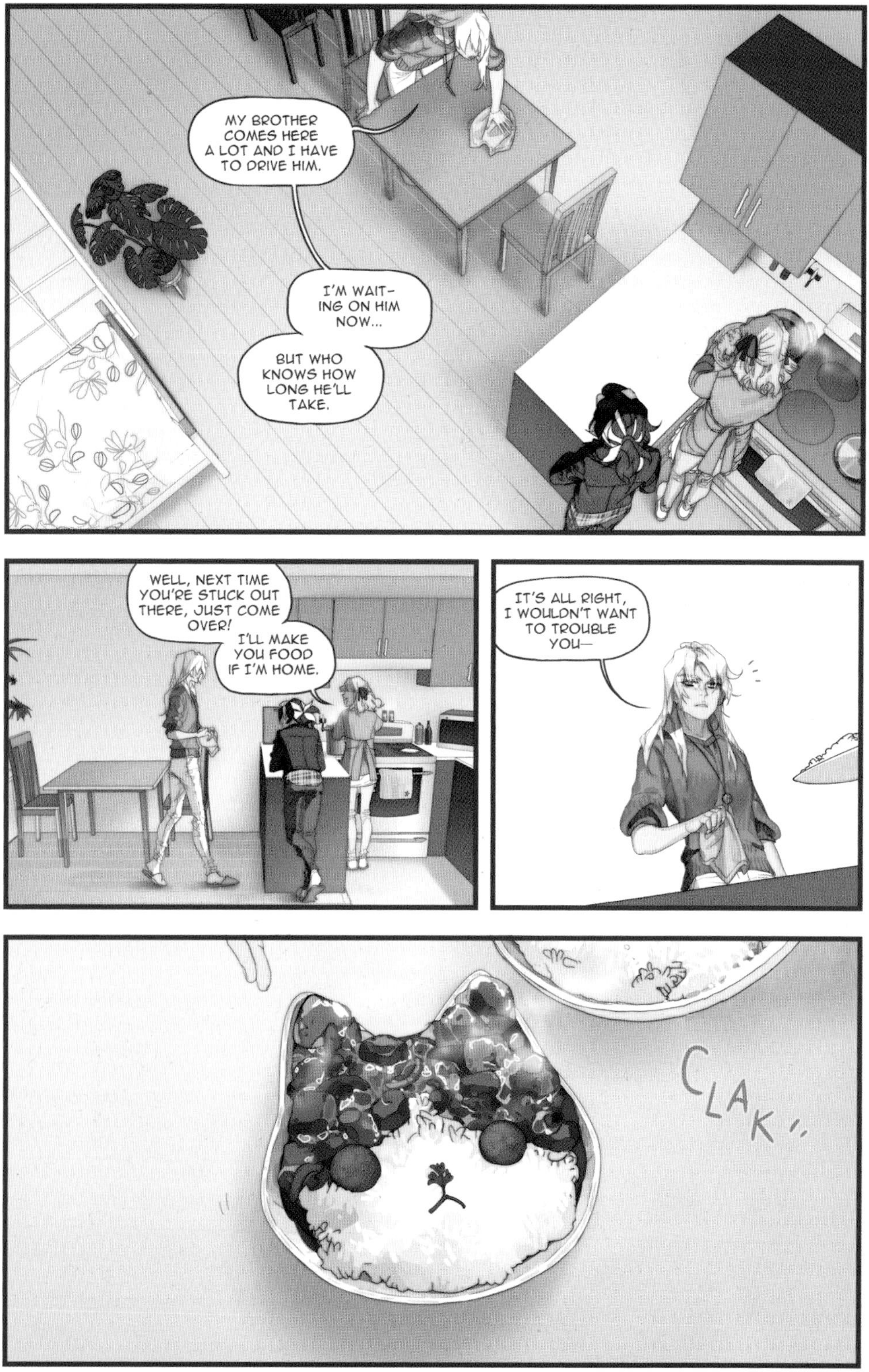
MY BROTHER COMES HERE A LOT AND I HAVE TO DRIVE HIM.
I'M WAITING ON HIM NOW...
BUT WHO KNOWS HOW LONG HE'LL TAKE.
WELL, NEXT TIME YOU'RE STUCK OUT THERE, JUST COME OVER!
I'LL MAKE YOU FOOD IF I'M HOME.
IT'S ALL RIGHT, I WOULDN'T WANT TO TROUBLE YOU—
CLAK

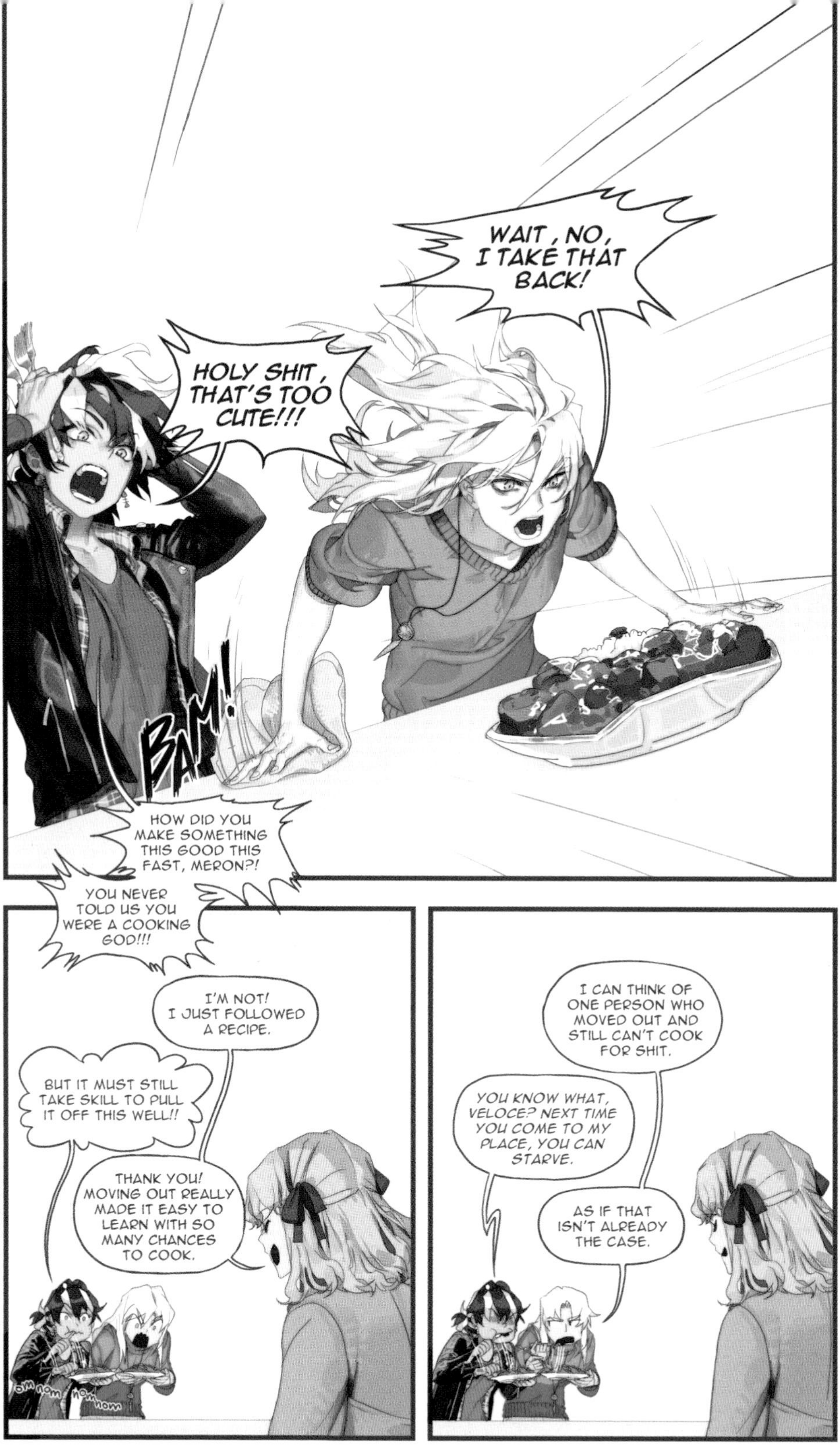
WAIT, NO, I TAKE THAT BACK!
HOLY SHIT, THAT'S TOO CUTE!!!
BAM!
HOW DID YOU MAKE SOMETHING THIS GOOD THIS FAST, MERON?!
YOU NEVER TOLD US YOU WERE A COOKING GOD!!!
I'M NOT! I JUST FOLLOWED A RECIPE.
BUT IT MUST STILL TAKE SKILL TO PULL IT OFF THIS WELL!!
THANK YOU! MOVING OUT REALLY MADE IT EASY TO LEARN WITH SO MANY CHANCES TO COOK.
nom nom nom nom
I CAN THINK OF ONE PERSON WHO MOVED OUT AND STILL CAN'T COOK FOR SHIT.
YOU KNOW WHAT, VELOCE? NEXT TIME YOU COME TO MY PLACE, YOU CAN STARVE.
AS IF THAT ISN'T ALREADY THE CASE.

10. Lunch (2)

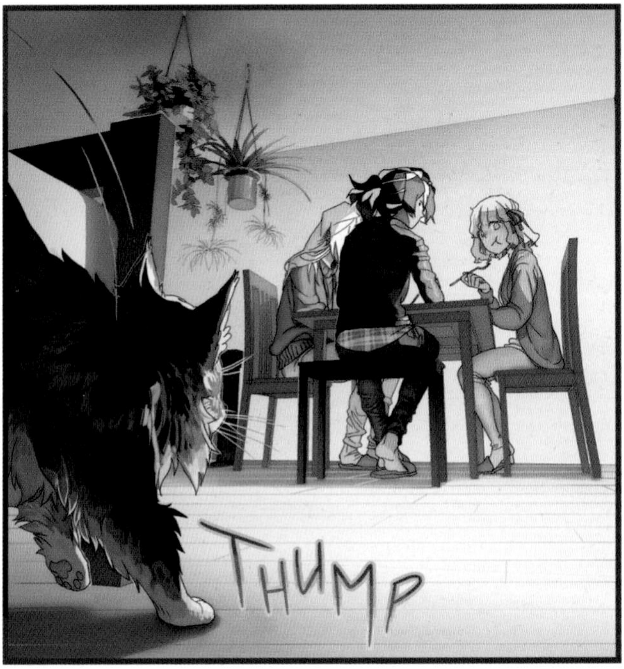
THUMP

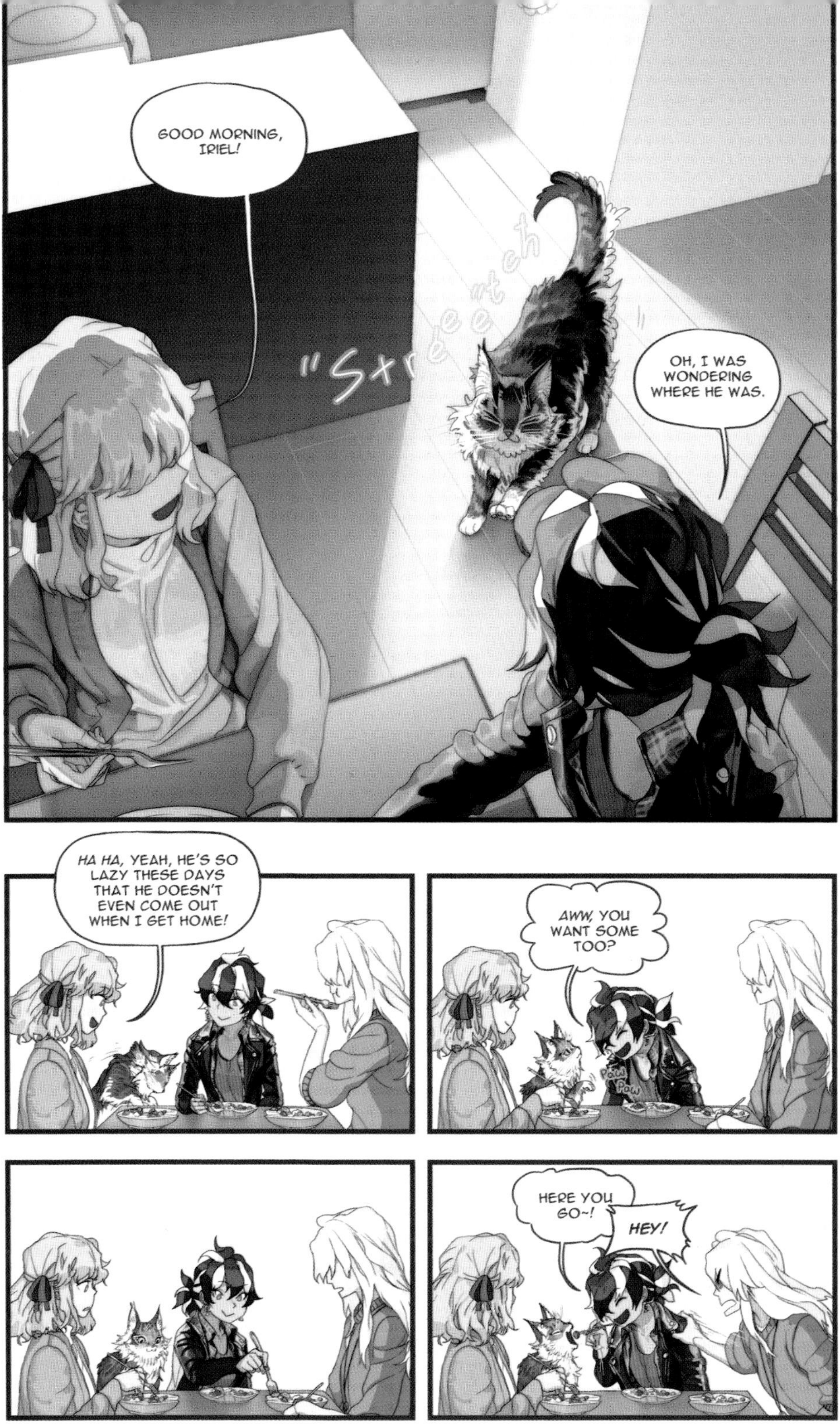
GOOD MORNING, IRIEL!
"Streeetch"
OH, I WAS WONDERING WHERE HE WAS.
HA HA, YEAH, HE'S SO LAZY THESE DAYS THAT HE DOESN'T EVEN COME OUT WHEN I GET HOME!
AWW, YOU WANT SOME TOO?
Paw Paw
HERE YOU GO~!
HEY!

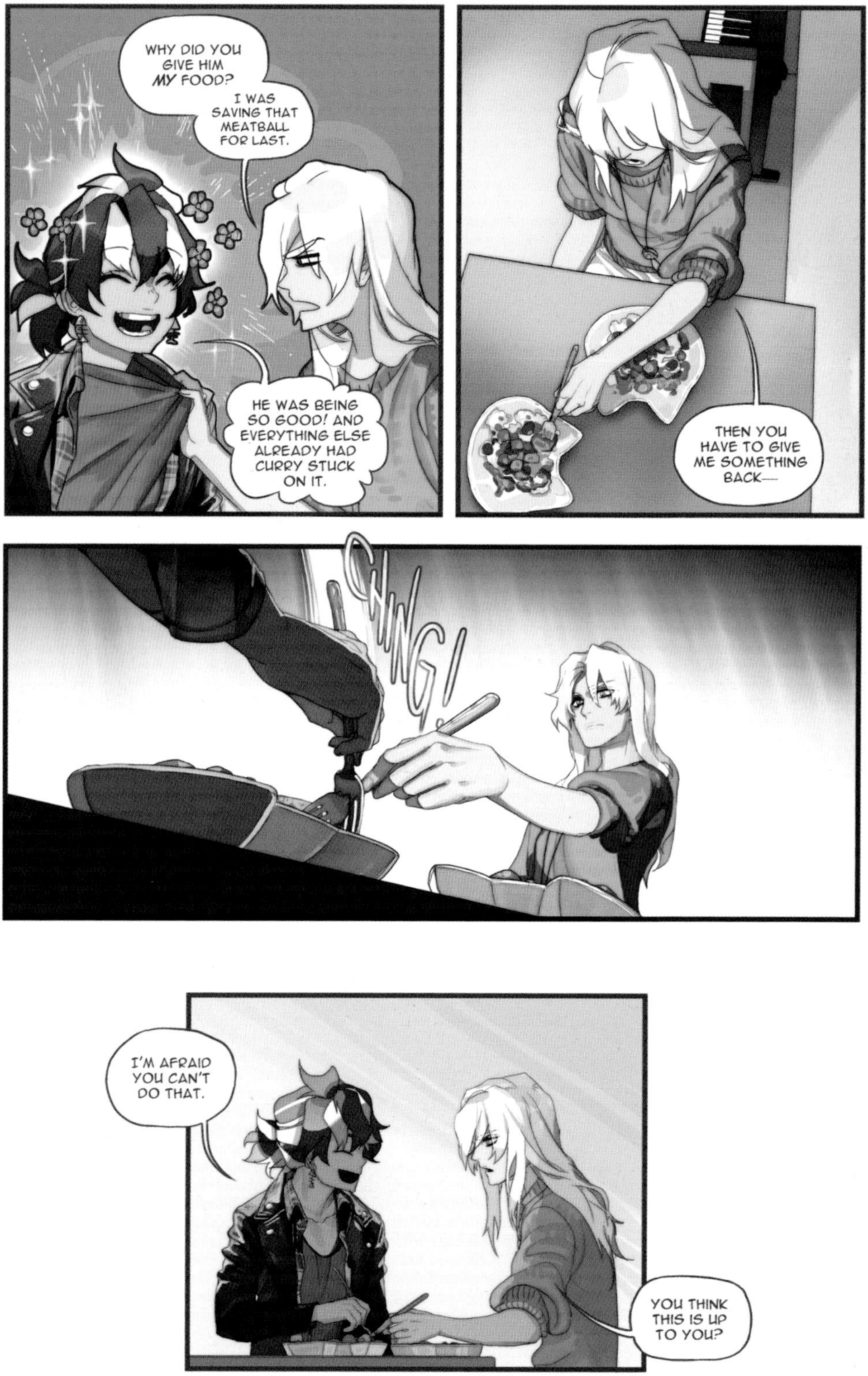
WHY DID YOU GIVE HIM MY FOOD?
I WAS SAVING THAT MEATBALL FOR LAST.
HE WAS BEING SO GOOD! AND EVERYTHING ELSE ALREADY HAD CURRY STUCK ON IT.
THEN YOU HAVE TO GIVE ME SOMETHING BACK—
CHING!
I'M AFRAID YOU CAN'T DO THAT.
YOU THINK THIS IS UP TO YOU?

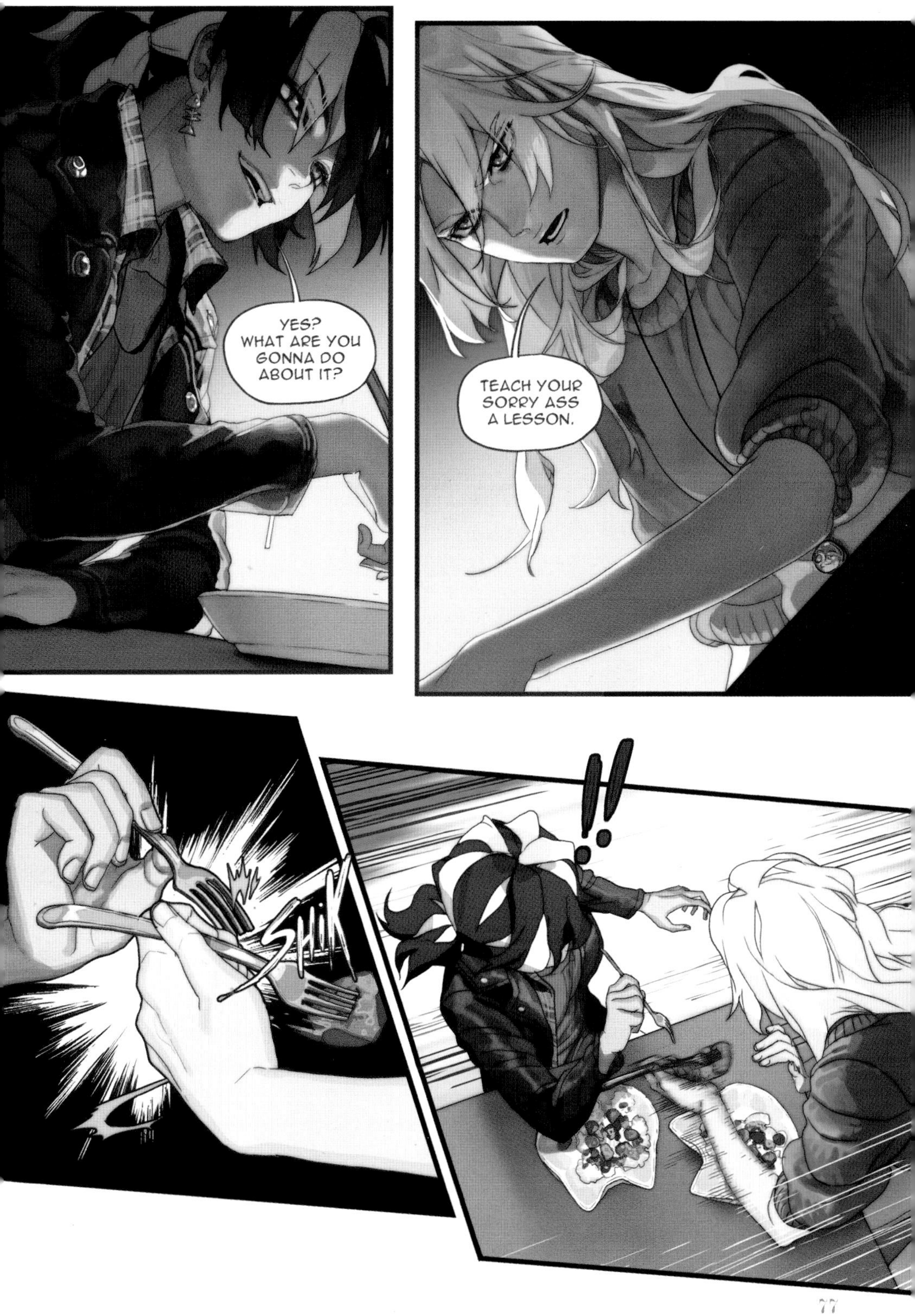
YES? WHAT ARE YOU GONNA DO ABOUT IT?
TEACH YOUR SORRY ASS A LESSON.
SHIK
!!

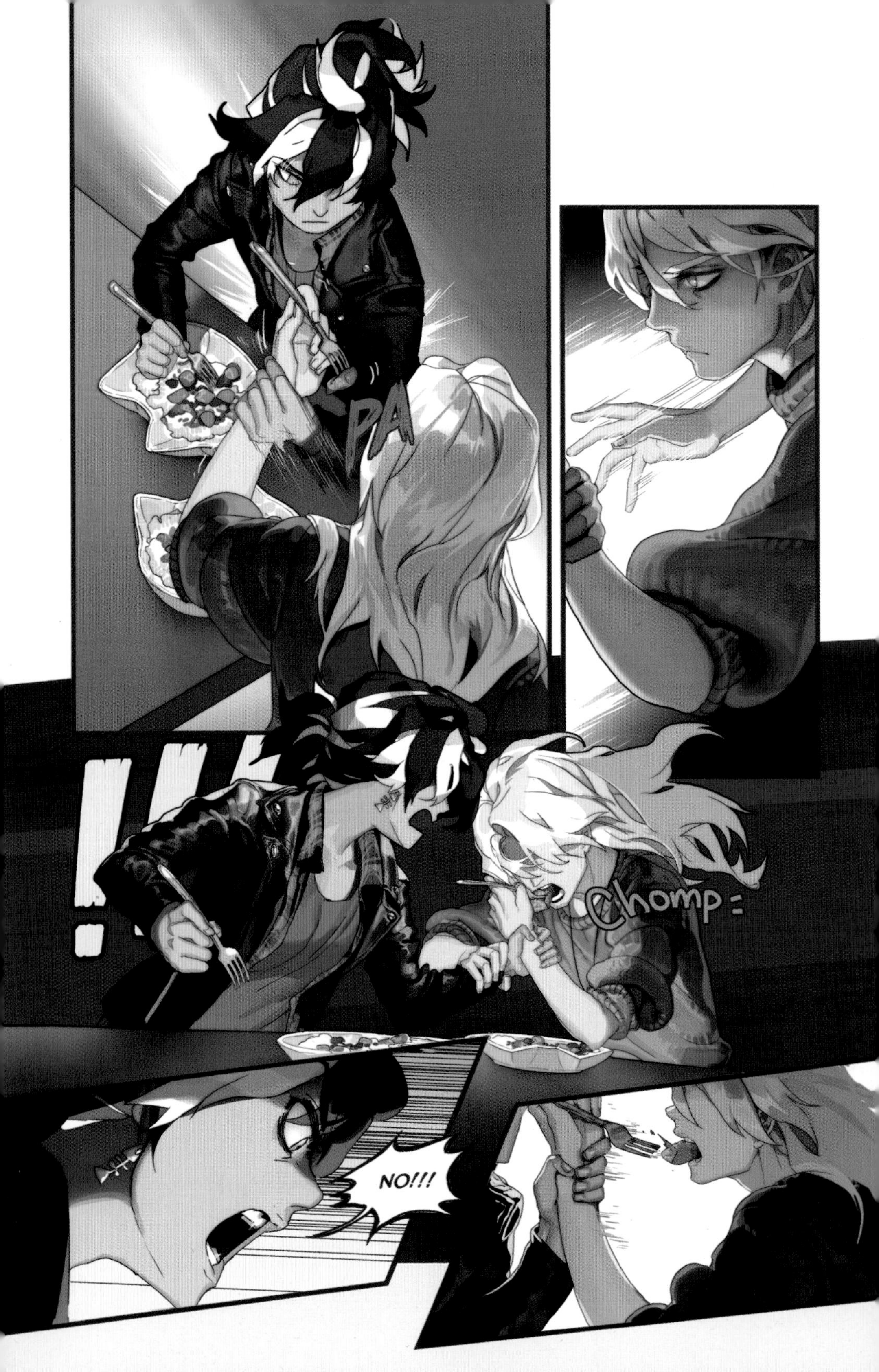
PA
!!!
Chomp
NO!!!

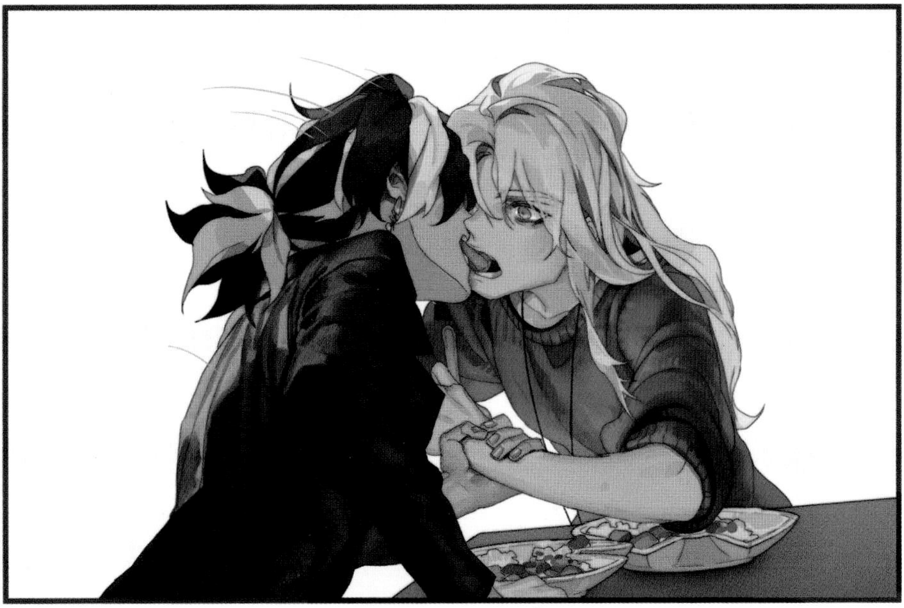

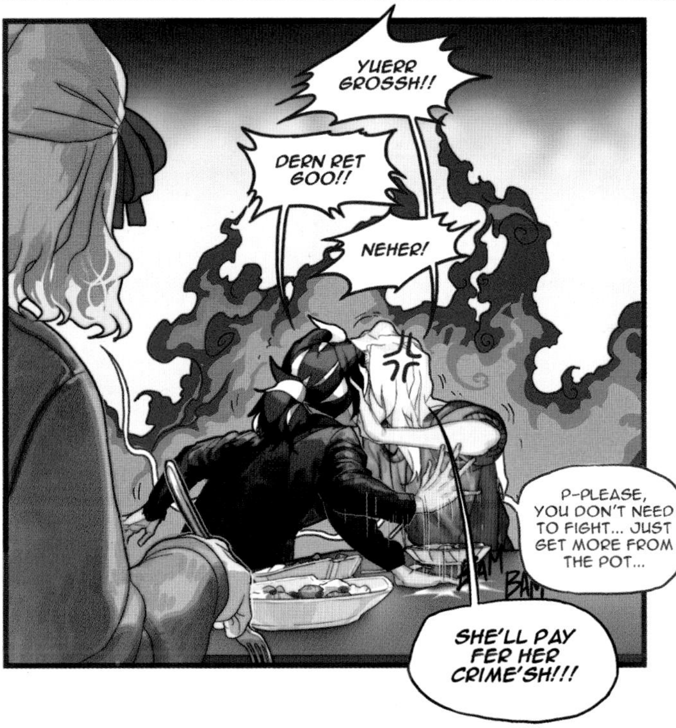
YUERR GROSSH!!
DERN RET GOO!!
NEHER!
P-PLEASE, YOU DON'T NEED TO FIGHT... JUST GET MORE FROM THE POT...
BAM BAM
SHE'LL PAY FER HER CRIME'SH!!!

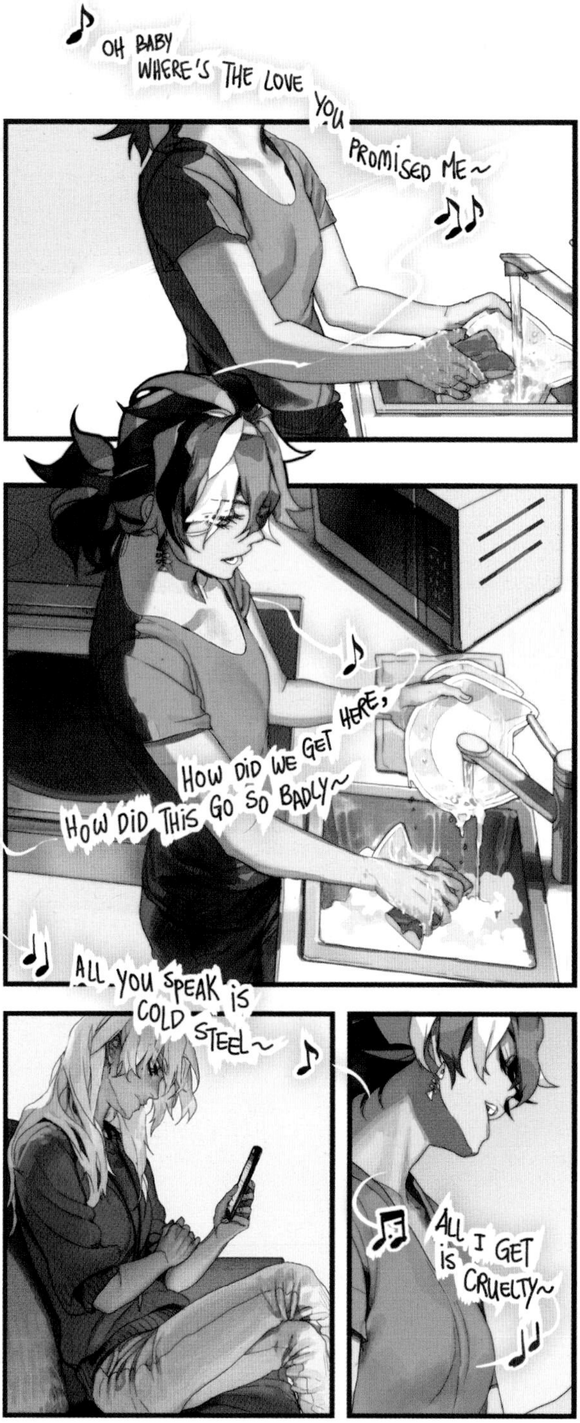
OH BABY WHERE'S THE LOVE YOU PROMISED ME~
HOW DID WE GET HERE,
HOW DID THIS GO SO BADLY~
ALL YOU SPEAK IS COLD STEEL~
ALL I GET IS CRUELTY~

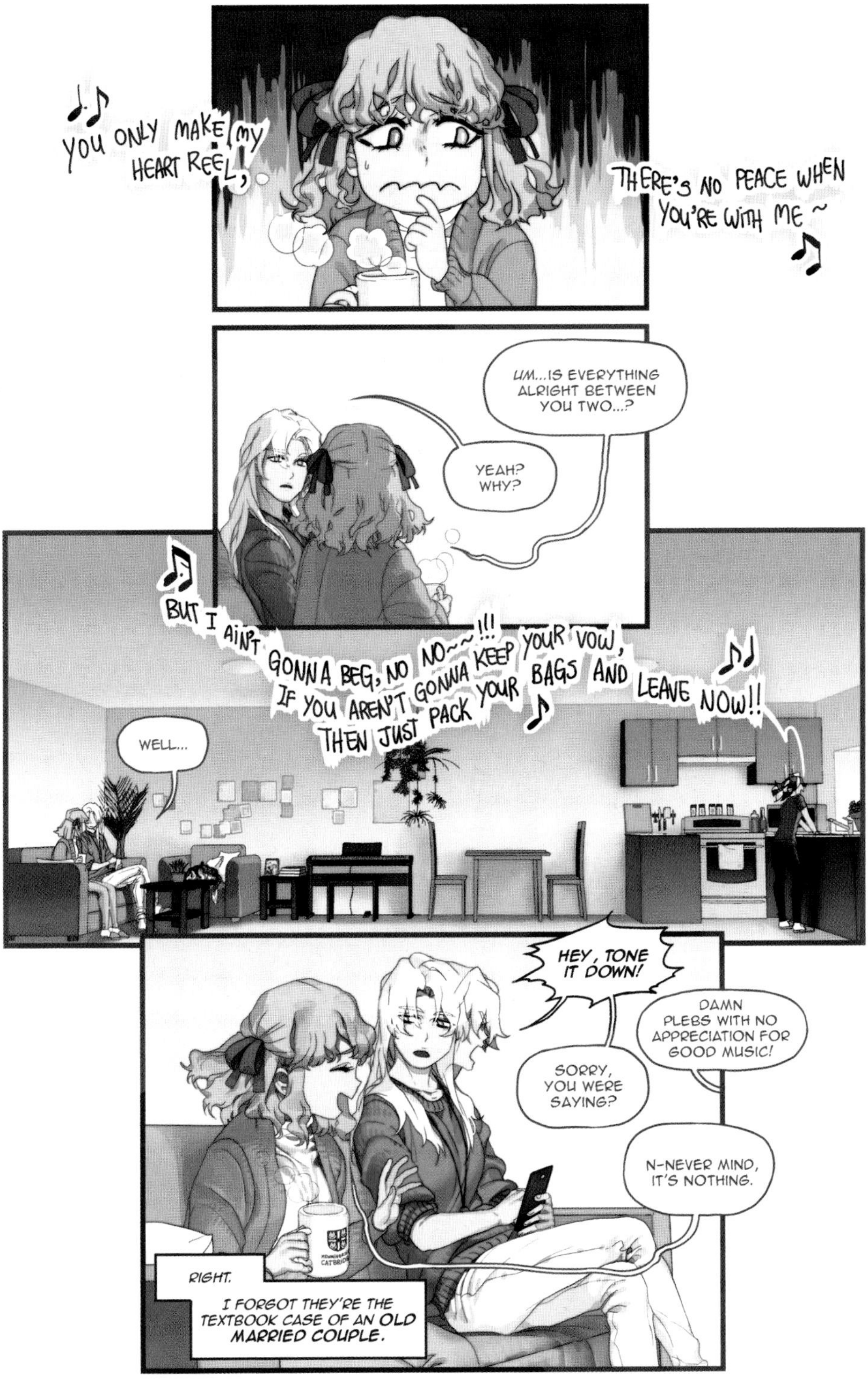
YOU ONLY MAKE MY HEART REEL,
THERE'S NO PEACE WHEN YOU'RE WITH ME ~
UM...IS EVERYTHING ALRIGHT BETWEEN YOU TWO...?
YEAH? WHY?
BUT I AIN'T GONNA BEG, NO NO~~!!!
IF YOU AREN'T GONNA KEEP YOUR VOW,
THEN JUST PACK YOUR BAGS AND LEAVE NOW!!
WELL...
HEY, TONE IT DOWN!
DAMN PLEBS WITH NO APPRECIATION FOR GOOD MUSIC!
SORRY, YOU WERE SAYING?
N-NEVER MIND, IT'S NOTHING.
RIGHT.
I FORGOT THEY'RE THE TEXTBOOK CASE OF AN OLD MARRIED COUPLE.

12. An Invitation

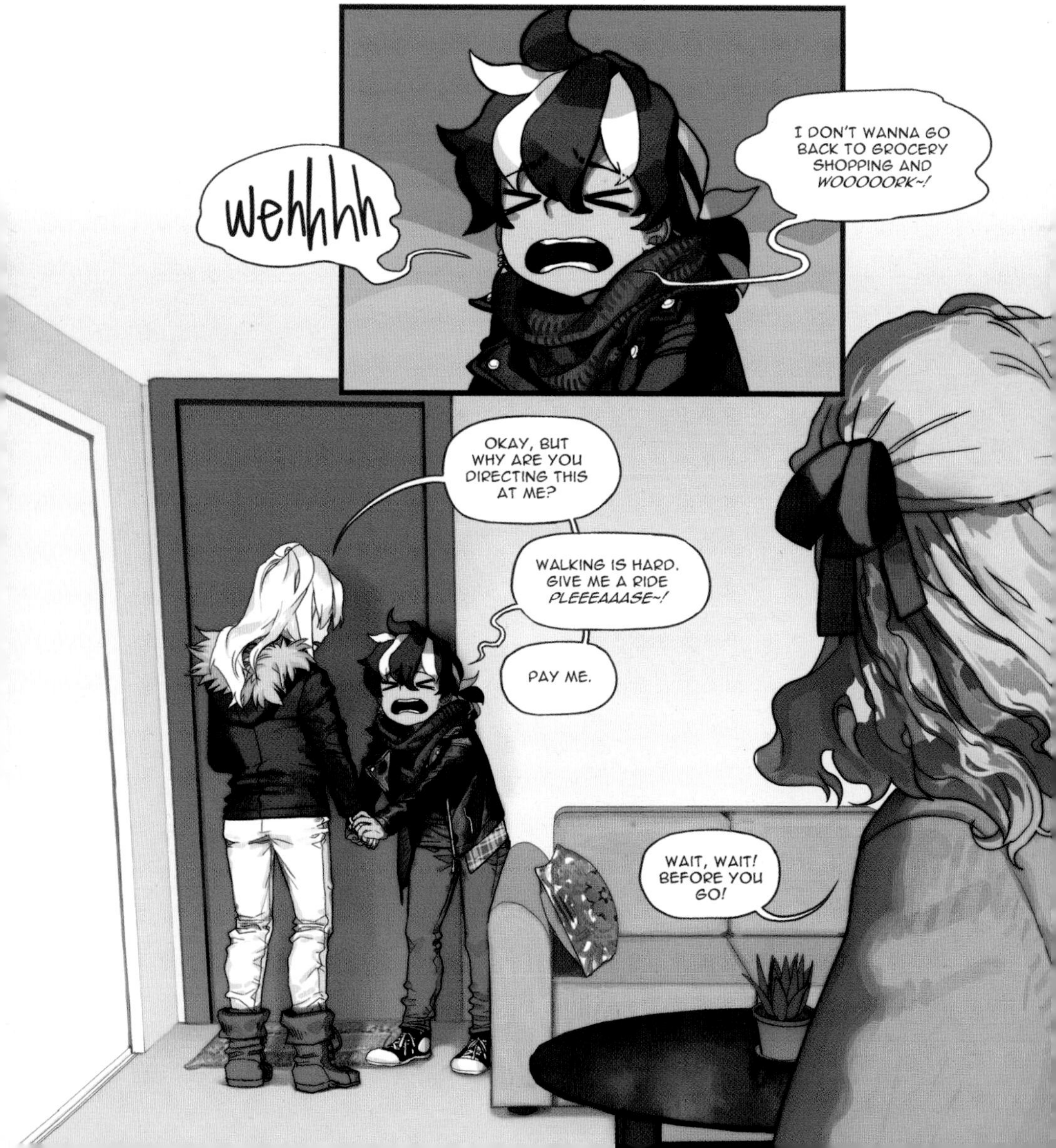
wehhh
I DON'T WANNA GO BACK TO GROCERY SHOPPING AND *WOOOOORK~!*
OKAY, BUT WHY ARE YOU DIRECTING THIS AT ME?
WALKING IS HARD. GIVE ME A RIDE *PLEEEAAASE~!*
PAY ME.
WAIT, WAIT! BEFORE YOU GO!

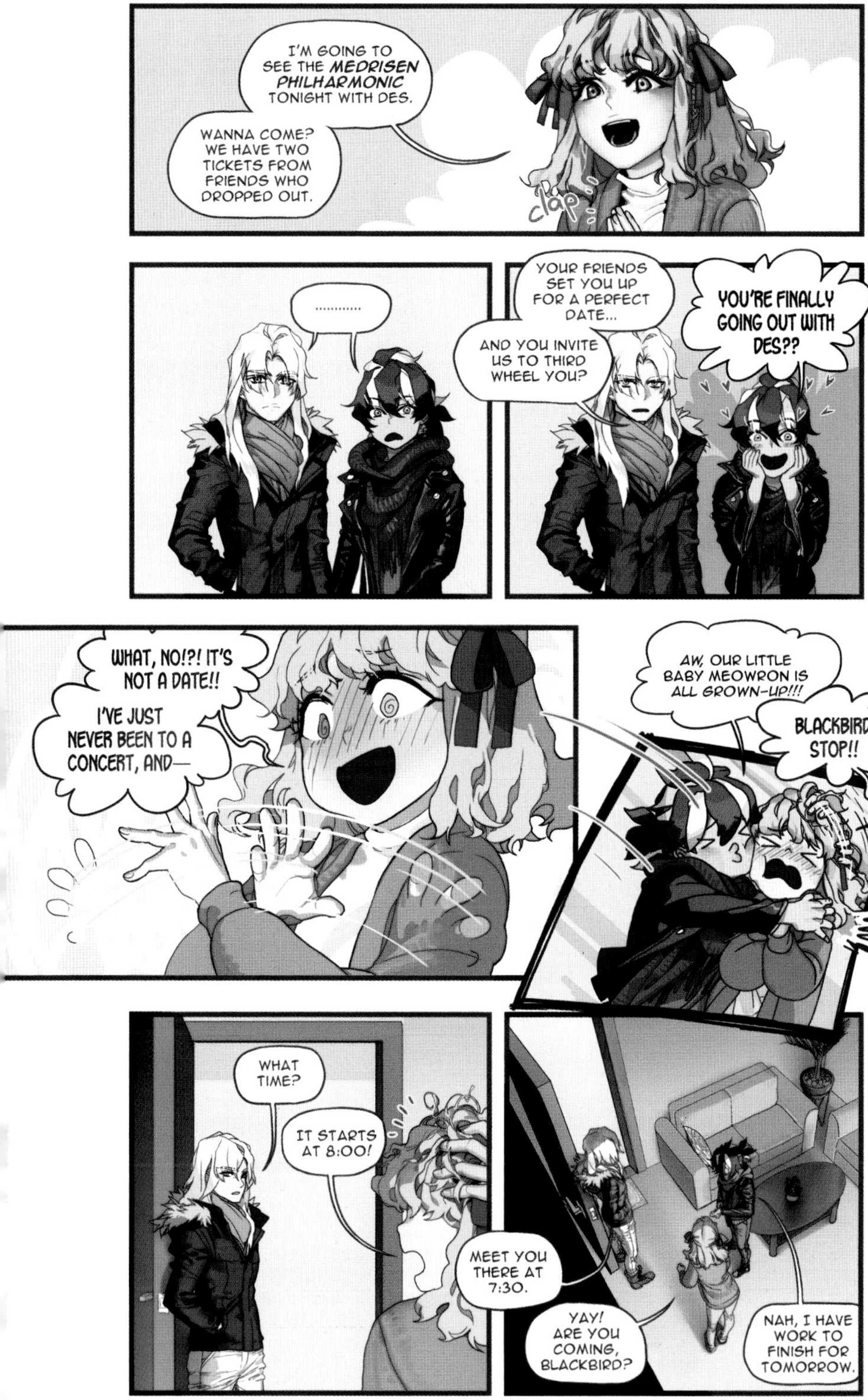

I'M GOING TO SEE THE MEDRISEN PHILHARMONIC TONIGHT WITH DES.
WANNA COME? WE HAVE TWO TICKETS FROM FRIENDS WHO DROPPED OUT.
clap
....
YOUR FRIENDS SET YOU UP FOR A PERFECT DATE...
AND YOU INVITE US TO THIRD WHEEL YOU?
YOU'RE FINALLY GOING OUT WITH DES??
WHAT, NO!?! IT'S NOT A DATE!!
I'VE JUST NEVER BEEN TO A CONCERT, AND—
AW, OUR LITTLE BABY MEOWRON IS ALL GROWN-UP!!!
BLACKBIRD, STOP!!
WHAT TIME?
IT STARTS AT 8:00!
MEET YOU THERE AT 7:30.
YAY! ARE YOU COMING, BLACKBIRD?
NAH, I HAVE WORK TO FINISH FOR TOMORROW.

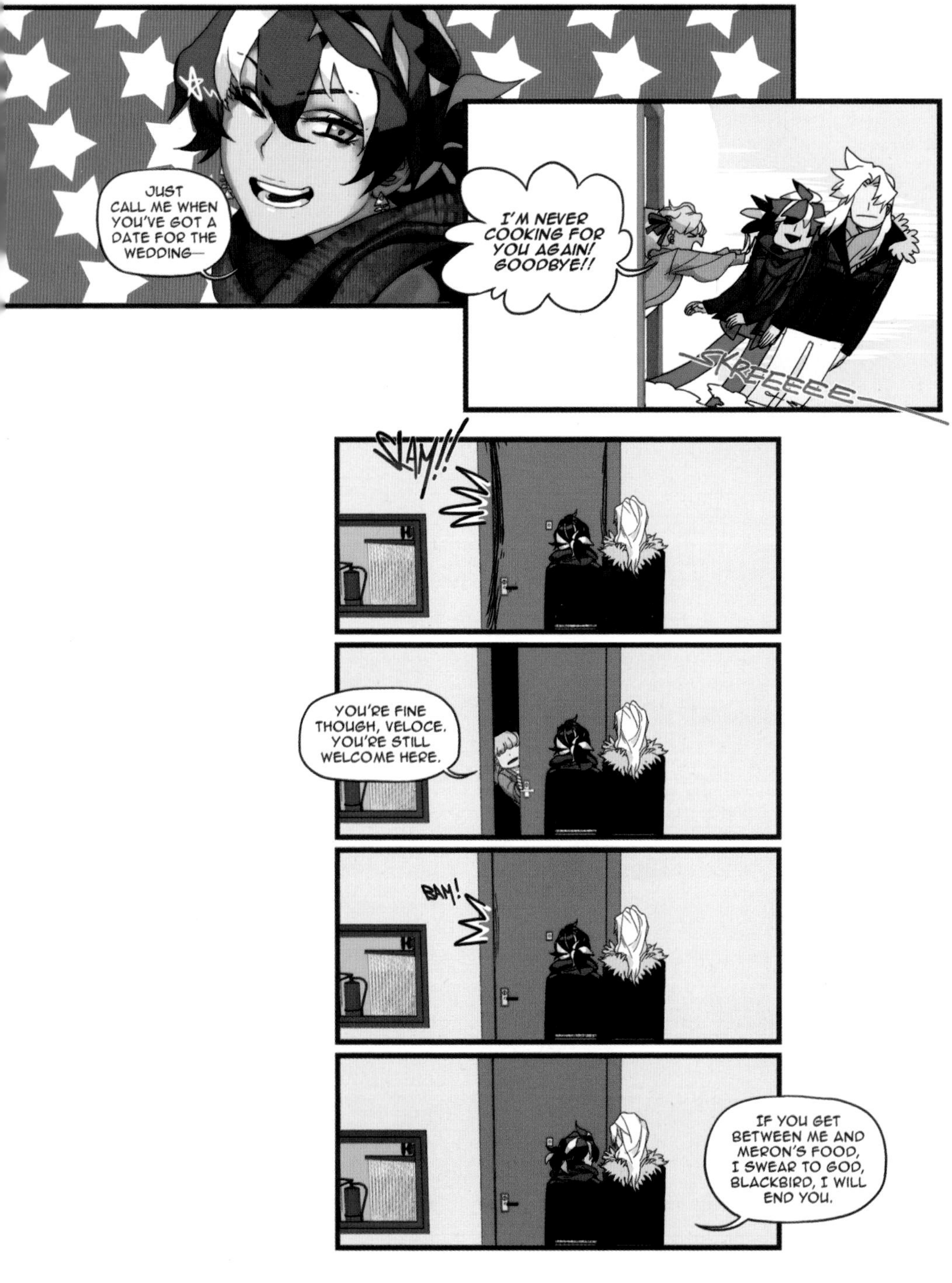
JUST CALL ME WHEN YOU'VE GOT A DATE FOR THE WEDDING—
I'M NEVER COOKING FOR YOU AGAIN! GOODBYE!!
SKREEEEEE—
SLAM!!
YOU'RE FINE THOUGH, VELOCE. YOU'RE STILL WELCOME HERE.
BAM!
IF YOU GET BETWEEN ME AND MERON'S FOOD, I SWEAR TO GOD, BLACKBIRD, I WILL END YOU.

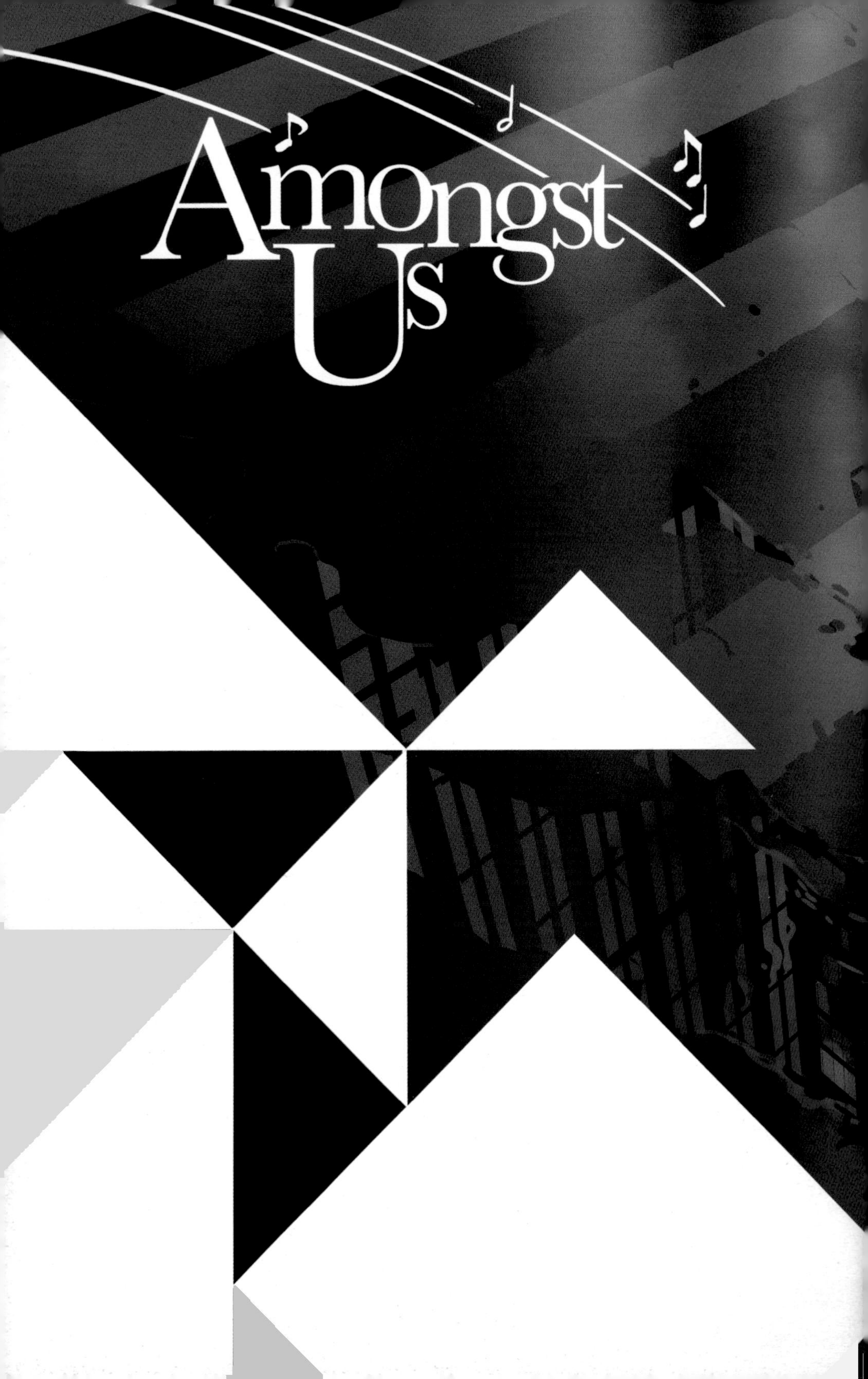
Amongst Us

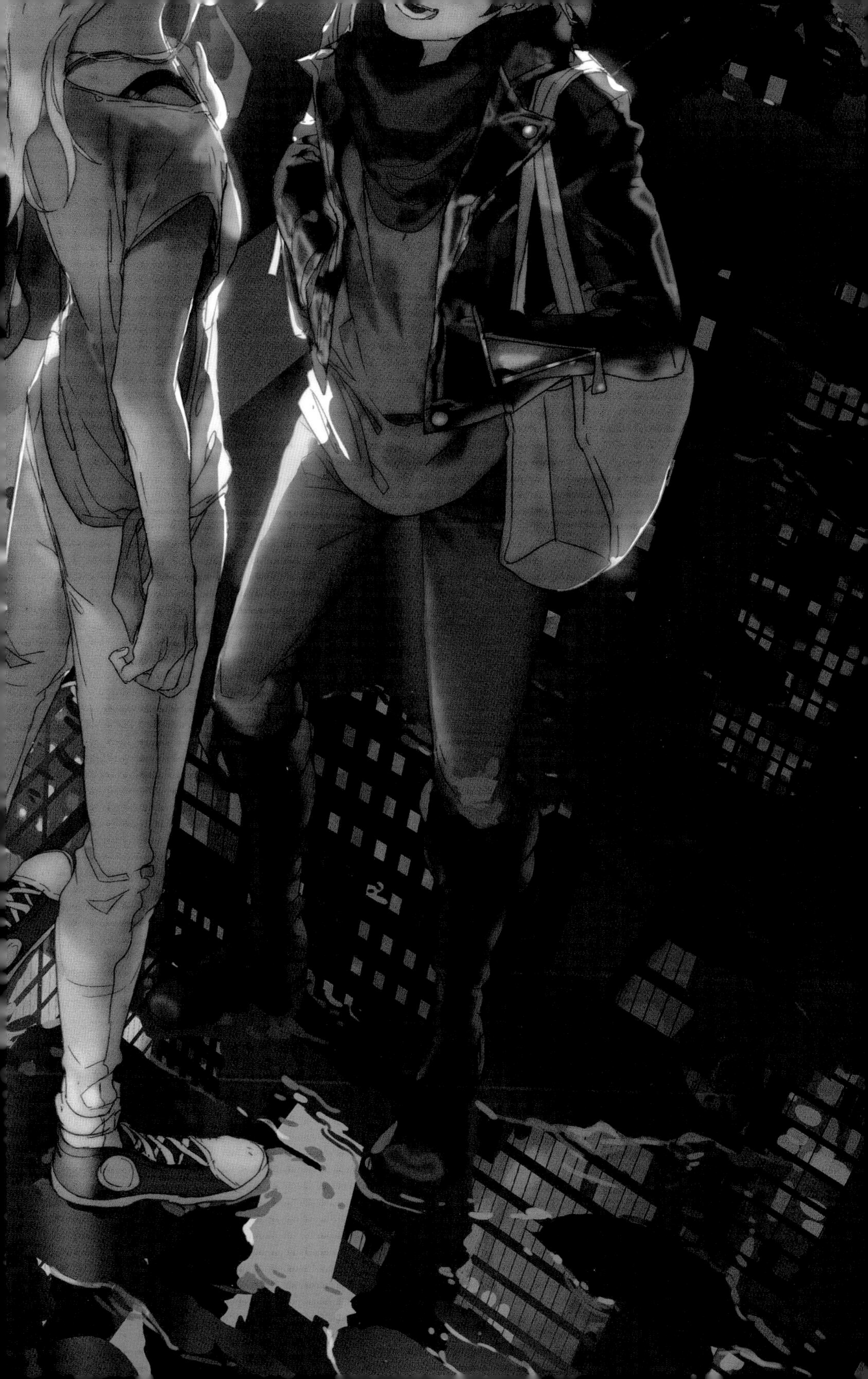

HONK
HONNNK
TOK
TOK
TOK

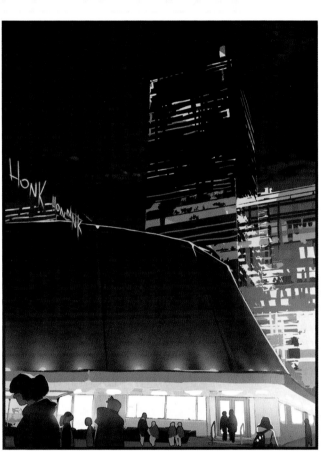

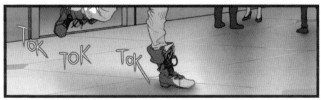

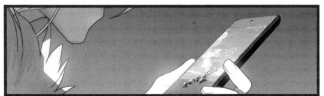

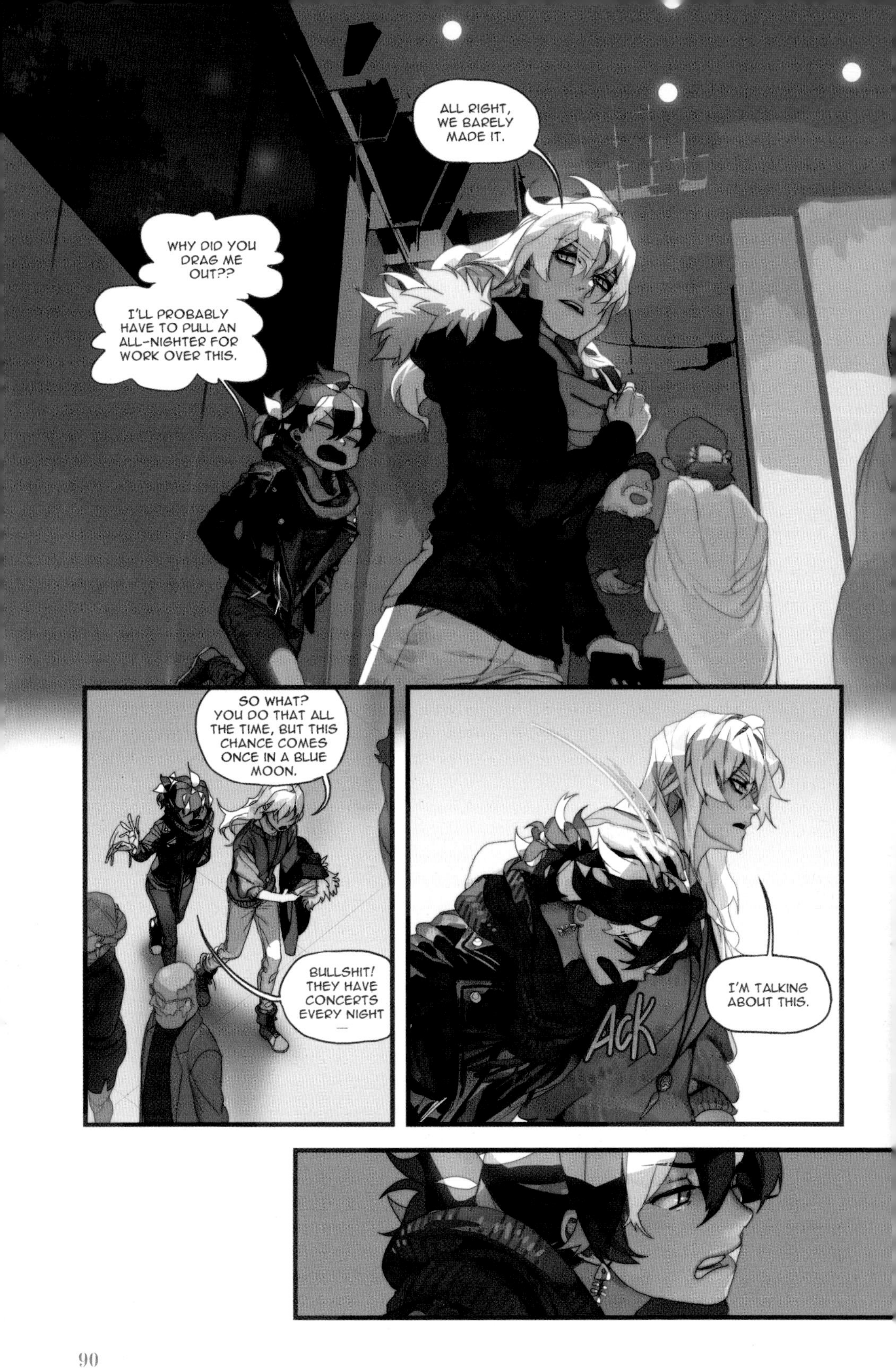
ALL RIGHT, WE BARELY MADE IT.
WHY DID YOU DRAG ME OUT??
I'LL PROBABLY HAVE TO PULL AN ALL-NIGHTER FOR WORK OVER THIS.
SO WHAT? YOU DO THAT ALL THE TIME, BUT THIS CHANCE COMES ONCE IN A BLUE MOON.
BULLSHIT! THEY HAVE CONCERTS EVERY NIGHT —
ACK
I'M TALKING ABOUT THIS.

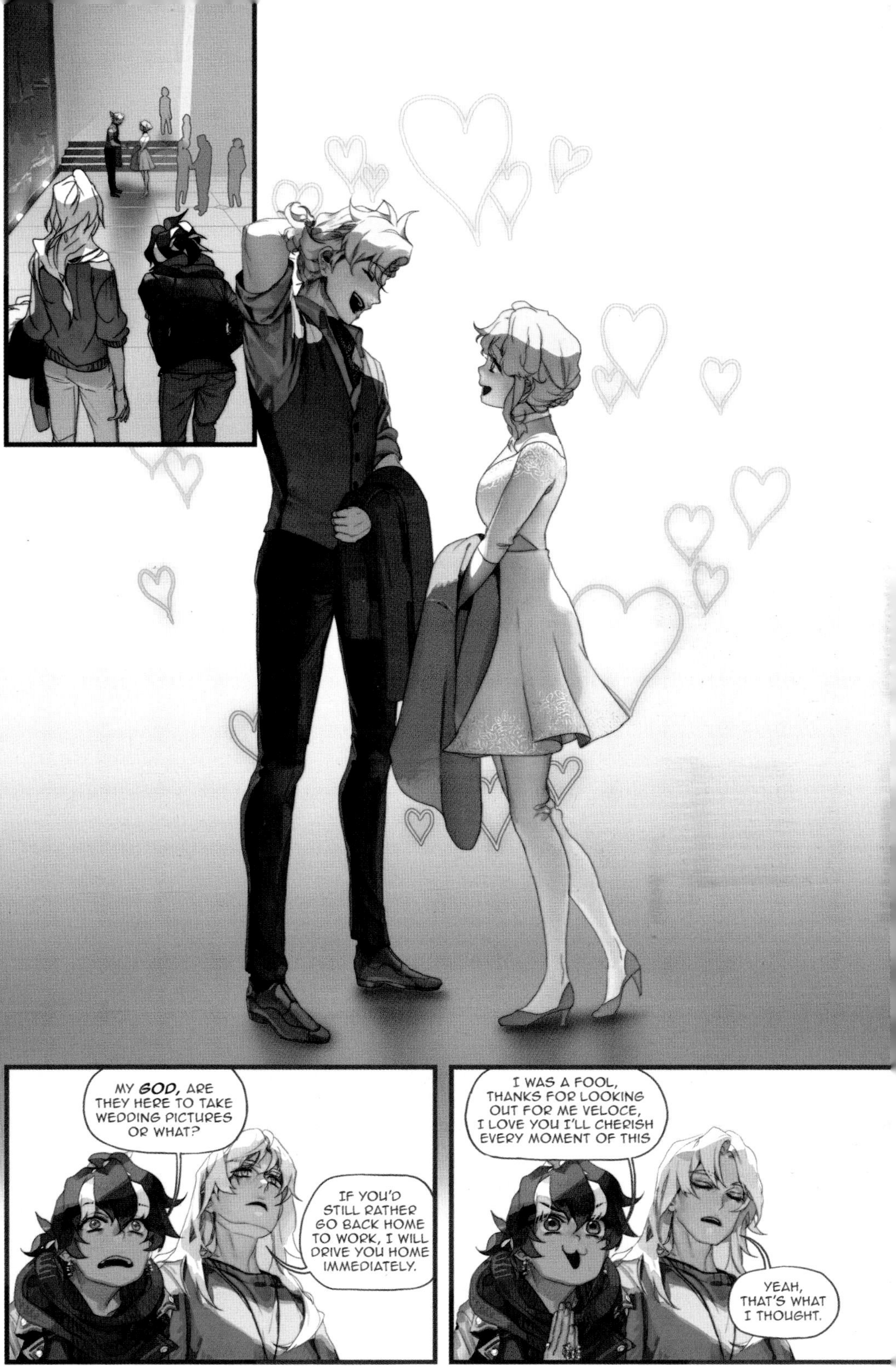
MY GOD, ARE THEY HERE TO TAKE WEDDING PICTURES OR WHAT?
IF YOU'D STILL RATHER GO BACK HOME TO WORK, I WILL DRIVE YOU HOME IMMEDIATELY.
I WAS A FOOL, THANKS FOR LOOKING OUT FOR ME VELOCE, I LOVE YOU I'LL CHERISH EVERY MOMENT OF THIS
YEAH, THAT'S WHAT I THOUGHT.

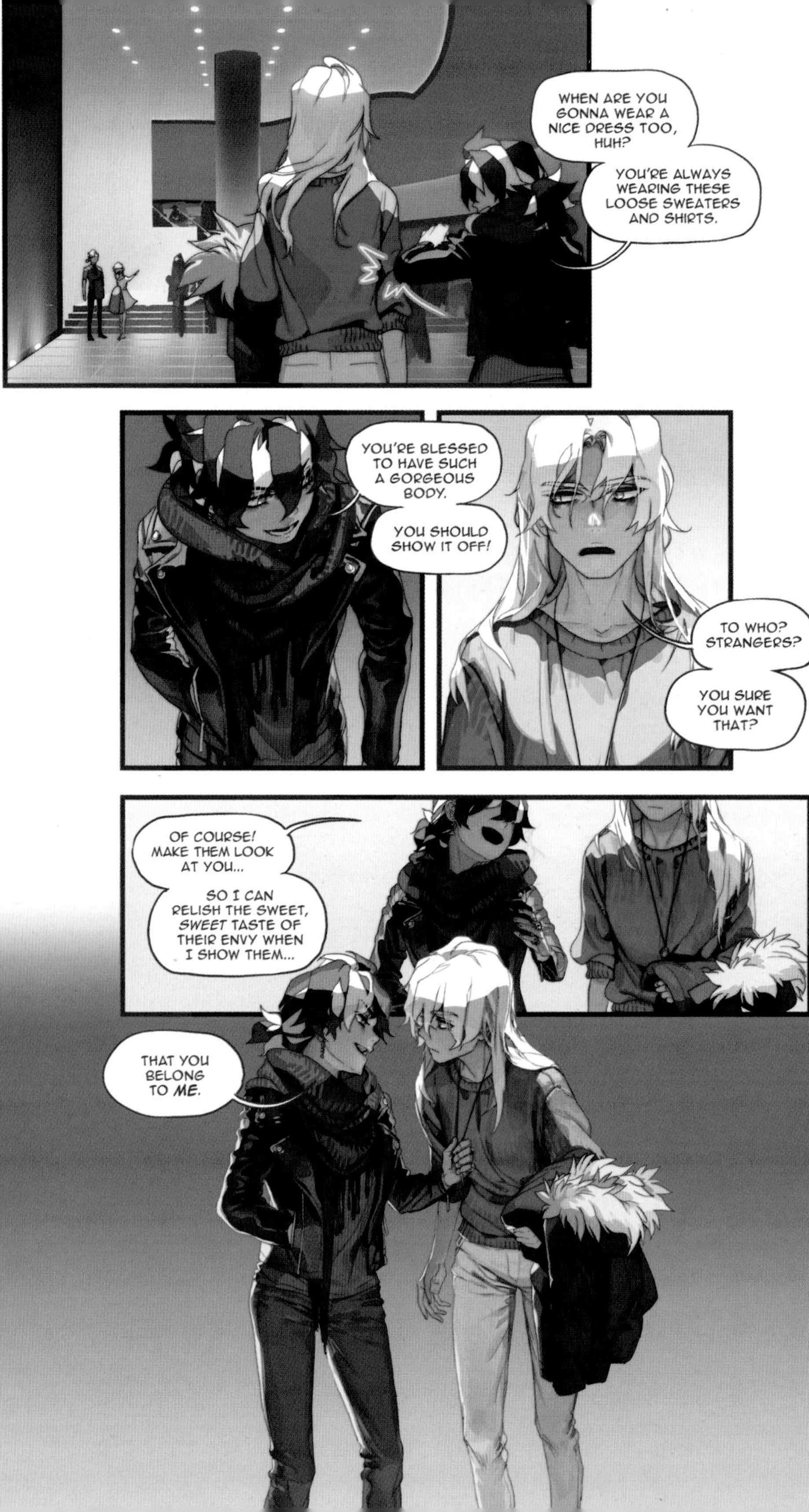
WHEN ARE YOU GONNA WEAR A NICE DRESS TOO, HUH?
YOU'RE ALWAYS WEARING THESE LOOSE SWEATERS AND SHIRTS.
YOU'RE BLESSED TO HAVE SUCH A GORGEOUS BODY.
YOU SHOULD SHOW IT OFF!
TO WHO? STRANGERS?
YOU SURE YOU WANT THAT?
OF COURSE! MAKE THEM LOOK AT YOU...
SO I CAN RELISH THE SWEET, *SWEET* TASTE OF THEIR ENVY WHEN I SHOW THEM...
THAT YOU BELONG TO *ME*.

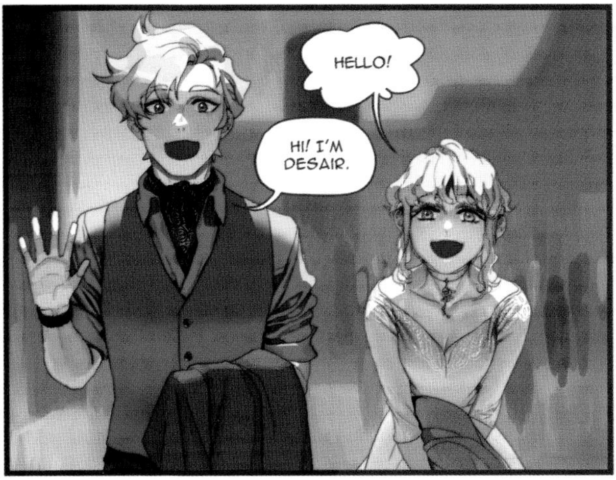
HELLO!
HI! I'M DESAIR.

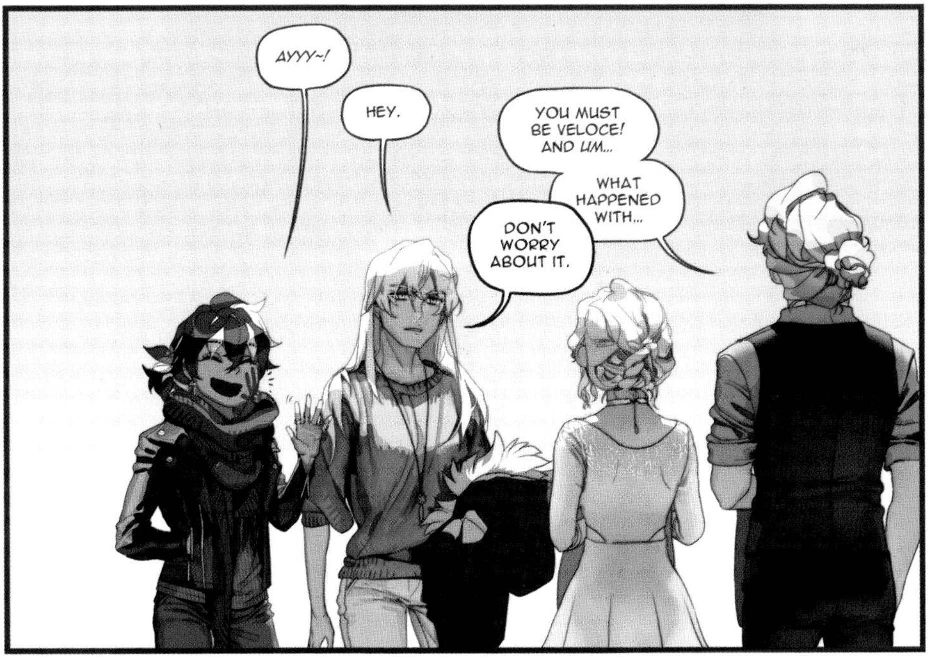
AYYY~!
HEY.
YOU MUST BE VELOCE! AND UM...
WHAT HAPPENED WITH...
DON'T WORRY ABOUT IT.

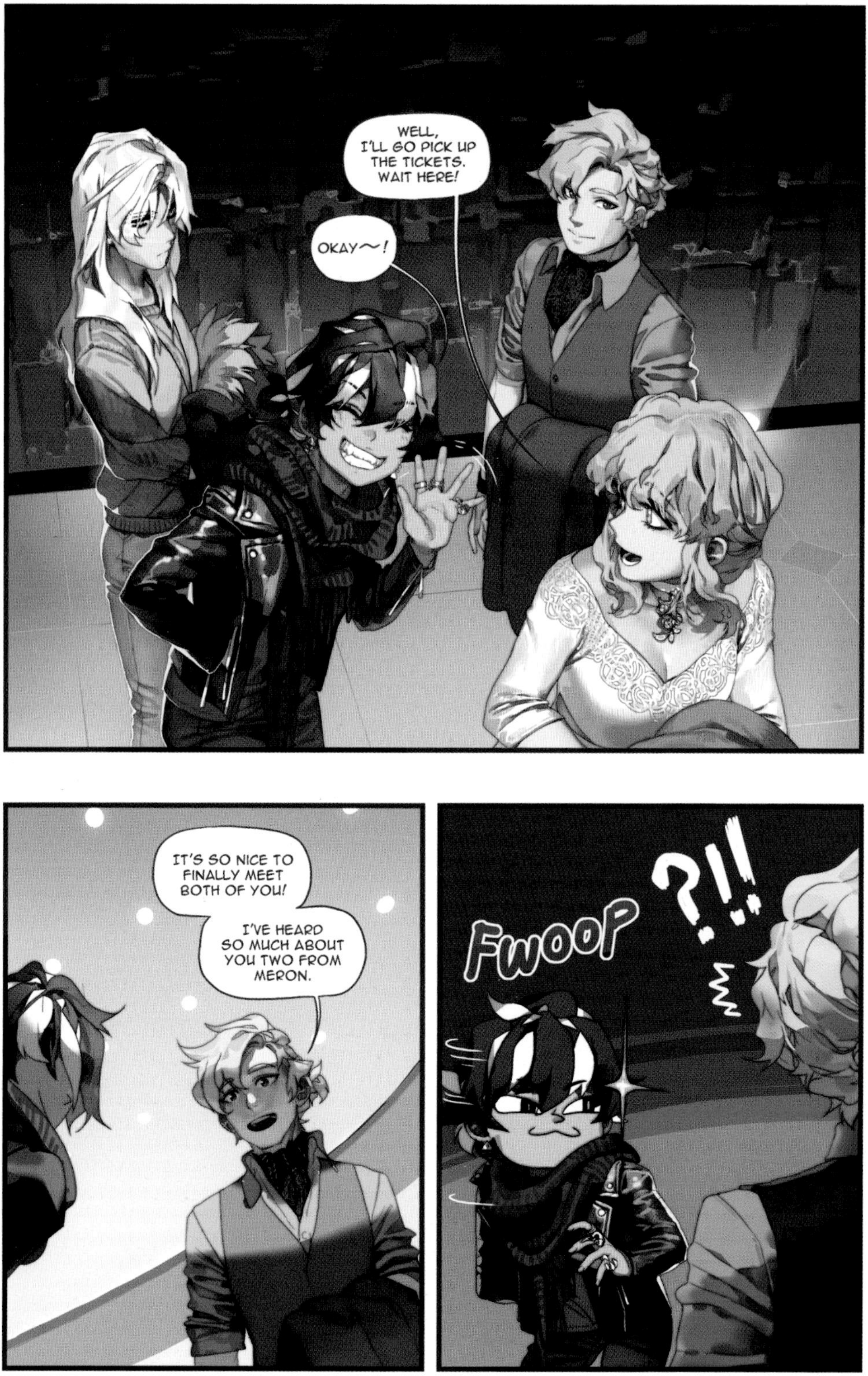
WELL, I'LL GO PICK UP THE TICKETS. WAIT HERE!
OKAY~!
IT'S SO NICE TO FINALLY MEET BOTH OF YOU!
I'VE HEARD SO MUCH ABOUT YOU TWO FROM MERON.
FWOOP
?!!

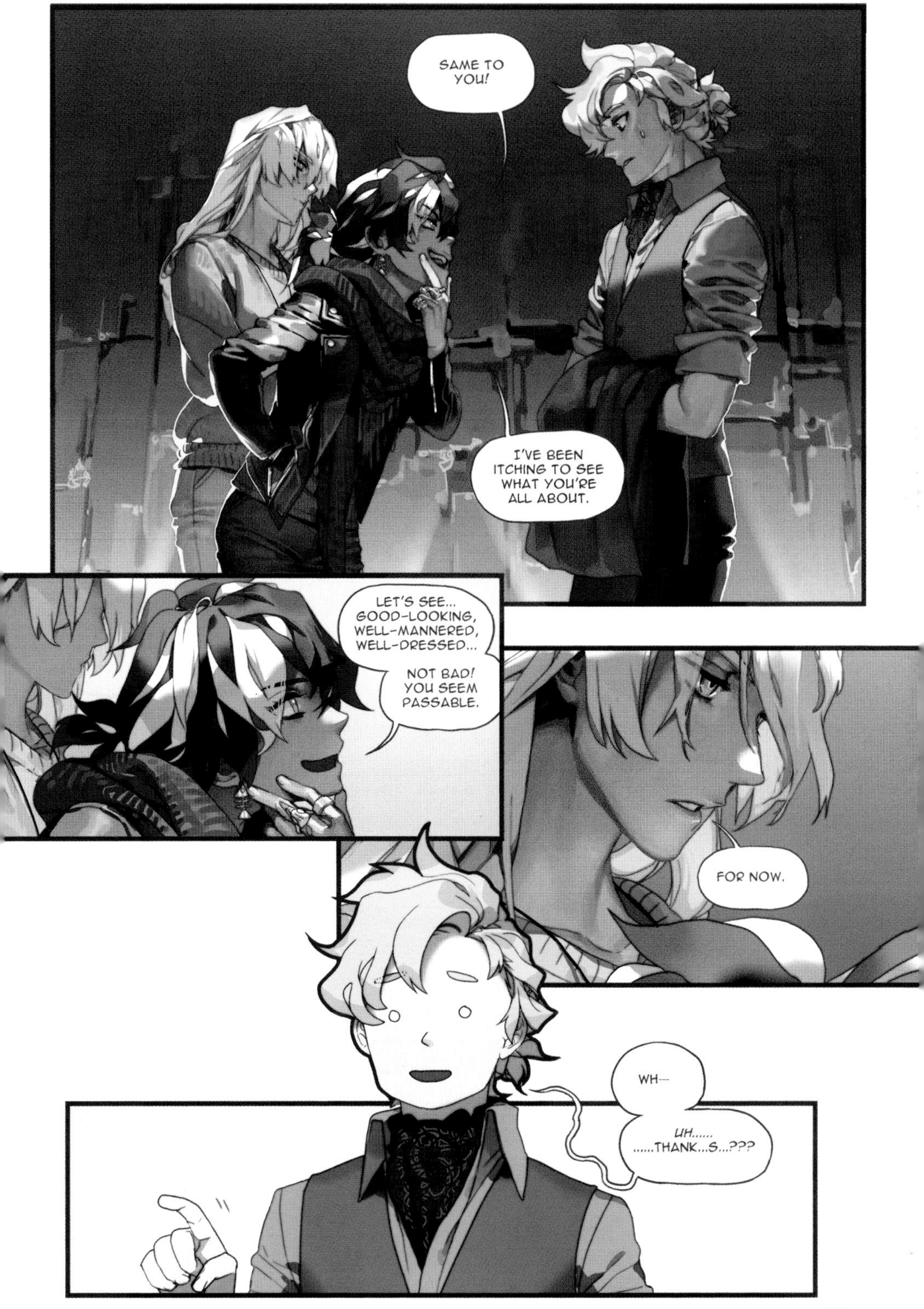
SAME TO YOU!
I'VE BEEN ITCHING TO SEE WHAT YOU'RE ALL ABOUT.
LET'S SEE... GOOD-LOOKING, WELL-MANNERED, WELL-DRESSED...
NOT BAD! YOU SEEM PASSABLE.
FOR NOW.
WH--
UH...... ......THANK...S...???

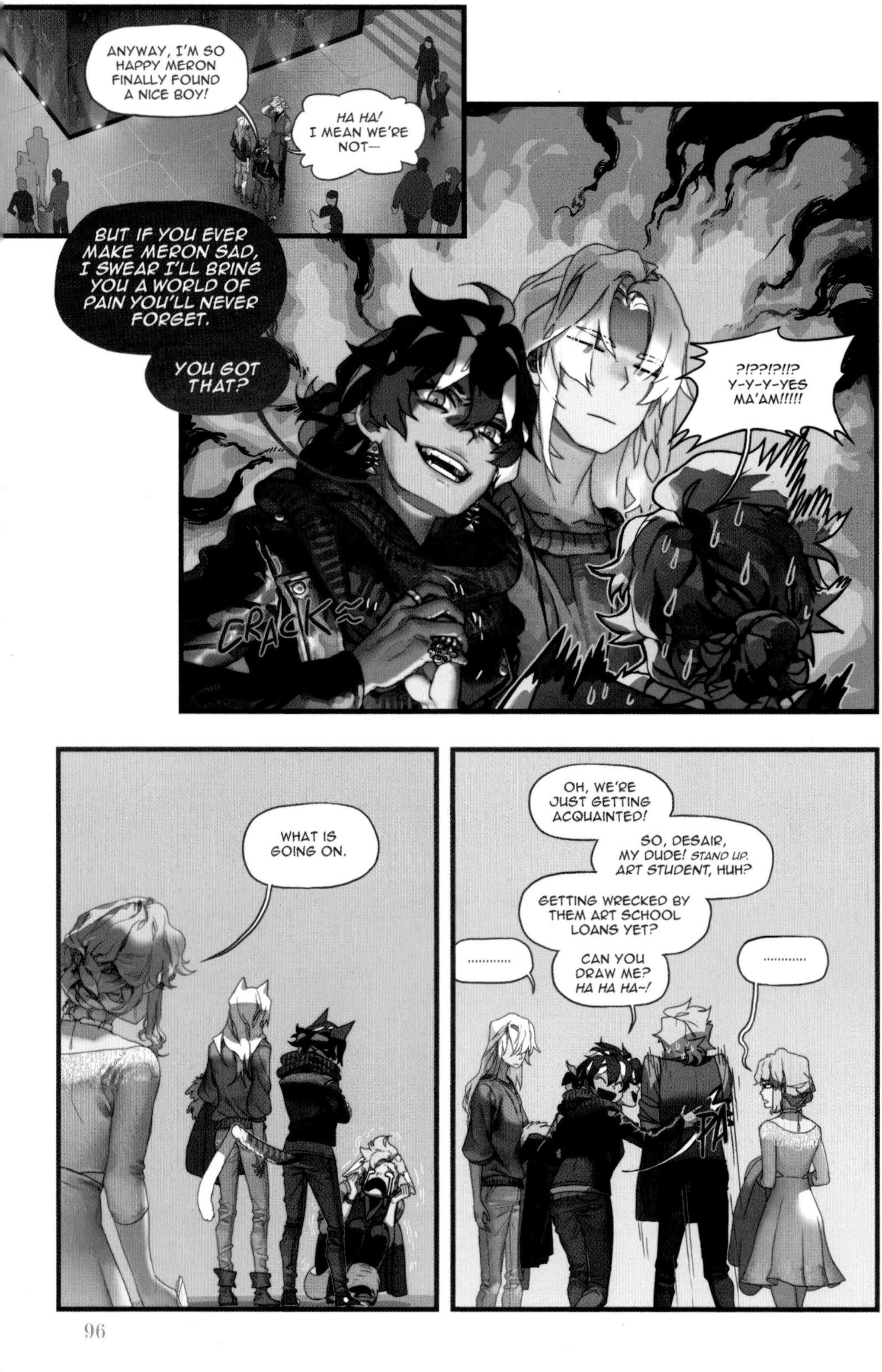
ANYWAY, I'M SO HAPPY MERON FINALLY FOUND A NICE BOY!
HA HA! I MEAN WE'RE NOT—
BUT IF YOU EVER MAKE MERON SAD, I SWEAR I'LL BRING YOU A WORLD OF PAIN YOU'LL NEVER FORGET.
YOU GOT THAT?
?!??!?!!? Y-Y-Y-YES MA'AM!!!!!
CRACK
WHAT IS GOING ON.
OH, WE'RE JUST GETTING ACQUAINTED!
SO, DESAIR, MY DUDE! STAND UP. ART STUDENT, HUH?
GETTING WRECKED BY THEM ART SCHOOL LOANS YET?
....
CAN YOU DRAW ME? HA HA HA~!
....

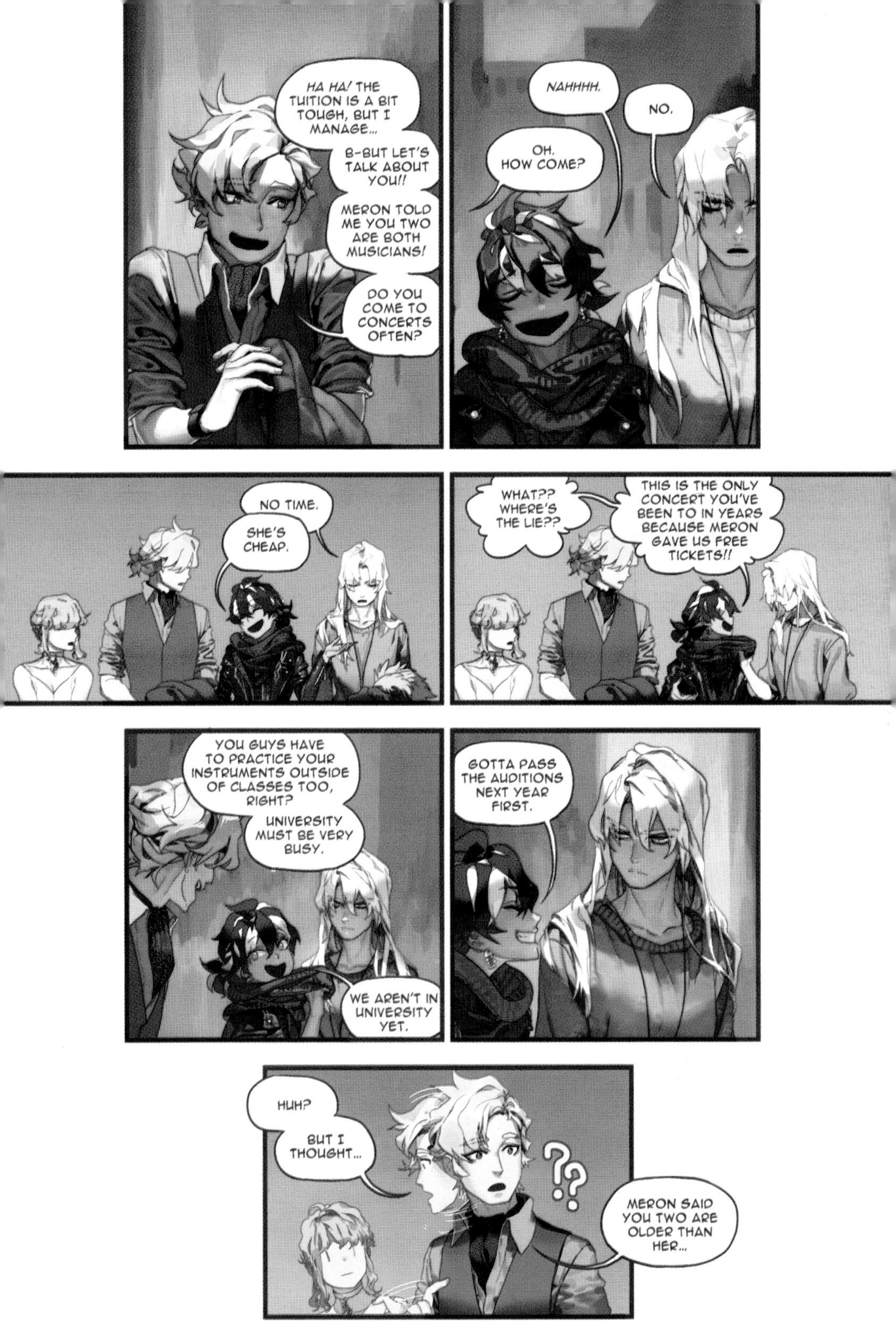
HA HA! THE TUITION IS A BIT TOUGH, BUT I MANAGE...
B-BUT LET'S TALK ABOUT YOU!!
MERON TOLD ME YOU TWO ARE BOTH MUSICIANS!
DO YOU COME TO CONCERTS OFTEN?
NAHHHH.
OH. HOW COME?
NO.
NO TIME.
SHE'S CHEAP.
WHAT?? WHERE'S THE LIE??
THIS IS THE ONLY CONCERT YOU'VE BEEN TO IN YEARS BECAUSE MERON GAVE US FREE TICKETS!!
YOU GUYS HAVE TO PRACTICE YOUR INSTRUMENTS OUTSIDE OF CLASSES TOO, RIGHT?
UNIVERSITY MUST BE VERY BUSY.
WE AREN'T IN UNIVERSITY YET.
GOTTA PASS THE AUDITIONS NEXT YEAR FIRST.
HUH?
BUT I THOUGHT...
??
MERON SAID YOU TWO ARE OLDER THAN HER...

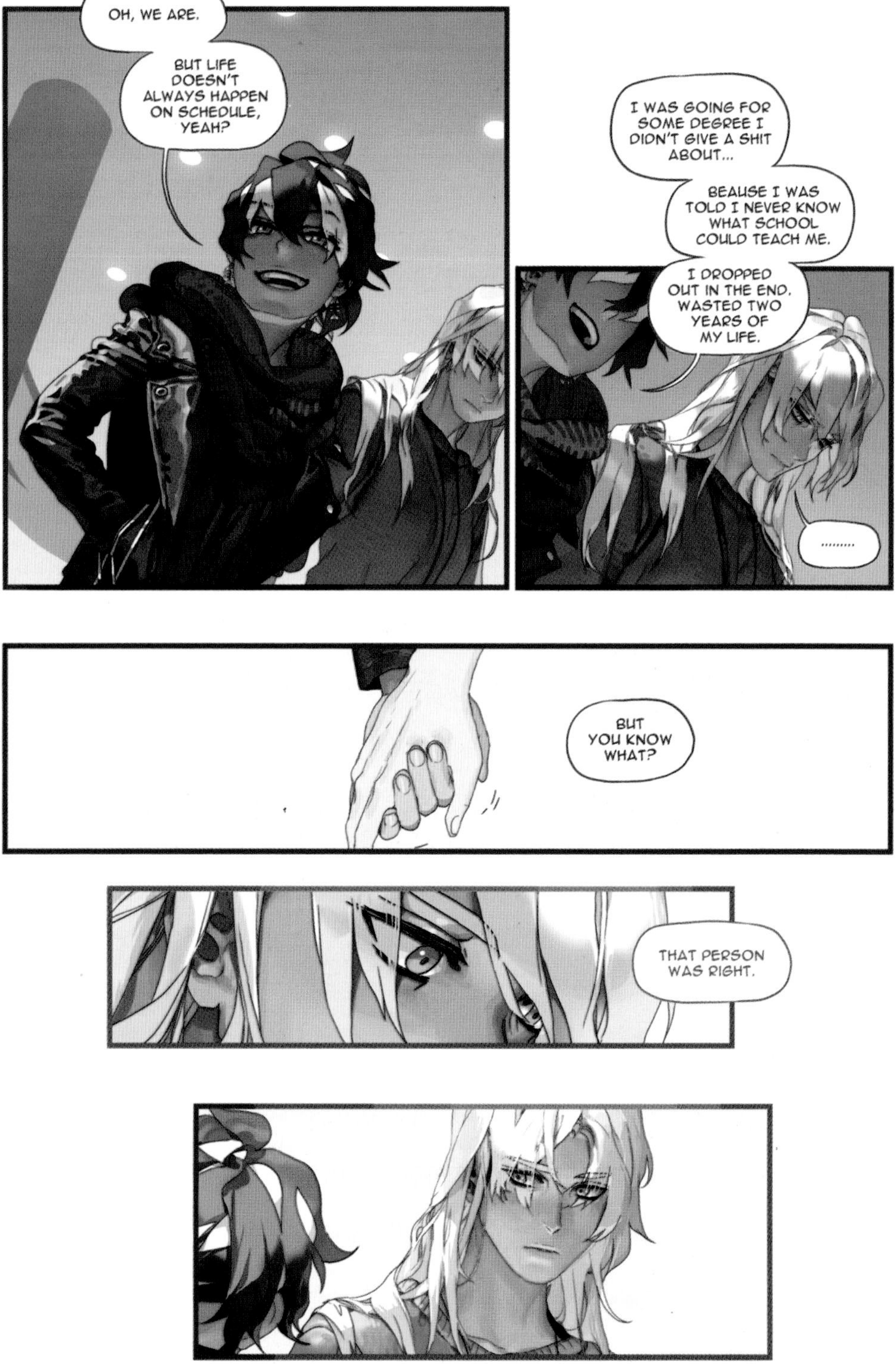
OH, WE ARE.
BUT LIFE DOESN'T ALWAYS HAPPEN ON SCHEDULE, YEAH?
I WAS GOING FOR SOME DEGREE I DIDN'T GIVE A SHIT ABOUT...
BEAUSE I WAS TOLD I NEVER KNOW WHAT SCHOOL COULD TEACH ME.
I DROPPED OUT IN THE END. WASTED TWO YEARS OF MY LIFE.
....
BUT YOU KNOW WHAT?
THAT PERSON WAS RIGHT.

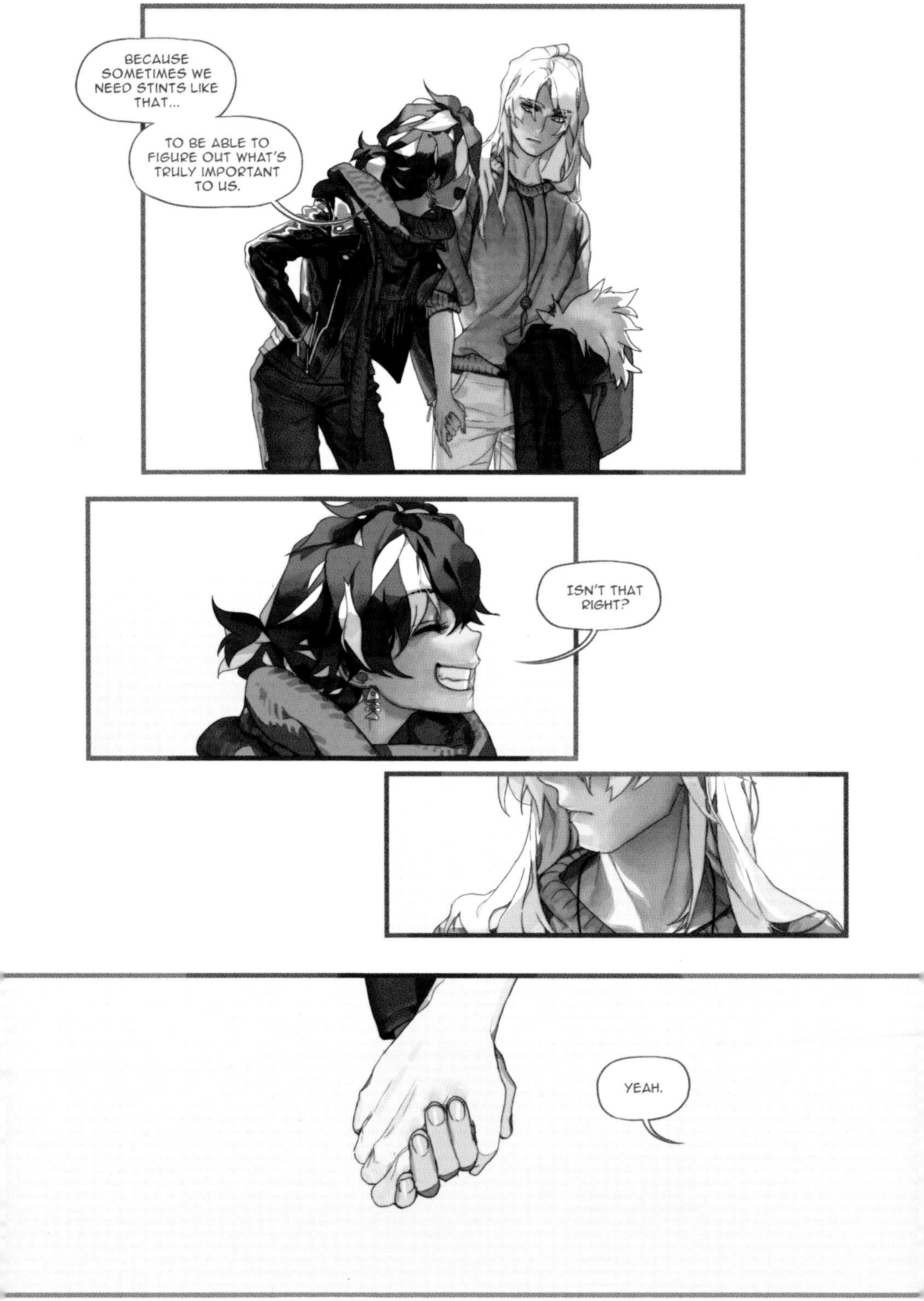
BECAUSE SOMETIMES WE NEED STINTS LIKE THAT...
TO BE ABLE TO FIGURE OUT WHAT'S TRULY IMPORTANT TO US.
ISN'T THAT RIGHT?
YEAH.

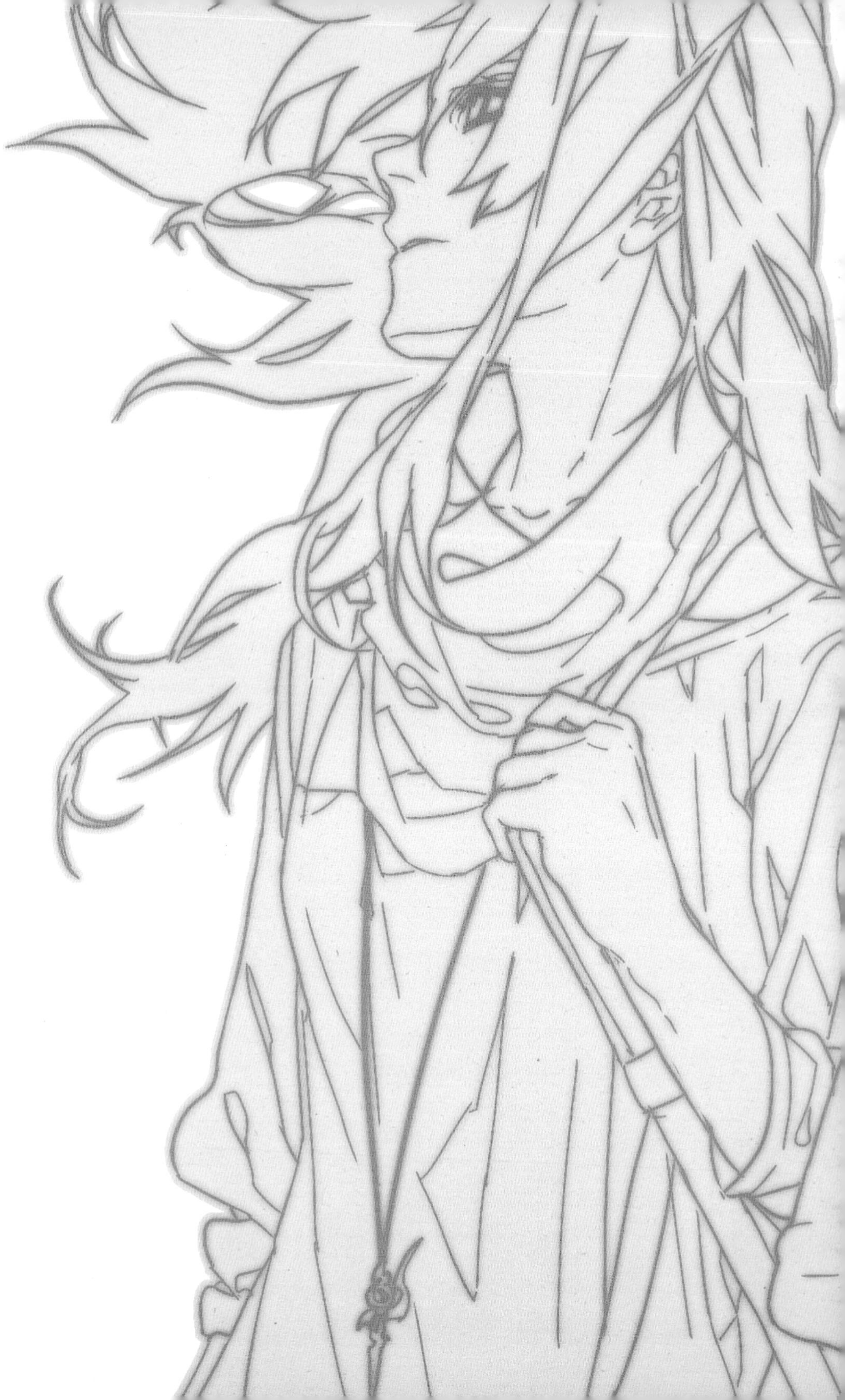

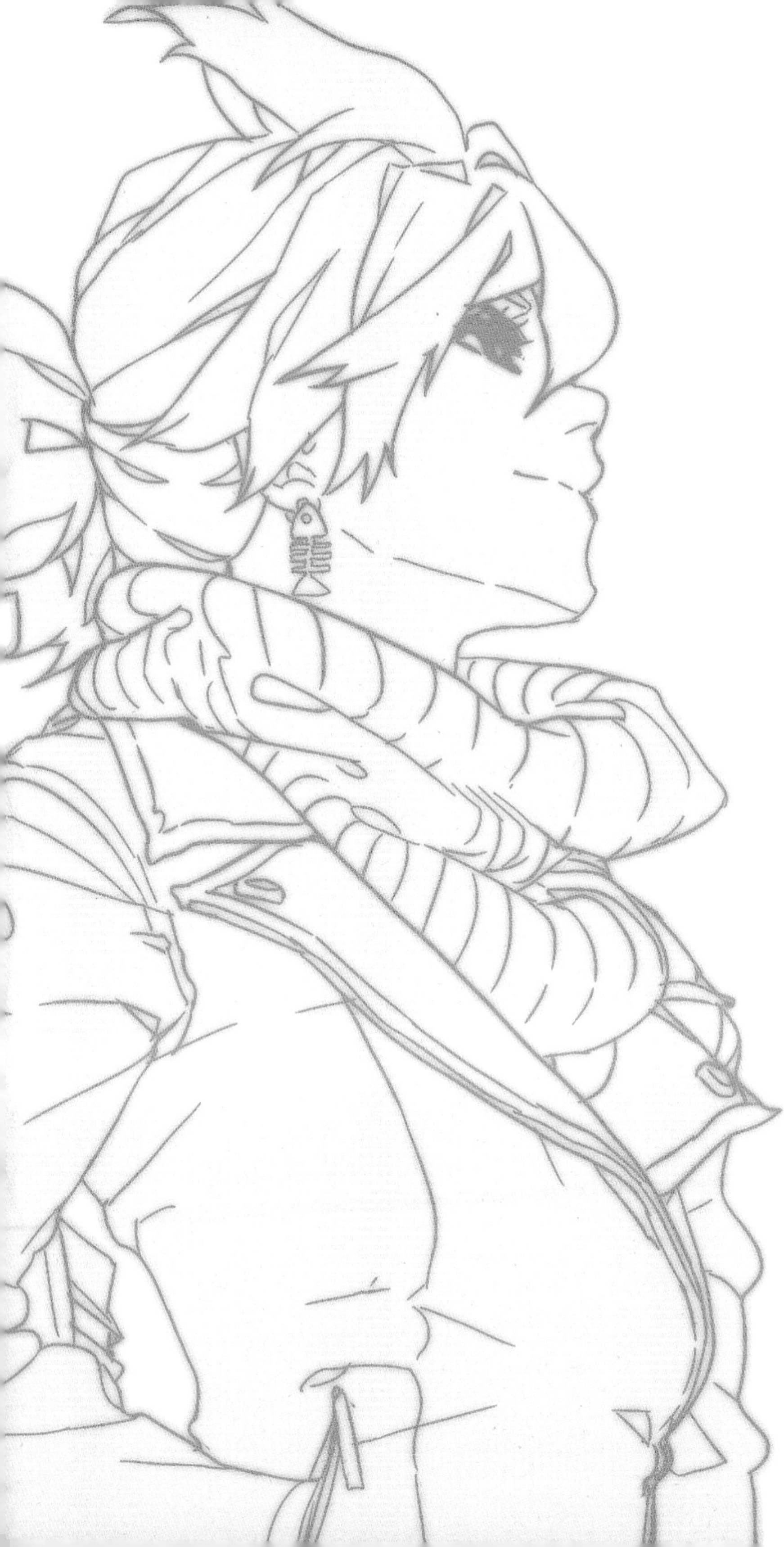

14. Ice cream

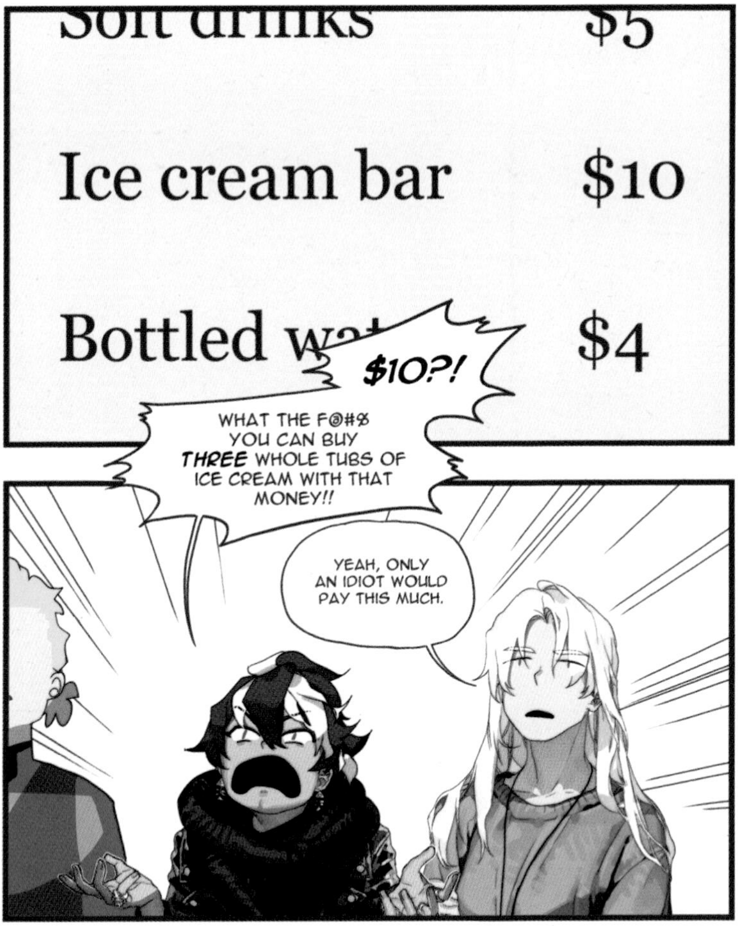

Ice cream bar $10
$10?!
WHAT THE F@#% YOU CAN BUY THREE WHOLE TUBS OF ICE CREAM WITH THAT MONEY!!
YEAH, ONLY AN IDIOT WOULD PAY THIS MUCH.

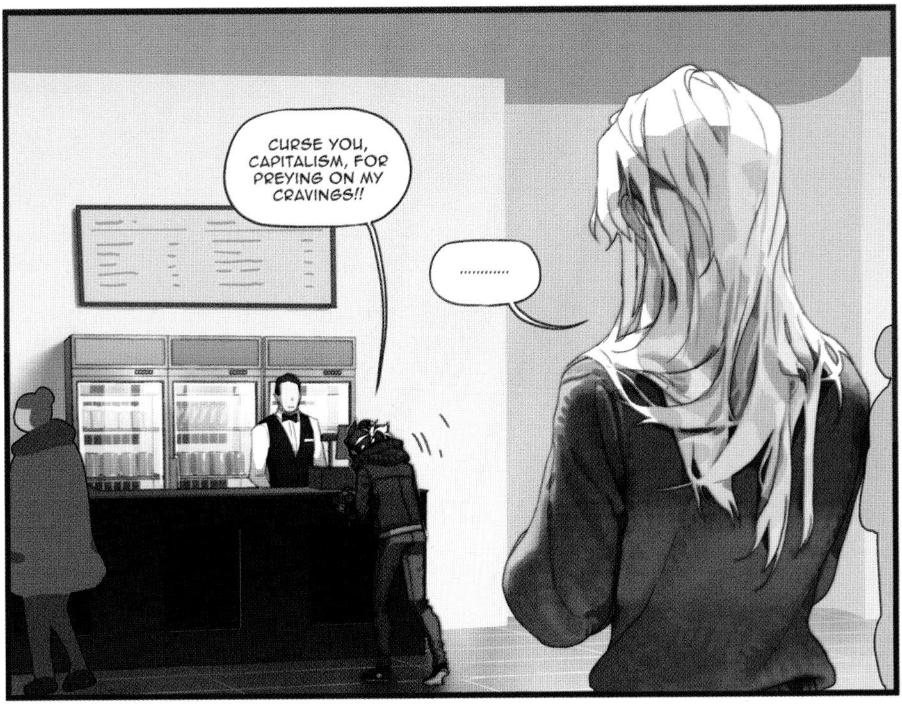
CURSE YOU, CAPITALISM, FOR PREYING ON MY CRAVINGS!!
....

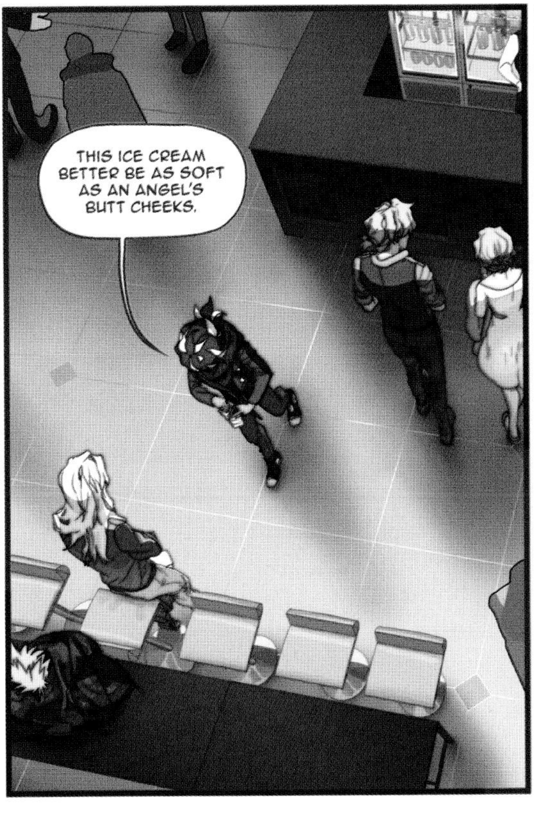
THIS ICE CREAM BETTER BE AS SOFT AS AN ANGEL'S BUTT CHEEKS.

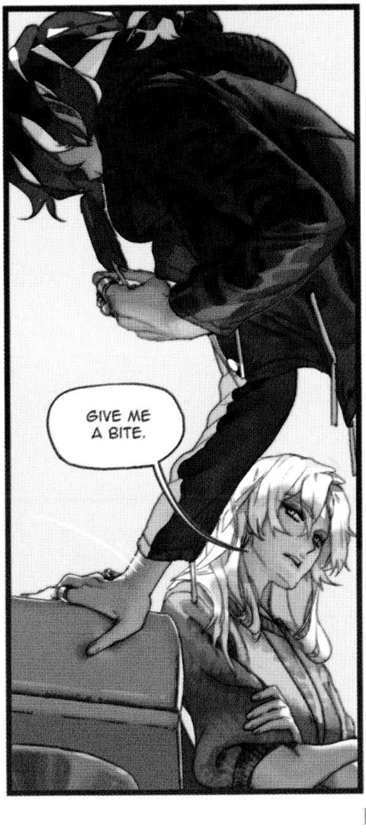
GIVE ME A BITE.

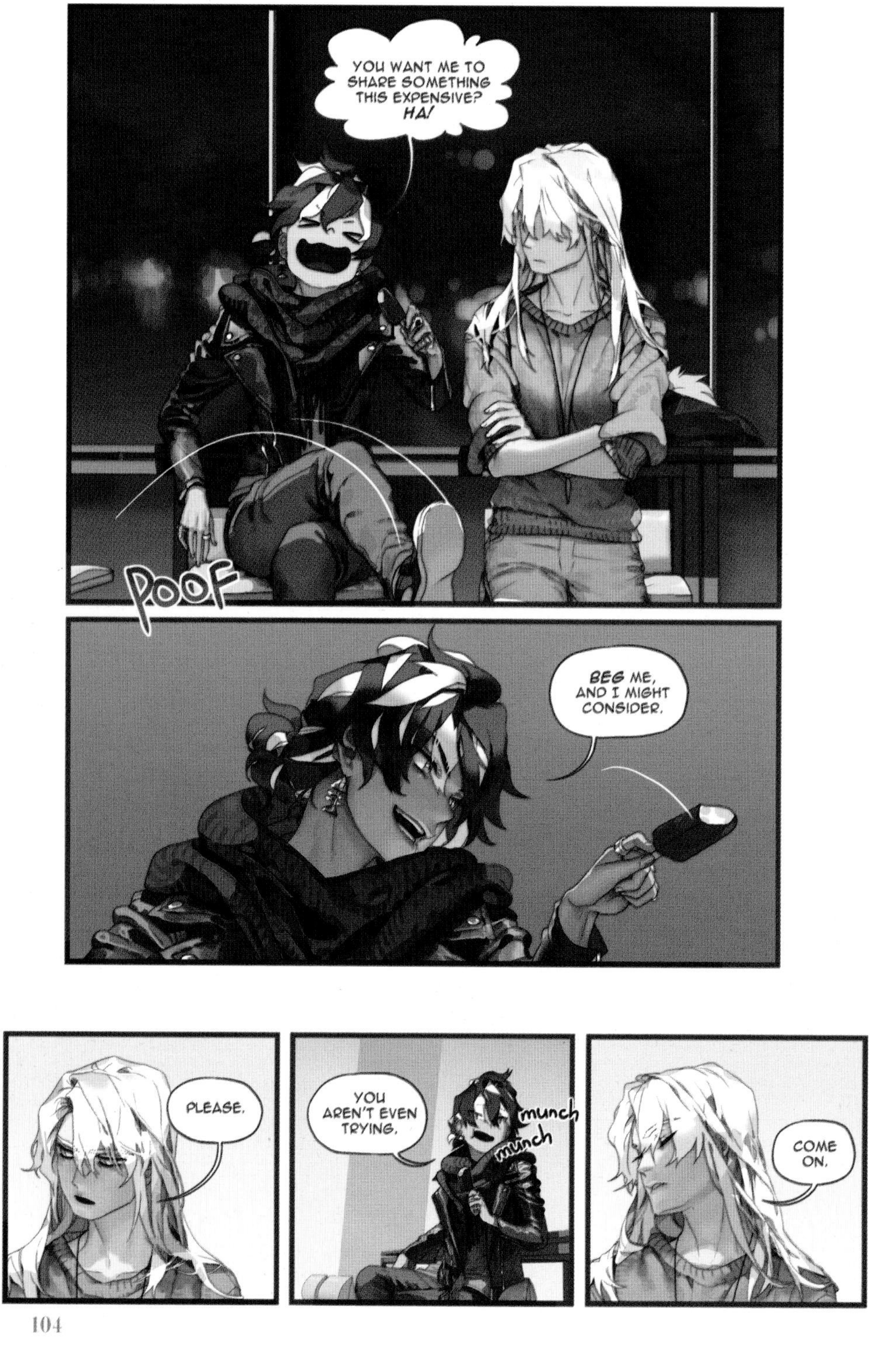
YOU WANT ME TO SHARE SOMETHING THIS EXPENSIVE? HA!
POOF
BEG ME, AND I MIGHT CONSIDER.
PLEASE.
YOU AREN'T EVEN TRYING.
munch
munch
COME ON.

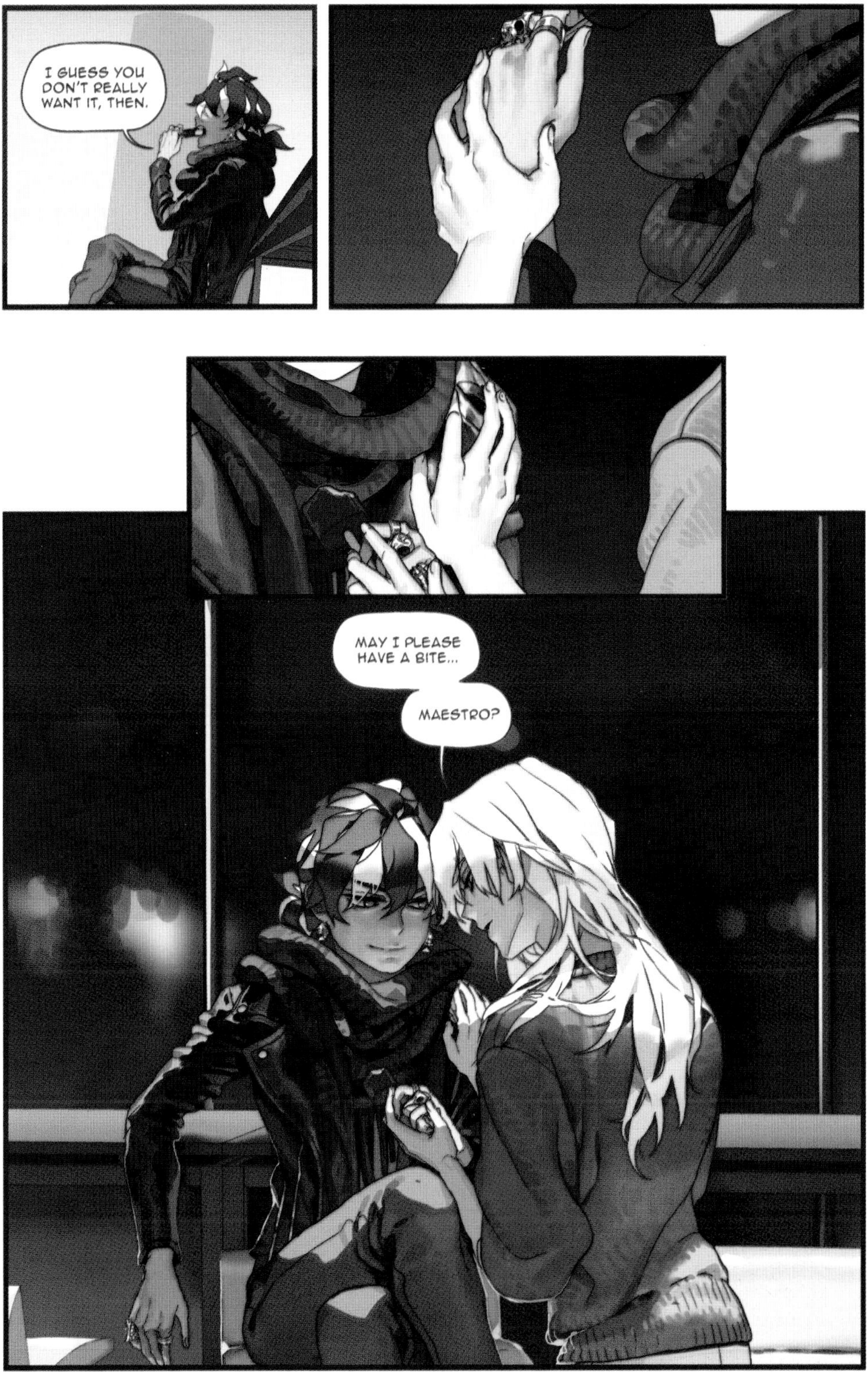
I GUESS YOU DON'T REALLY WANT IT, THEN.
MAY I PLEASE HAVE A BITE...
MAESTRO?

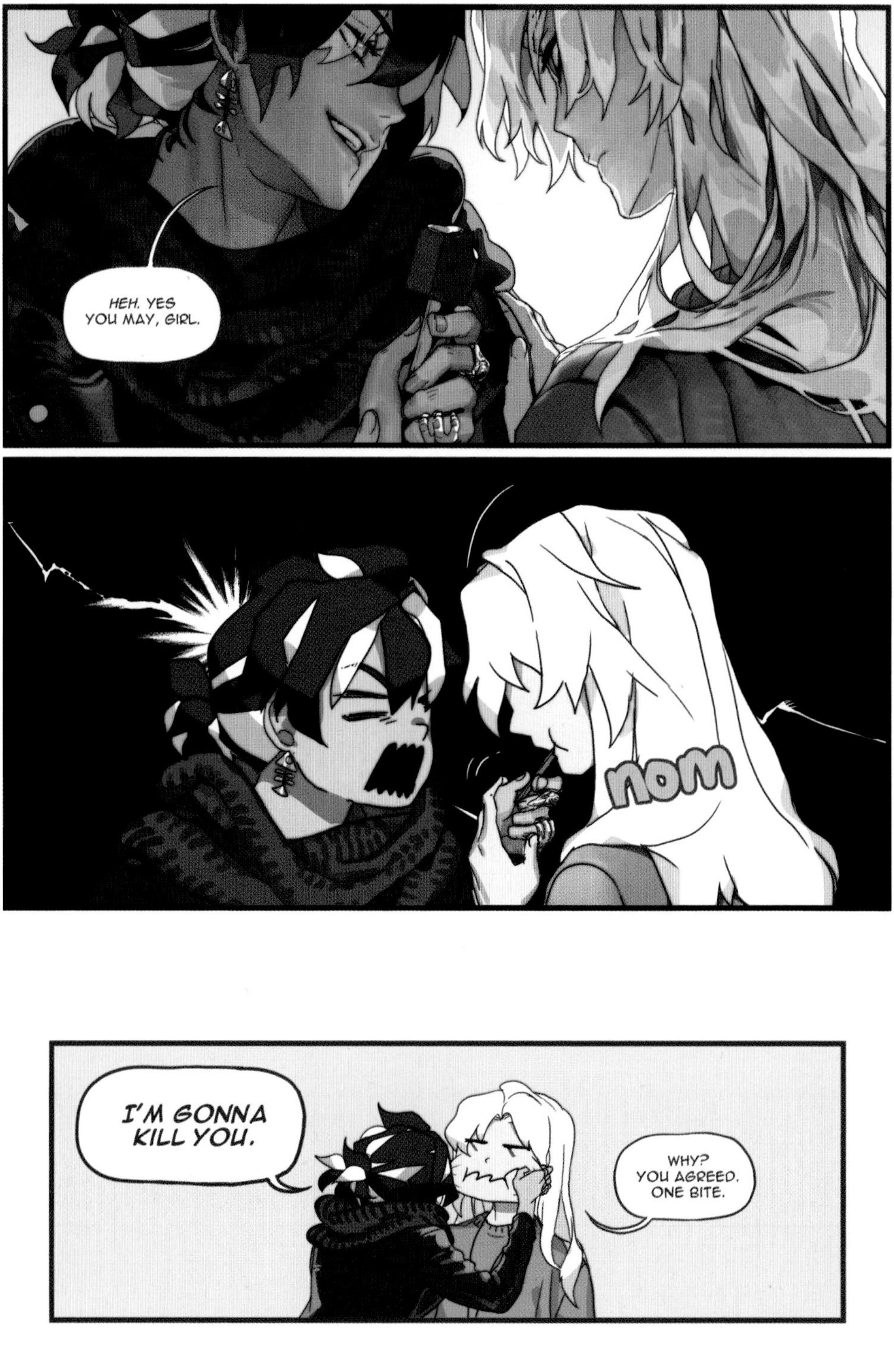
HEH. YES YOU MAY, GIRL.
nom
I'M GONNA KILL YOU.
WHY? YOU AGREED. ONE BITE.

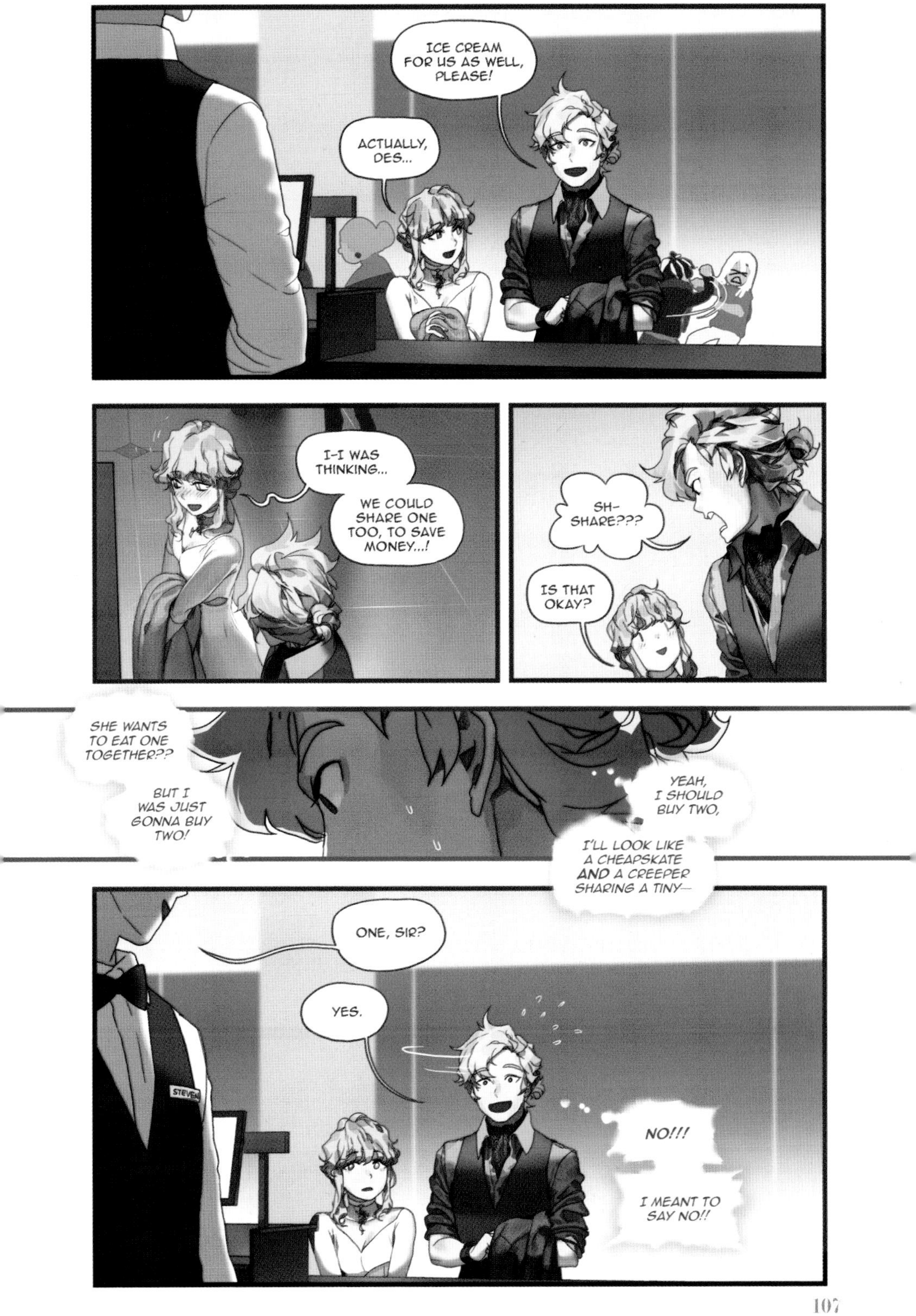
ICE CREAM FOR US AS WELL, PLEASE!
ACTUALLY, DES...
I-I WAS THINKING...
WE COULD SHARE ONE TOO, TO SAVE MONEY...!
SH- SHARE???
IS THAT OKAY?
SHE WANTS TO EAT ONE TOGETHER??
BUT I WAS JUST GONNA BUY TWO!
YEAH, I SHOULD BUY TWO,
I'LL LOOK LIKE A CHEAPSKATE AND A CREEPER SHARING A TINY—
ONE, SIR?
YES.
STEVEN
NO!!!
I MEANT TO SAY NO!!

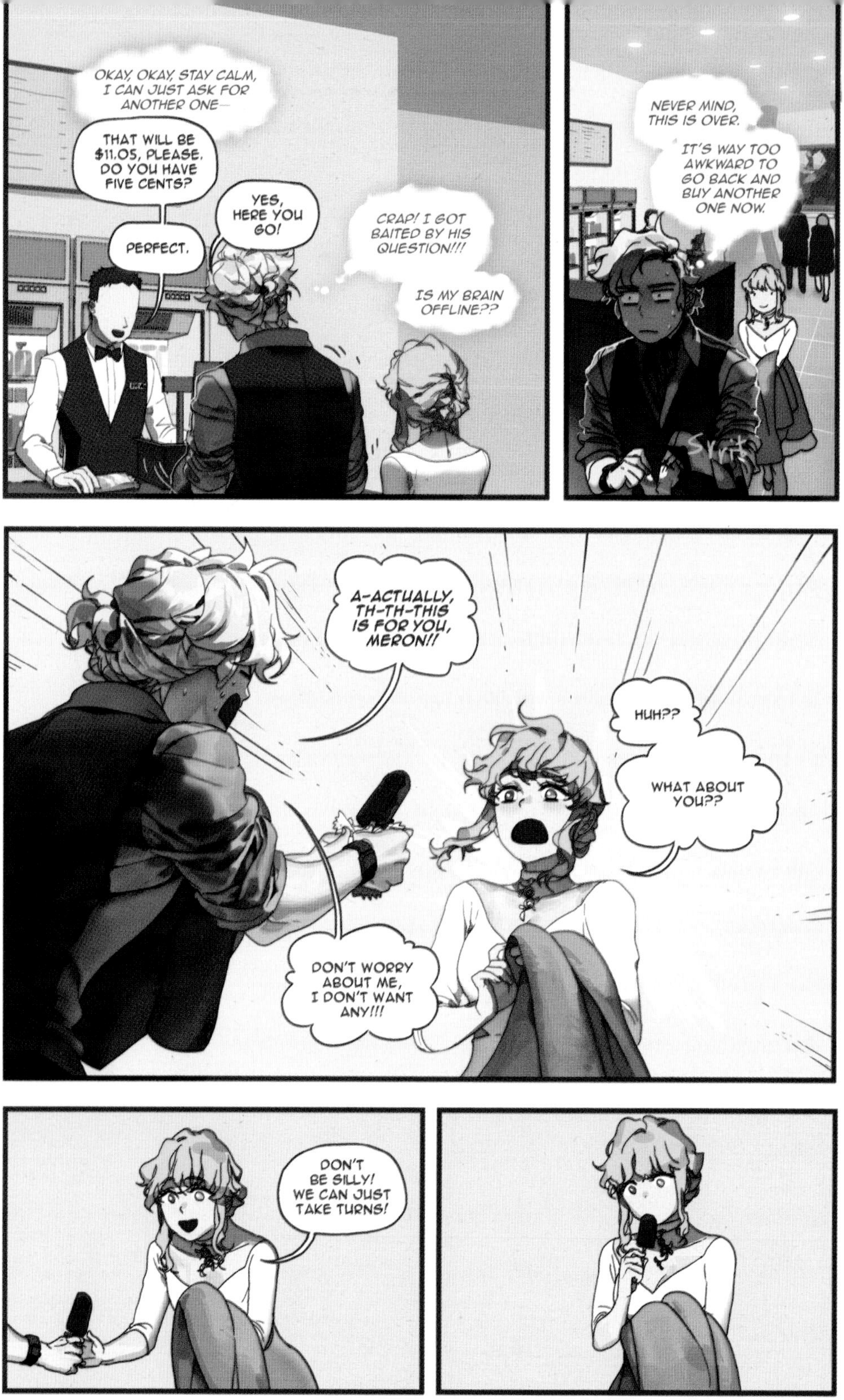
OKAY, OKAY, STAY CALM, I CAN JUST ASK FOR ANOTHER ONE—
THAT WILL BE $11.05, PLEASE. DO YOU HAVE FIVE CENTS?
YES, HERE YOU GO!
PERFECT.
CRAP! I GOT BAITED BY HIS QUESTION!!!
IS MY BRAIN OFFLINE??
NEVER MIND, THIS IS OVER.
IT'S WAY TOO AWKWARD TO GO BACK AND BUY ANOTHER ONE NOW.
A-ACTUALLY, TH-TH-THIS IS FOR YOU, MERON!!
HUH??
WHAT ABOUT YOU??
DON'T WORRY ABOUT ME, I DON'T WANT ANY!!!
DON'T BE SILLY! WE CAN JUST TAKE TURNS!

FATE IS INESCAPABLE.
HERE!

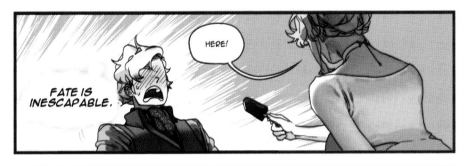

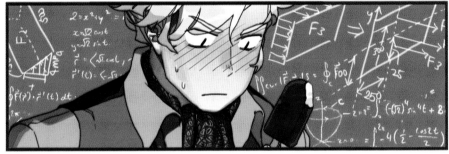

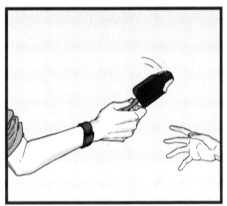

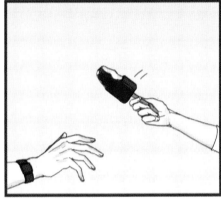

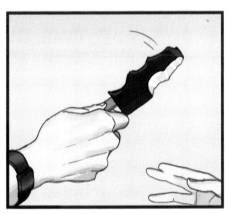

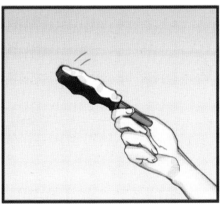

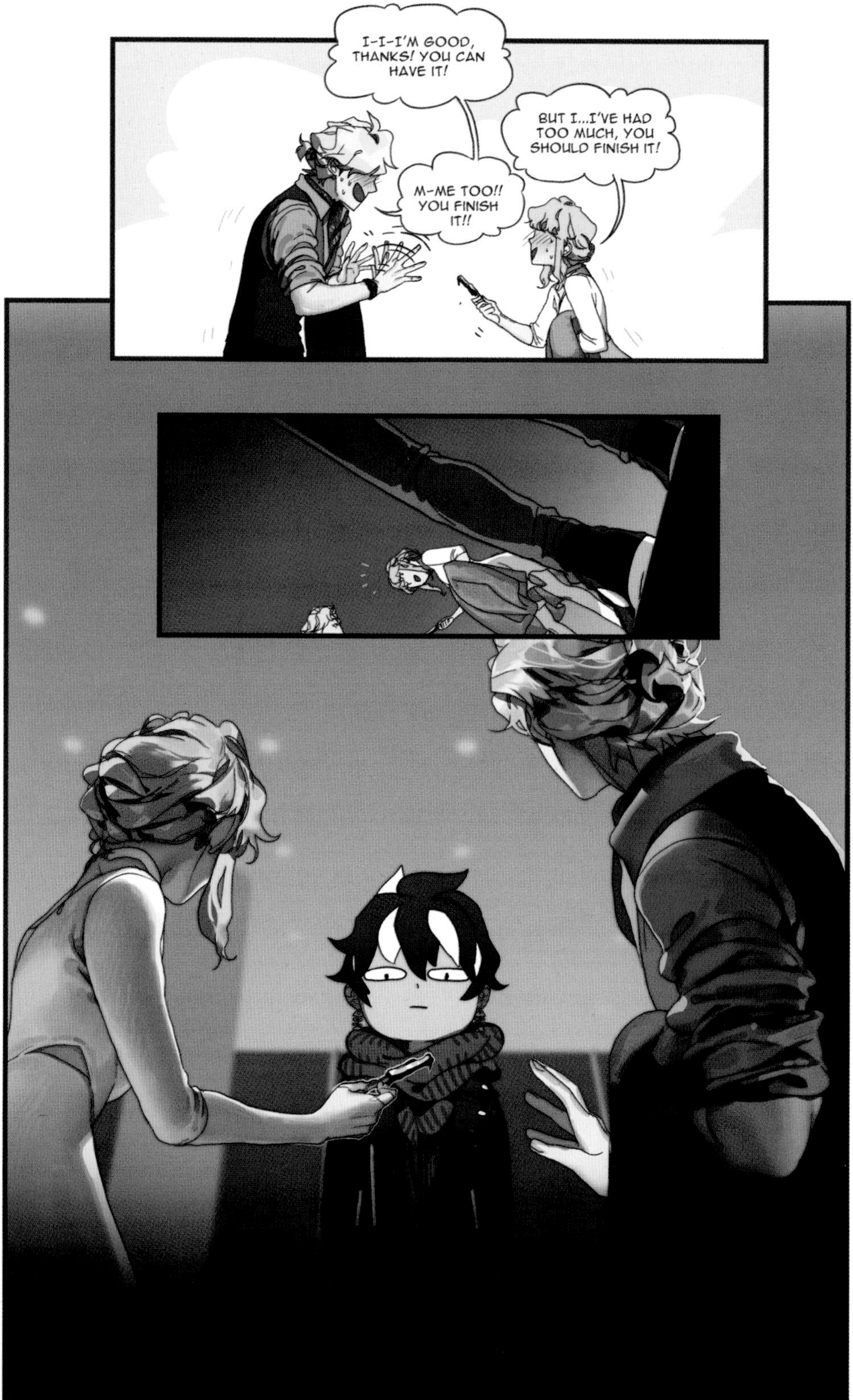
I-I-I'M GOOD, THANKS! YOU CAN HAVE IT!
BUT I...I'VE HAD TOO MUCH, YOU SHOULD FINISH IT!
M-ME TOO!! YOU FINISH IT!!

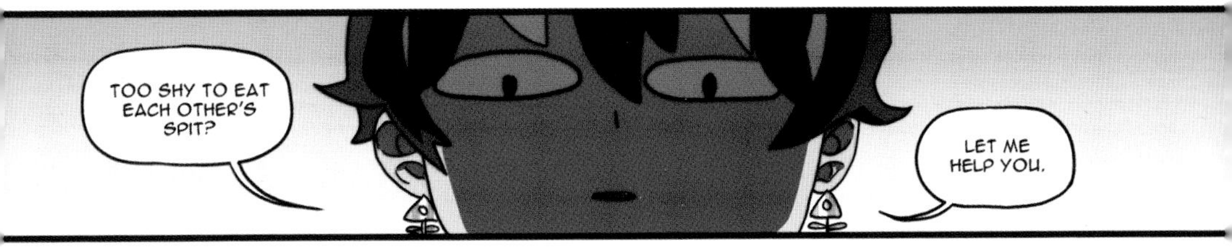
TOO SHY TO EAT EACH OTHER'S SPIT?
LET ME HELP YOU.

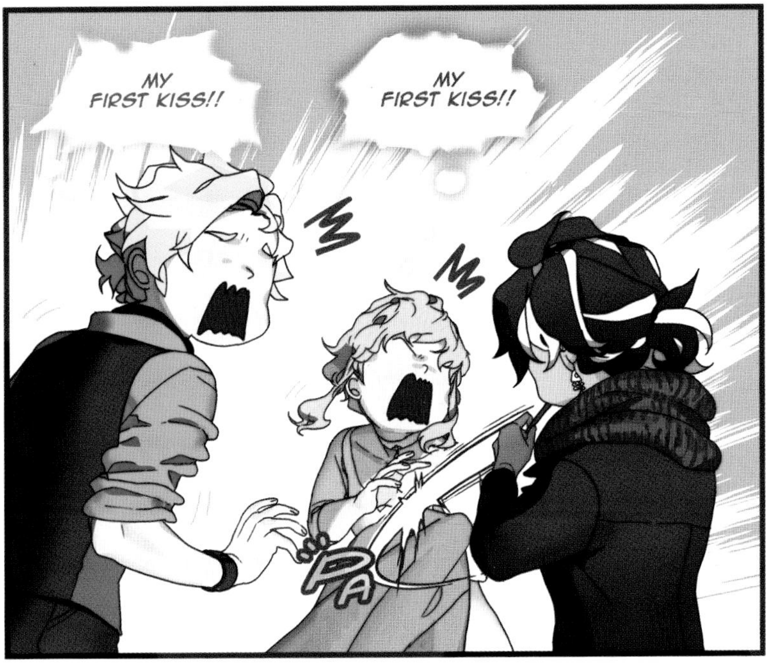
MY FIRST KISS!!
MY FIRST KISS!!
M
M
PA

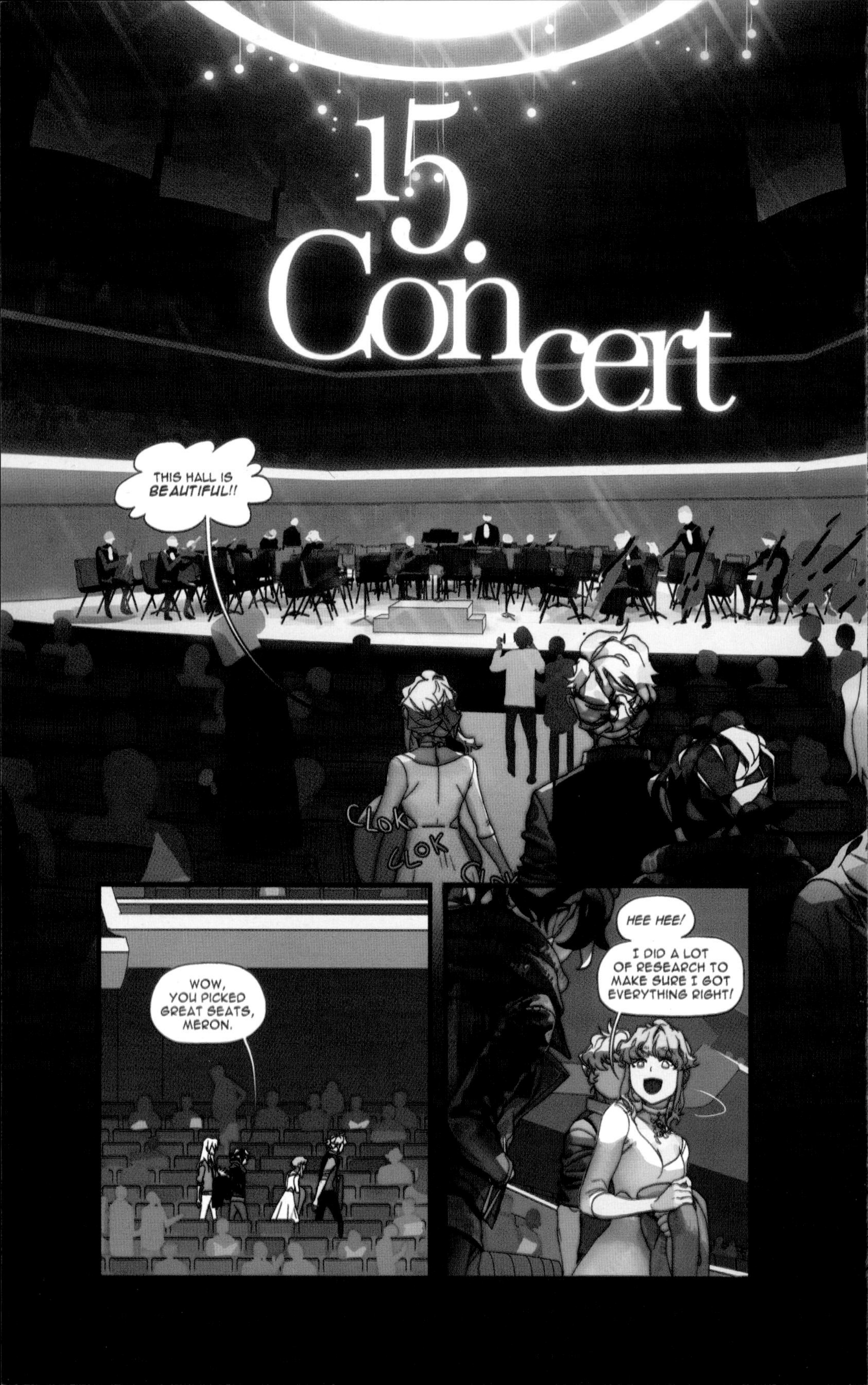
15. Concert
THIS HALL IS BEAUTIFUL!!
CLOK CLOK
WOW, YOU PICKED GREAT SEATS, MERON.
HEE HEE!
I DID A LOT OF RESEARCH TO MAKE SURE I GOT EVERYTHING RIGHT!

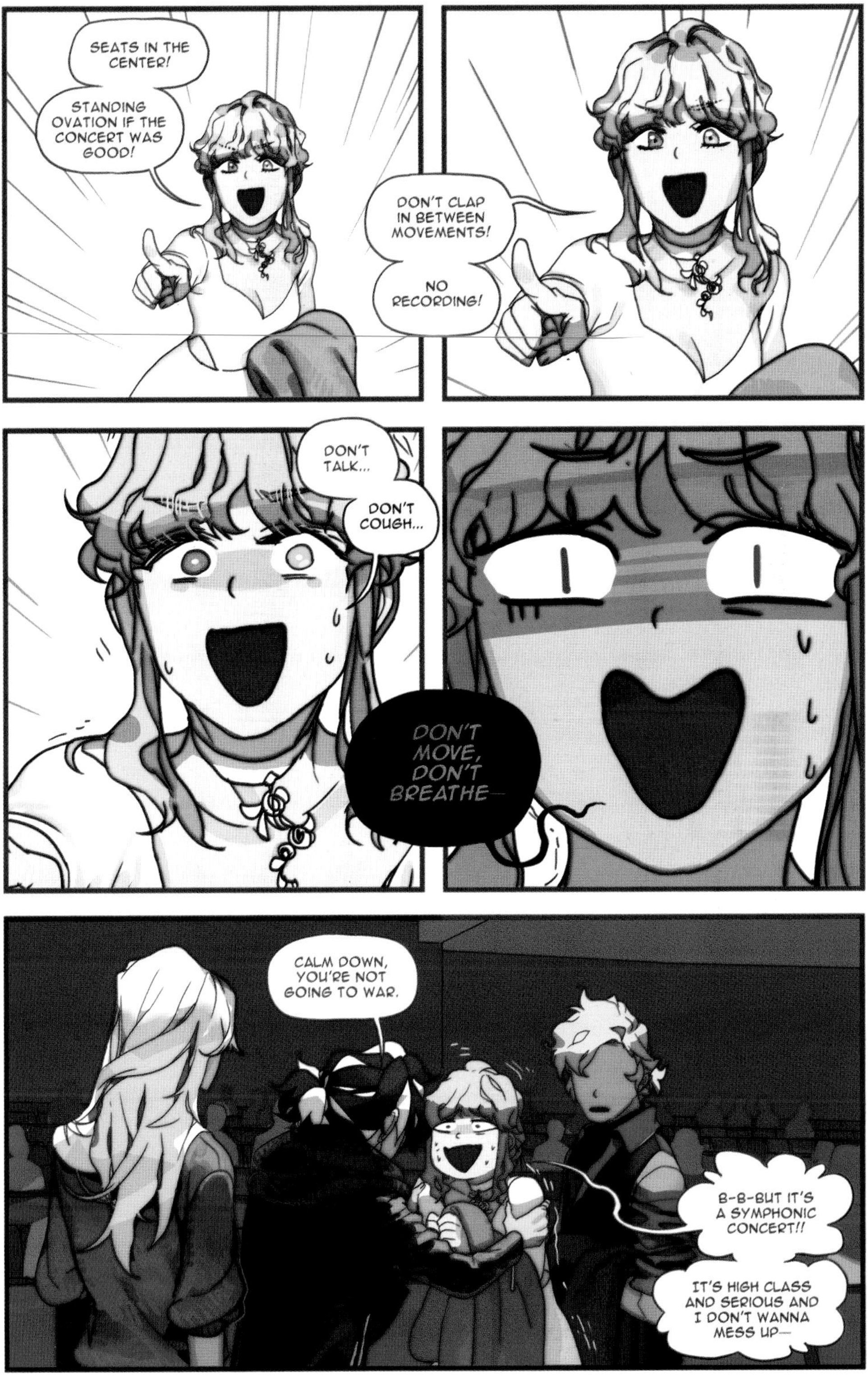
SEATS IN THE CENTER!
STANDING OVATION IF THE CONCERT WAS GOOD!
DON'T CLAP IN BETWEEN MOVEMENTS!
NO RECORDING!
DON'T TALK...
DON'T COUGH...
DON'T MOVE, DON'T BREATHE—
CALM DOWN, YOU'RE NOT GOING TO WAR.
B-B-BUT IT'S A SYMPHONIC CONCERT!!
IT'S HIGH CLASS AND SERIOUS AND I DON'T WANNA MESS UP—

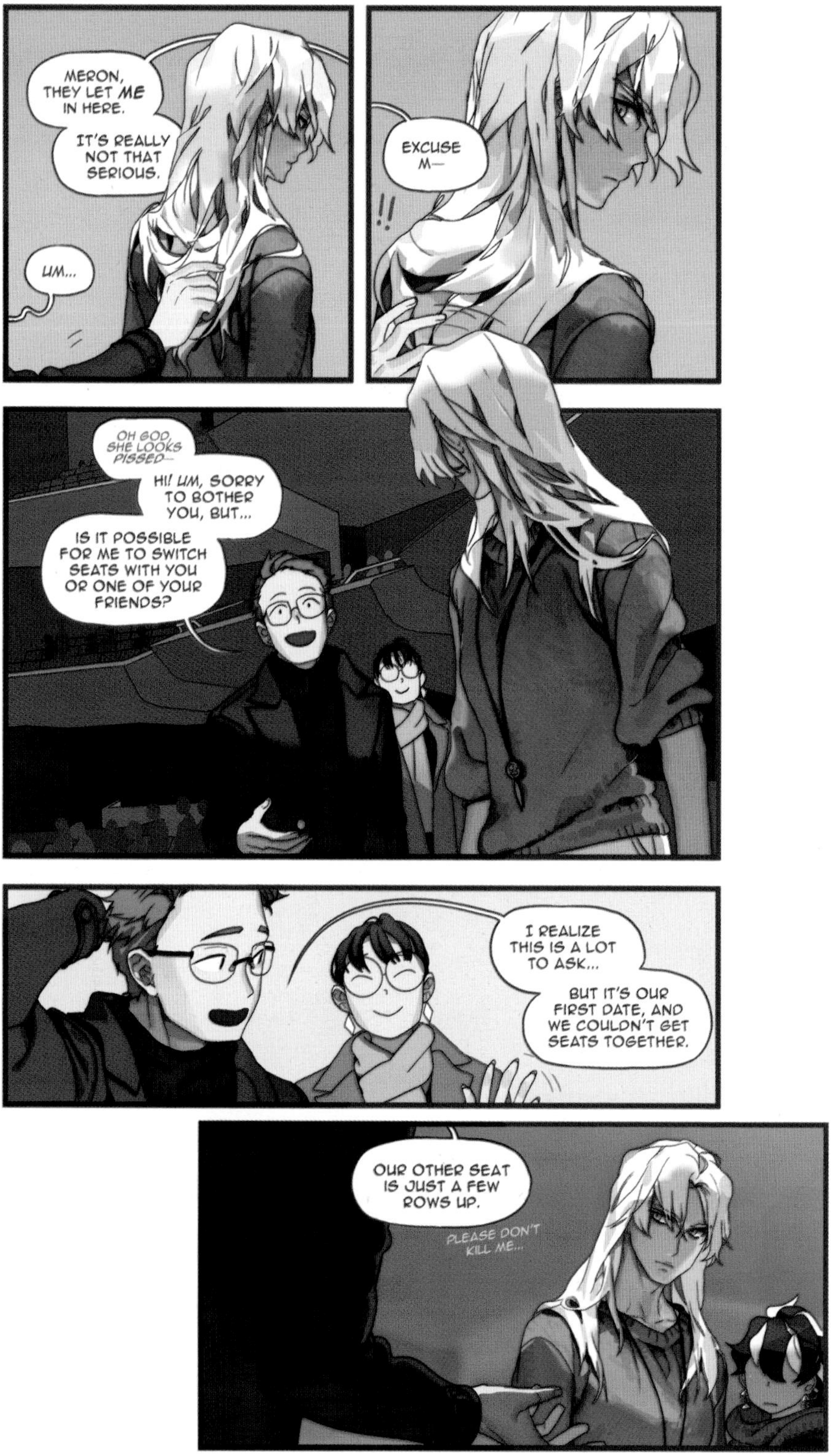
MERON, THEY LET *ME* IN HERE.
IT'S REALLY NOT THAT SERIOUS.
UM...
EXCUSE M—
!!
OH GOD, SHE LOOKS PISSED—
HI! *UM*, SORRY TO BOTHER YOU, BUT...
IS IT POSSIBLE FOR ME TO SWITCH SEATS WITH YOU OR ONE OF YOUR FRIENDS?
I REALIZE THIS IS A LOT TO ASK...
BUT IT'S OUR FIRST DATE, AND WE COULDN'T GET SEATS TOGETHER.
OUR OTHER SEAT IS JUST A FEW ROWS UP.
PLEASE DON'T KILL ME...

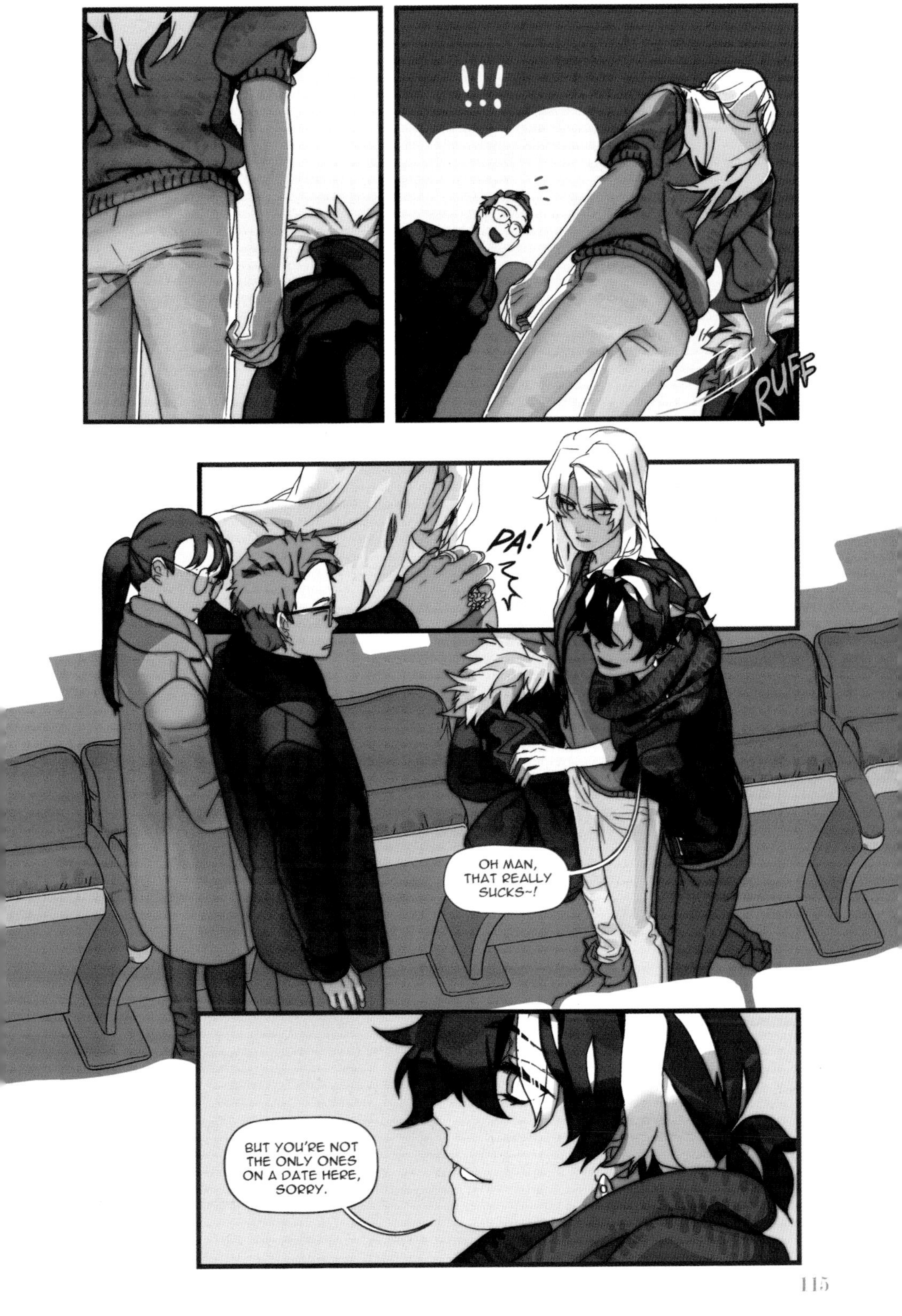
!!!
RUFF
PA!
OH MAN, THAT REALLY SUCKS~!
BUT YOU'RE NOT THE ONLY ONES ON A DATE HERE, SORRY.

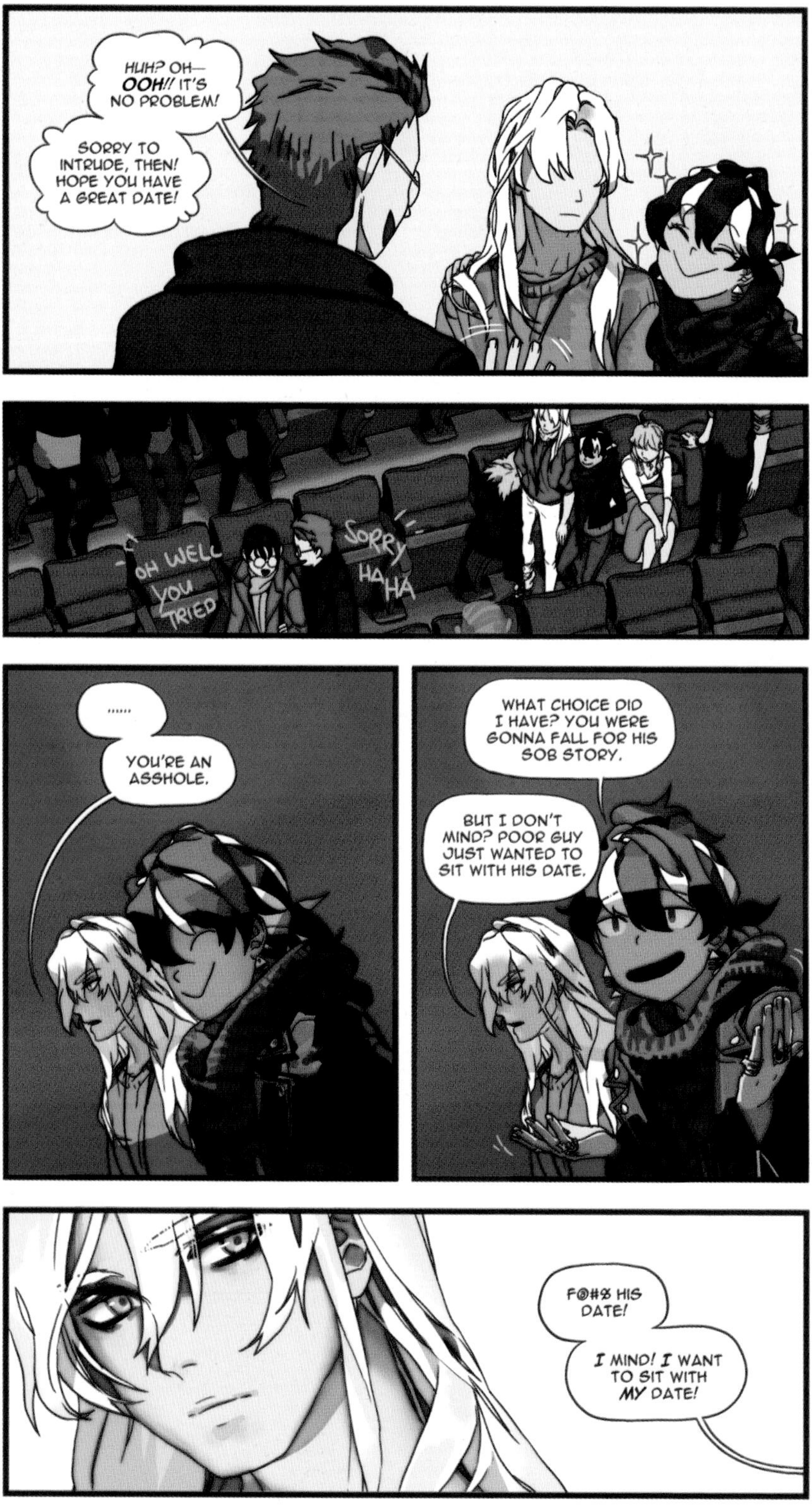
HUH? OH—
OOH!! IT'S NO PROBLEM!
SORRY TO INTRUDE, THEN! HOPE YOU HAVE A GREAT DATE!
OH WELL YOU TRIED
SORRY HAHA
......
YOU'RE AN ASSHOLE.
WHAT CHOICE DID I HAVE? YOU WERE GONNA FALL FOR HIS SOB STORY.
BUT I DON'T MIND? POOR GUY JUST WANTED TO SIT WITH HIS DATE.
F@#$ HIS DATE!
I MIND! I WANT TO SIT WITH MY DATE!

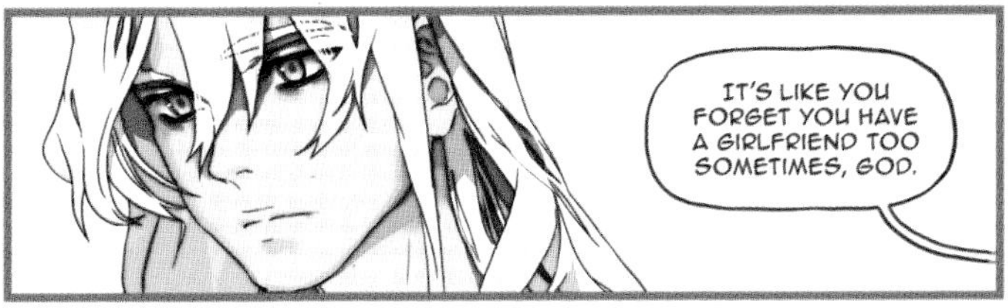
IT'S LIKE YOU FORGET YOU HAVE A GIRLFRIEND TOO SOMETIMES, GOD.

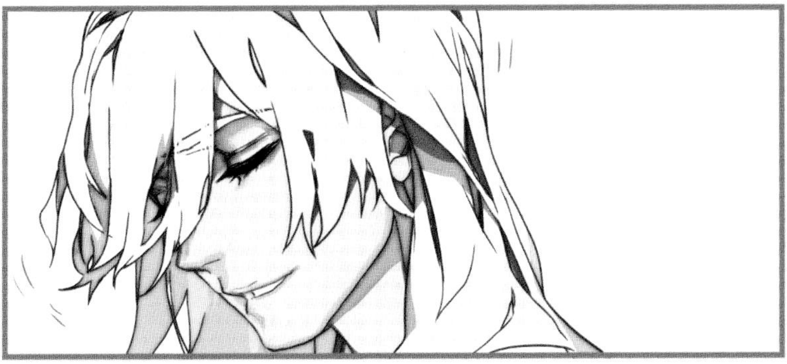

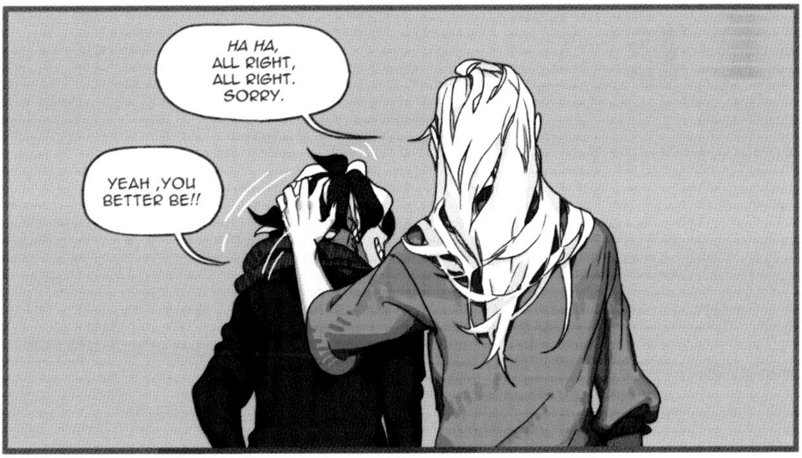
HA HA, ALL RIGHT, ALL RIGHT. SORRY.
YEAH ,YOU BETTER BE!!

IT MAY SOUND STRANGE, BUT I DO FORGET.

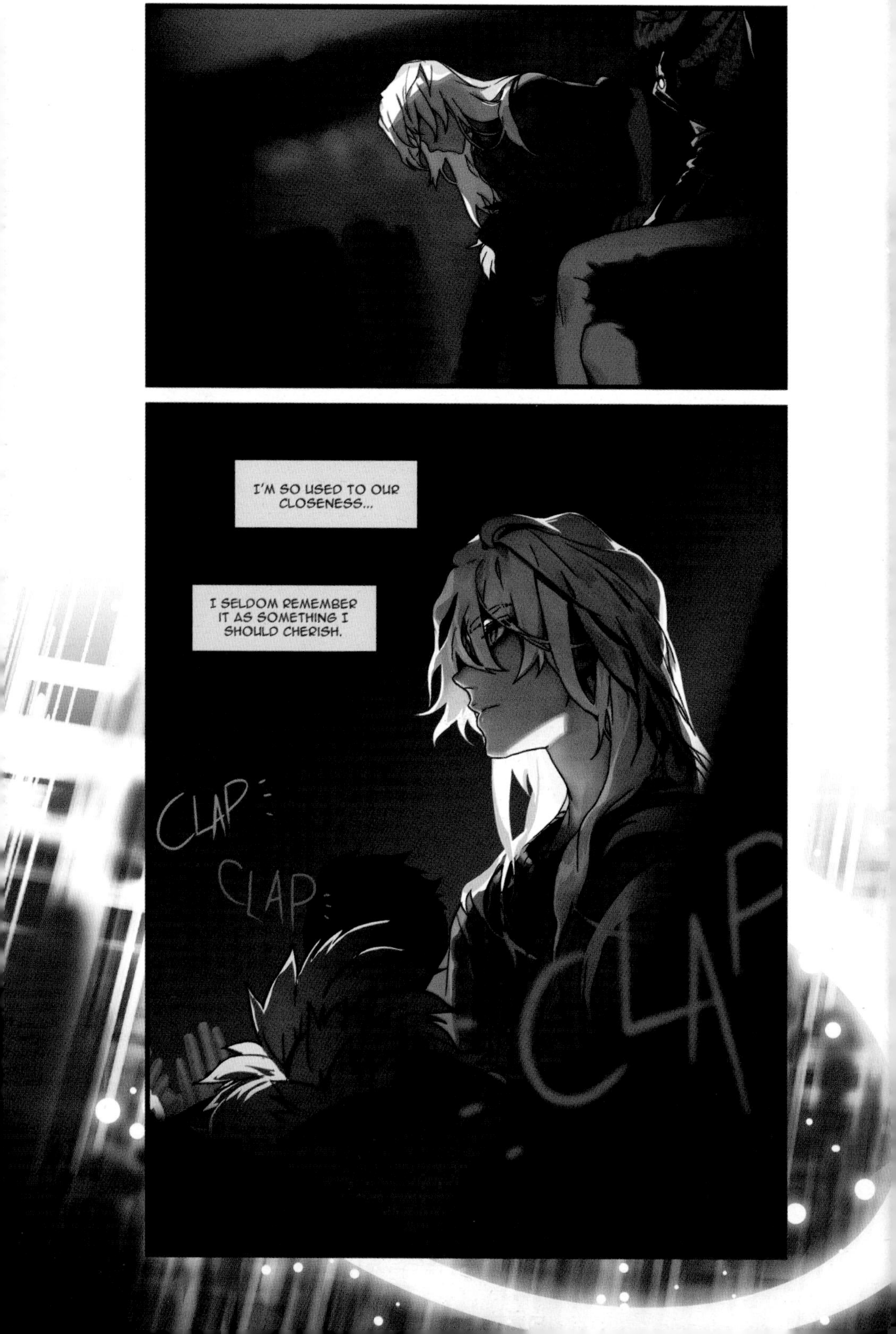
I'M SO USED TO OUR CLOSENESS...
I SELDOM REMEMBER IT AS SOMETHING I SHOULD CHERISH.
CLAP
CLAP
CLAP

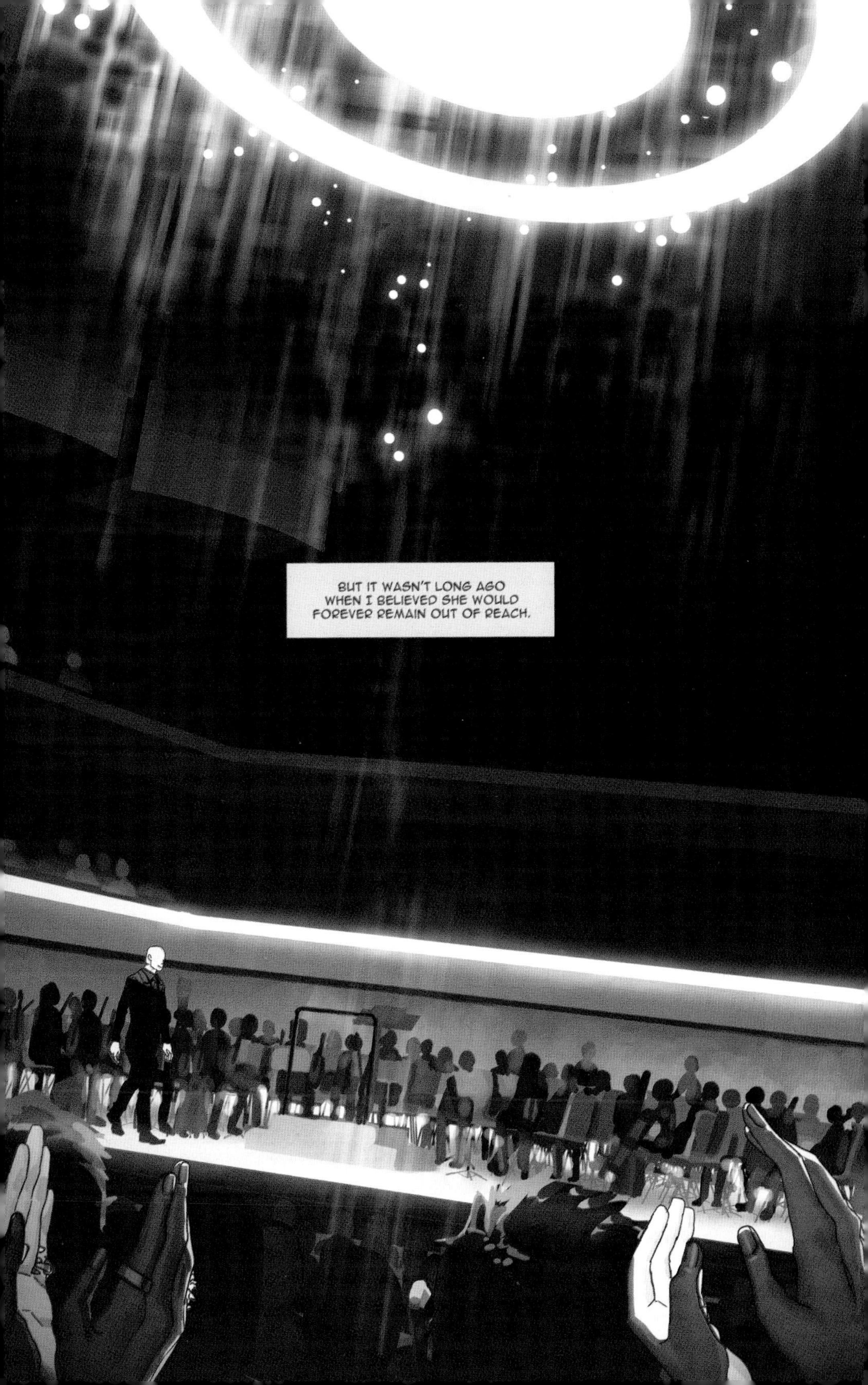
BUT IT WASN'T LONG AGO WHEN I BELIEVED SHE WOULD FOREVER REMAIN OUT OF REACH.

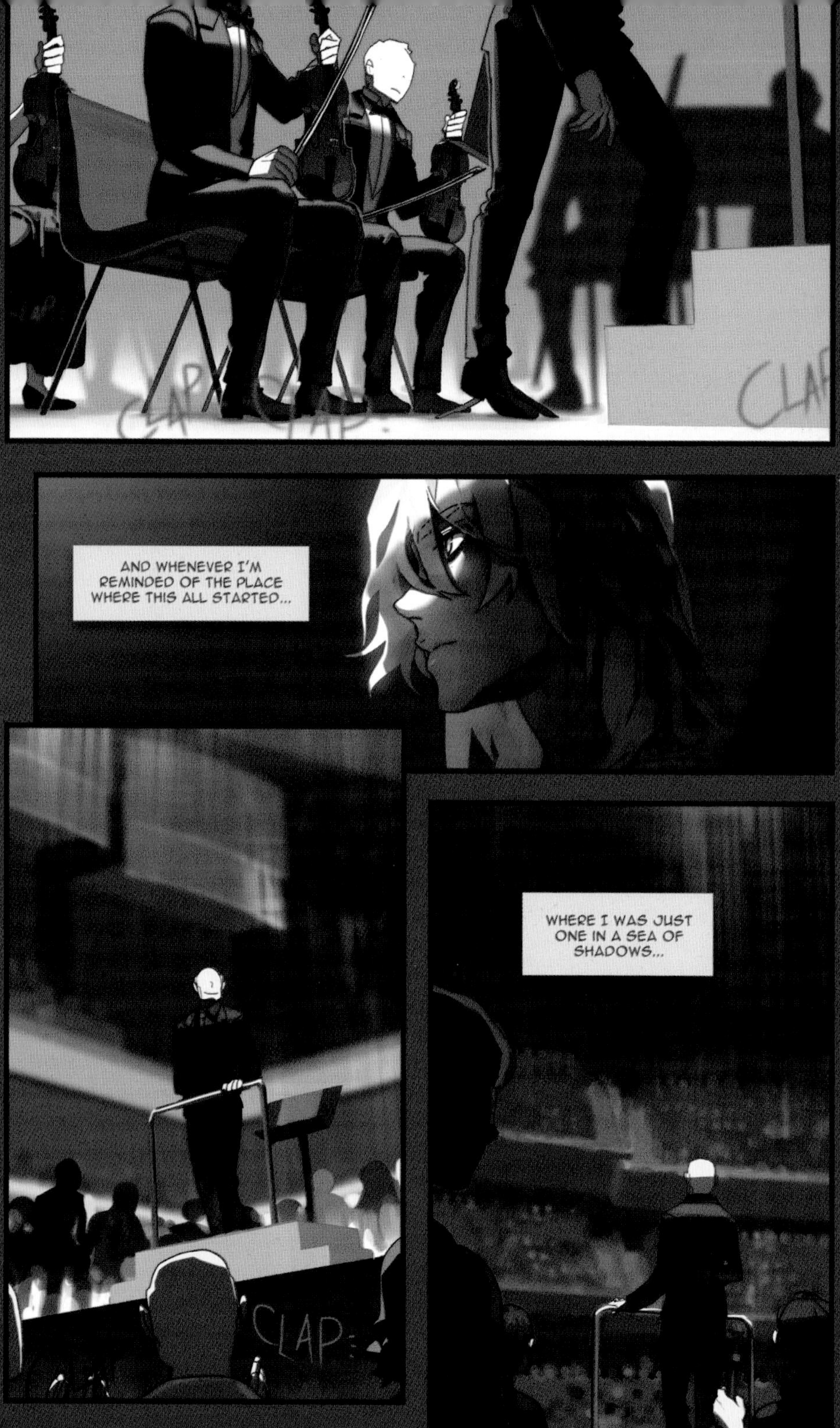
CLAP
CLAP
CLAP
AND WHENEVER I'M REMINDED OF THE PLACE WHERE THIS ALL STARTED...
CLAP
WHERE I WAS JUST ONE IN A SEA OF SHADOWS...

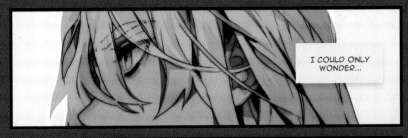

I COULD ONLY
WONDER...

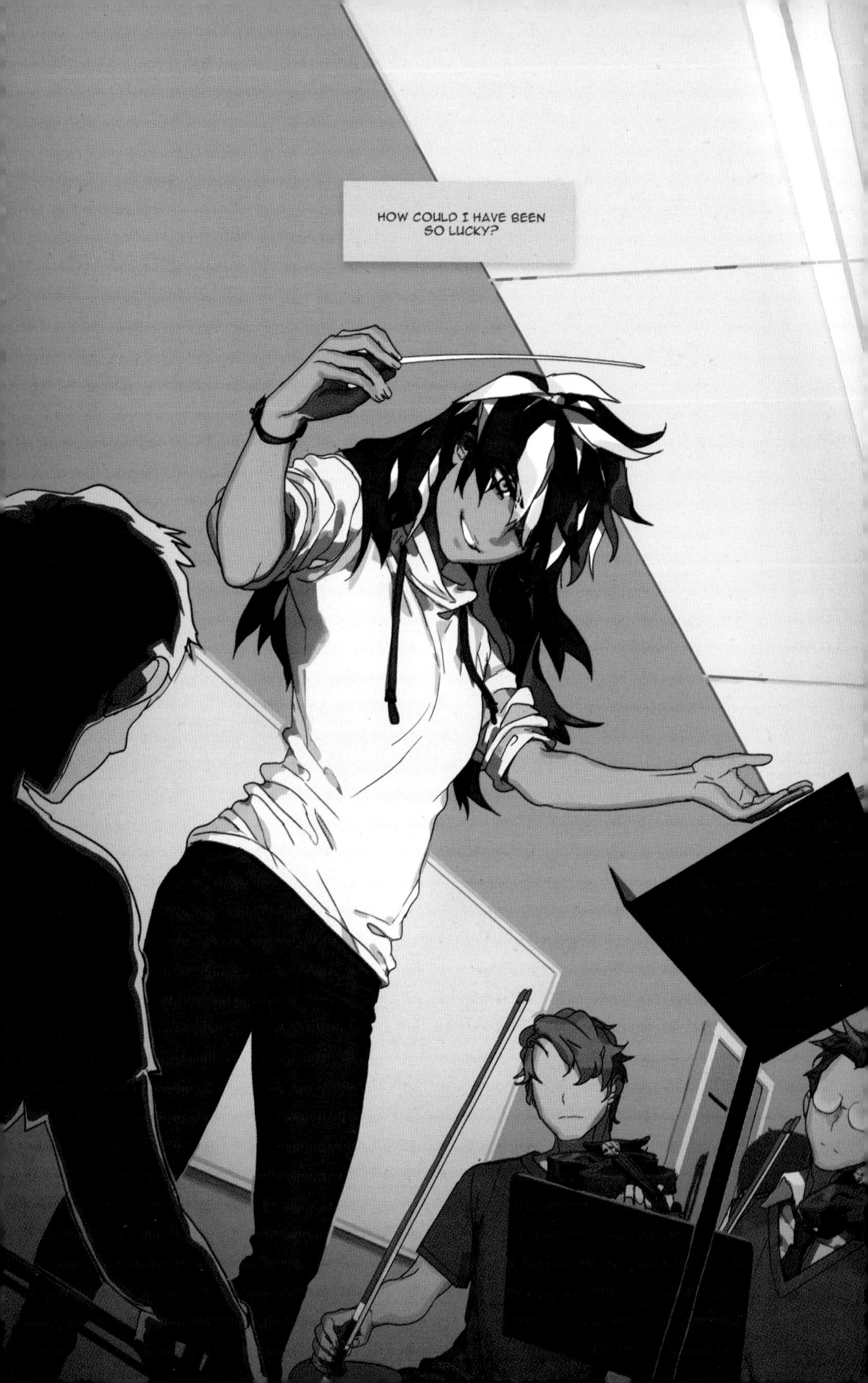
HOW COULD I HAVE BEEN SO LUCKY?

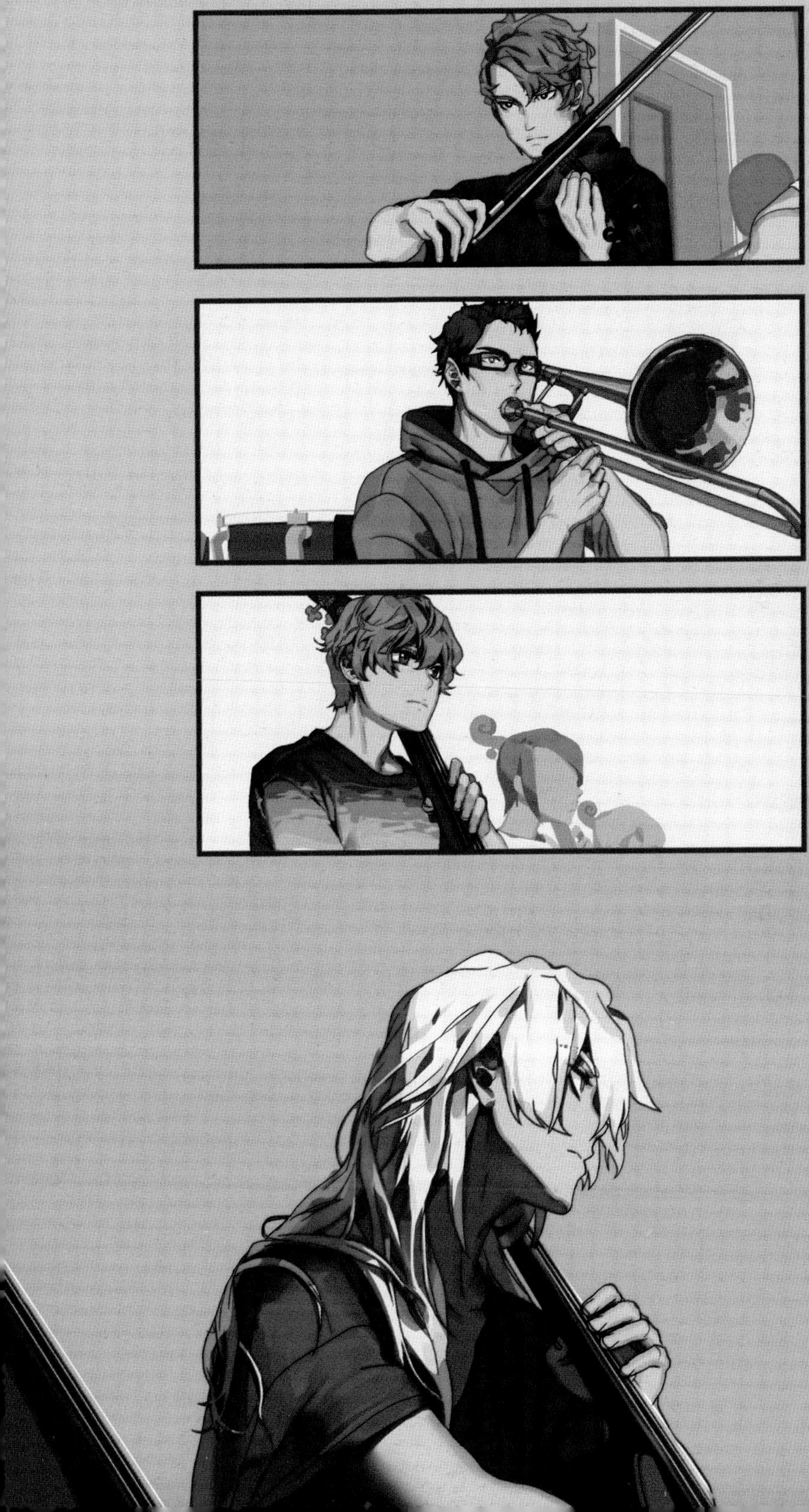

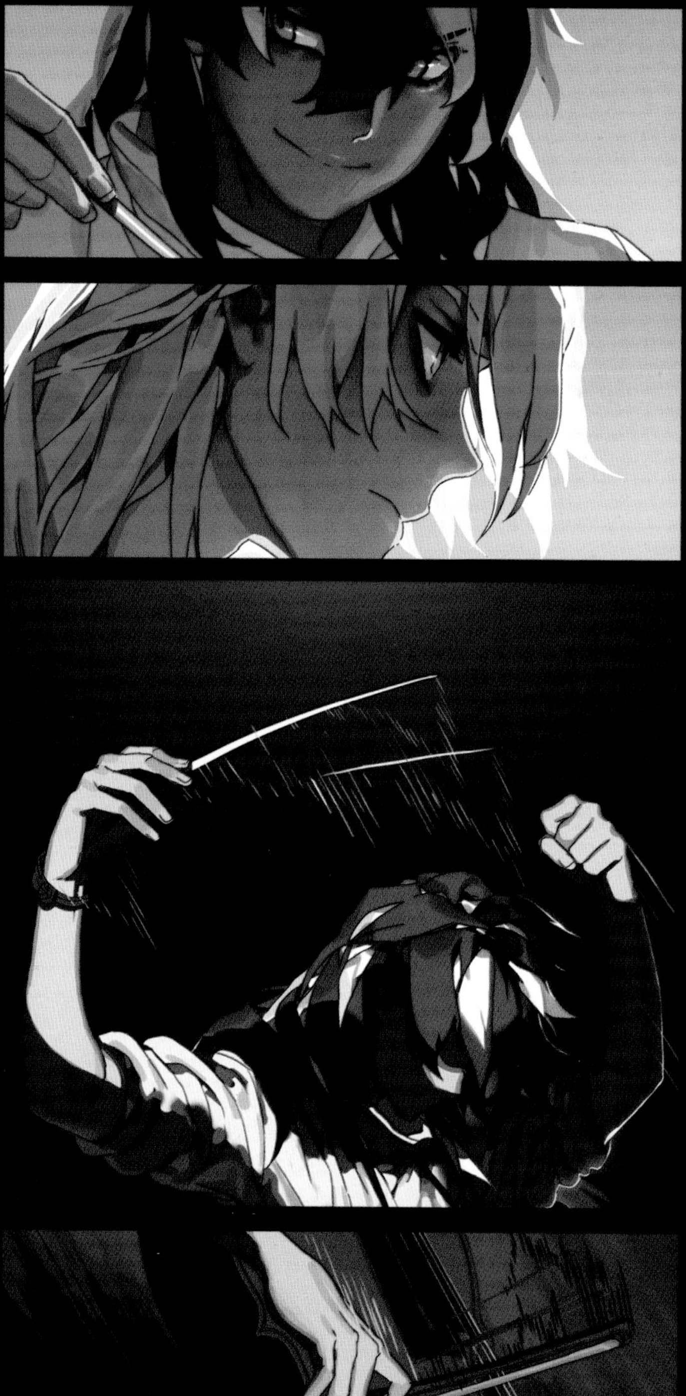

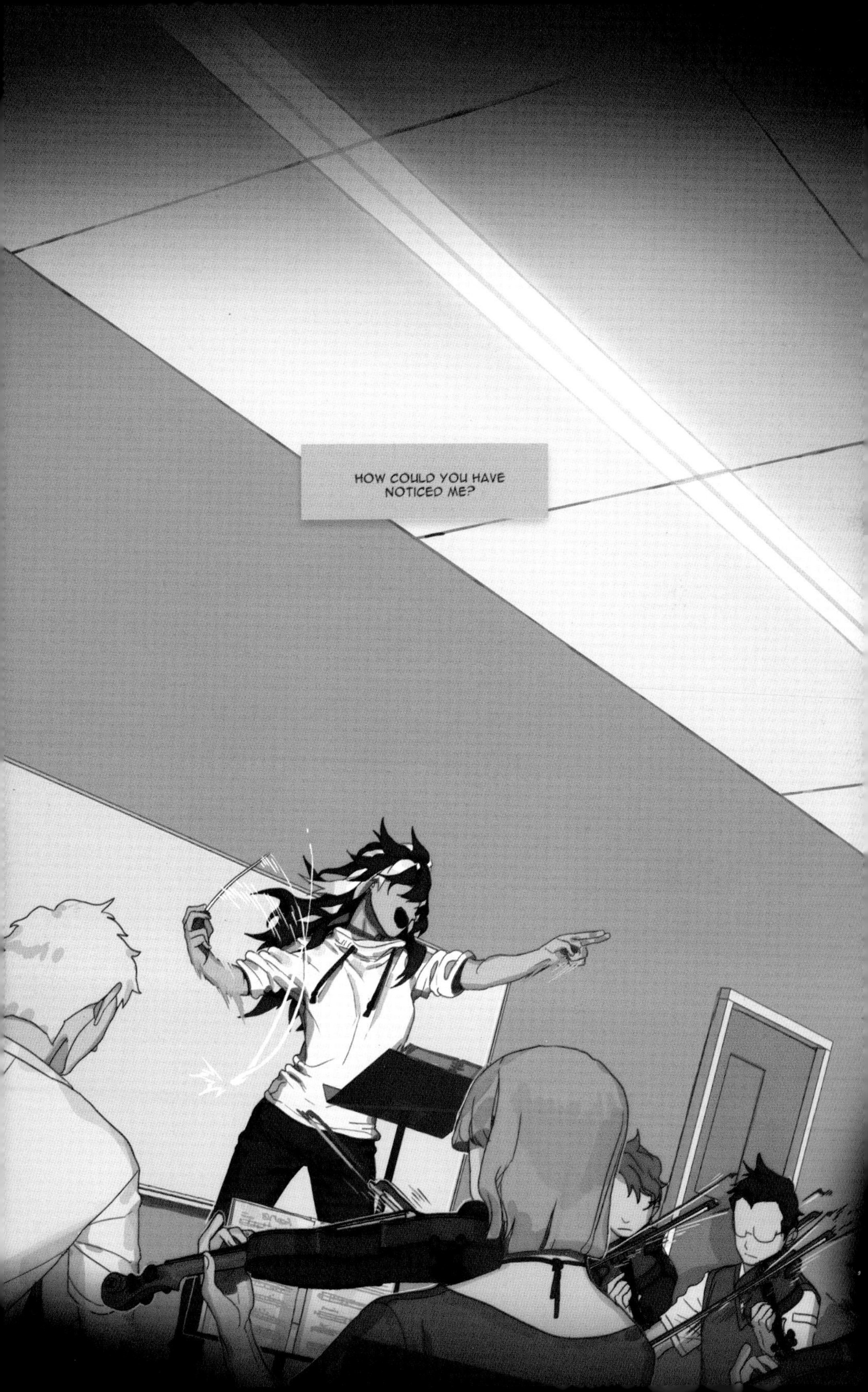
HOW COULD YOU HAVE NOTICED ME?

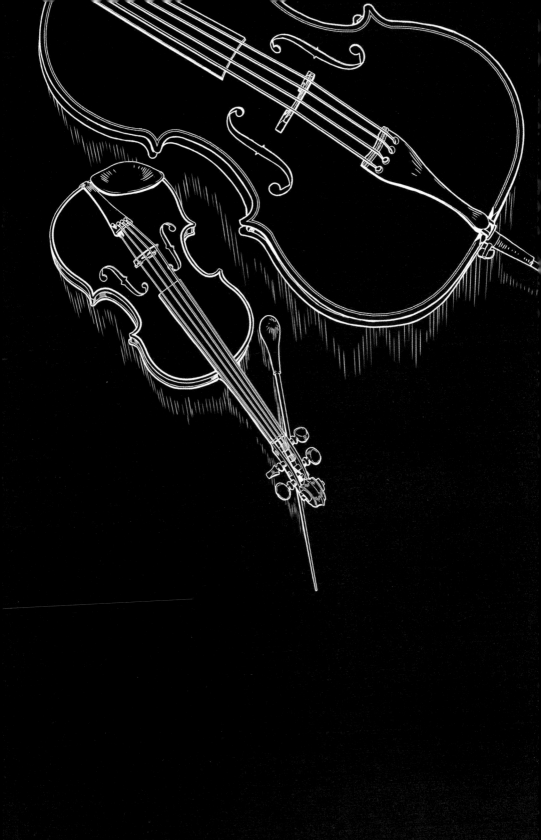

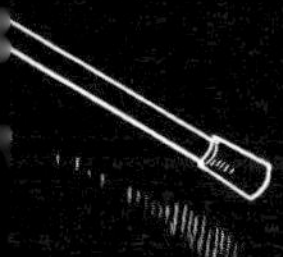

To be continued...

About the Creator

Shilin is an artist from Canada who
loves writing stories and drawing
comics. Once upon a time, she studied
music; now she happily lives through
the little orchestra gremlins she
brings to life on paper.